# The
# Nehrus
# of India

*BEATRICE PITNEY LAMB*

# The
# Nehrus
# of India

## THREE GENERATIONS OF LEADERSHIP

The Macmillan Company · New York

Photographs by the author appear on the following pages: 129 (top), 129
(bottom), 130 (top), 130 (bottom), 131 (top), 131 (bottom), 132 (bottom),
238 (bottom), 239 (top), 240 (top), 240 (bottom), 241 (bottom), 242 (top),
242 (bottom), 244 (bottom left). Other photographs courtesy of: Government of India Tourist Office, 127 (top); Keystone Press Agency, Ltd., 241
(top), 243 (bottom); Press Information Bureau, Government of India, 126
(bottom), 127 (bottom), 128 (top), 237 (top), 243 (top), 244 (top right),
244 (bottom right); Nehru Memorial Museum and Library, New Delhi, 125
(top), 125 (bottom), 126 (top left), 128 (bottom), 237 (bottom); Radio
Times Hulton Picture Library, 126 (top right), 244 (top left); Wide World
Photos, 132 (top), 238 (top). Picture editing by Patricia Crum.

The author wishes to thank the following for permission to reproduce copy-
righted material: HARCOURT, BRACE & WORLD, INC., for *After Nehru, Who?* by
Welles Hangen, copyright © 1963 by Welles Hangen. HOLT, RINEHART AND
WINSTON, INC., for "How Hard It Is to Keep·from Being King When It's in
You and in the Situation" from *In the Clearing* by Robert Frost, copyright ©
1962 by Robert Frost. THE JOHN DAY COMPANY, INC., for *The Nehrus* by B.
R. Nanda, copyright © 1962 by George Allen & Unwin Ltd.; *The Discovery
of India* by Jawaharlal Nehru, copyright © 1946 by The John Day Com-
pany; *Glimpses of World History* by Jawaharlal Nehru, copyright © 1942 by
The John Day Company; *Independence and After, Collection of Speeches
1946-49* by Jawaharlal Nehru; *Toward Freedom* by Jawaharlal Nehru, copyright © 1941 by The John Day Company; *With No Regrets, An Autobiography* by Krishna Nehru, copyright © 1945 by Asia Press, Inc.; and *Nehru,
The First Sixty Years* by Dorothy Norman, copyright © 1965 by Indira
Nehru Gandhi. THE MACMILLAN COMPANY for "Gitanjali," *The Collected
Poems and Plays of Rabindranath Tagore,* copyright by Rabindranath Tagore
and by The Macmillan Company. ARNOLD MICHAELIS and THE MCCALL COR-
PORATION for "Interview with Indira Gandhi" by Arnold Michaelis, *McCall's,*
April 1966, copyright © 1966 by The McCall Corporation. OXFORD UNIVER-
SITY PRESS for *Nehru, A Political Biography* by Michael Brecher, copyright
© 1959 by Oxford University Press.

# Foreword

IF NOT LIMITED by the present subtitle, *Three Generations of Leadership*, a book entitled *The Nehrus of India* would necessarily have to deal with at least several more prominent Nehrus in addition to the three whose interrelated story is the theme of this work.

Among the other Nehrus of stature is, of course, Prime Minister Nehru's sister, Madame Vijaya Lakshmi Pandit, who served as Indian Ambassador to the United States and the Soviet Union and was the first woman to be elected President of the General Assembly of the United Nations.

Another is Braj Kumar Nehru, a cousin of the Prime Minister, who has had a long and prominent career in Indian government service culminating in a fruitful term as Indian Ambassador to the United States. Still another cousin, Ratan Kumar Nehru, served as Indian Ambassador to various nations including China, and later became Vice Chancellor of the University of Allahabad.

Two women members of the family have become well-known writers, Mrs. Krishna Nehru Hutheesingh and Mrs. Tara Sahgal.

The complete saga of the entire family deserves to be told but is beyond the scope of this book.

First among the three Nehrus on whom I concentrate here is Motilal, a powerful, dynamic, irrepressible person whose leadership was such that he would clearly have become prime minister of India if India had attained independence before his death in 1931. Unfortunately, I never had the chance to meet him and must rely entirely on the reports of others as to what he was like. I have followed in the main the account of his life written by B. R. Nanda in *The Nehrus: Motilal and Jawaharlal*. I am indebted to Dr. Nanda also for the personal help he has given me.

From Motilal, leadership passed, of course, to his far better known son, Jawaharlal, whom I had the privilege of meeting for the first time in 1949 and with whom I talked thereafter on several other occasions. It was in 1949 also that I first met his daughter, Mrs. Indira Gandhi.

Without knowing either prime minister well, I carry with me a vivid impression of them both and have been glad to have this chance to convey what I have seen in them.

In this foreword, I should like to express also my gratitude to several persons without whose help and assistance I might not have been able to complete the preparation of this book.

First my thanks go to Ambassador B. K. Nehru who found time in his busy schedule to go over my manuscript with me chapter by chapter, making most helpful detailed comments, and in places suggesting additions based on his own recollections of the family life of the Nehrus.

I am also greatly indebted to Mr. Y. Sharada Prasad, Deputy Information Officer to the Prime Minister, who located for me much valuable material especially regarding the early life of Her Excellency Mrs. Indira Gandhi, and who checked the finished manuscript for possible factual errors.

Mr. Nirmal Singh, Indian Information Officer in New York City, spared no pains to secure for me rapidly any information that I needed and he also went over the finished manuscript making thoughtful suggestions. Mr. Anand Mohun, also of the Indian Information Office in New York City, gave me similar assistance and in the same cooperative spirit.

Mr. Sevaklal M. Master, Librarian-Bibliographer of the School of International Studies of Columbia University, located for me many useful articles in back issues of Indian magazines which I might otherwise have failed to find, and he helped me in many other ways also.

Last but not least, I thank Mrs. Shirley Denner who has not only typed and retyped my manuscript in its successive drafts, but has also given me even more important assistance—steadying me when I grew discouraged with my work.

BEATRICE PITNEY LAMB

# Contents

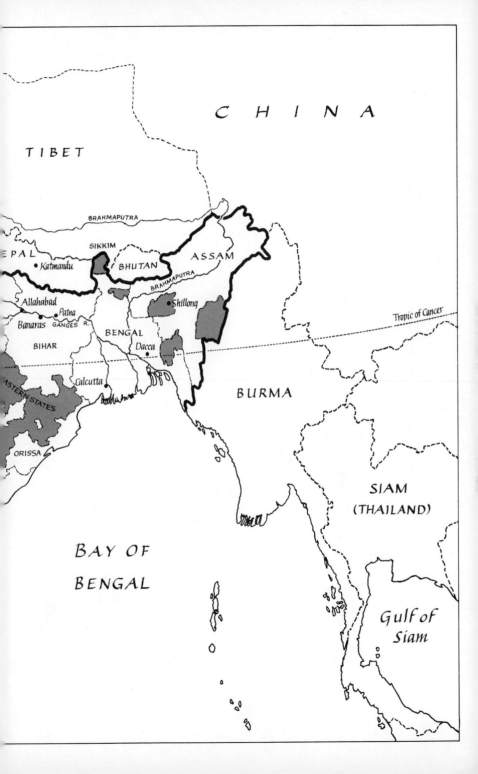

# Introduction

The political map of the world has always changed frequently, but within the last quarter of a century it has changed in an especially remarkable way. In the early twentieth century, large sections of Asia, the Far East, and Africa were included in the empires of Great Britain and other European nations. Today the idea of an overseas empire is so much in disfavor that many have forgotten how strong a hold it had over British and European thinking even a few decades ago.

When India, previously under British rule, won her independence in 1947, she was the first colonial land to do so, except for the Philippines which the United States had freed the preceding year. The American acquisition of the Philippines in 1898 at the end of the Spanish-American War had always been opposed by a considerable section of American opinion. The attainment of freedom by the Philippines, therefore, was not an arresting development. The British, on the other hand, had tenaciously cherished India as "the brightest jewel of the British Empire." India's success, occurring as it

1

did after decades of British opposition to Indian nationalist aspirations, was far more dramatic. It led subject peoples the world over to question the inevitability of their own subjection, and it made it easier for them to win freedom later. More than half of the nations of the world today attained their independence only after India won hers.

In this phenomenal worldwide movement for national independence, outstanding roles were played by three leaders in successive generations of a single family: the Nehrus of India. The eminence of Prime Minister Jawaharlal Nehru and of his daughter, Prime Minister Indira Gandhi, is well known. It is not so well known that Jawaharlal's father, Motilal, also played an essential role in the independence movement.

Together the lives of father, son, and granddaughter span more than one hundred years, during which significant changes have taken place in India, as in the entire world. Modern India, the largest democracy in the world, cannot be understood without reference to the activities of these three leaders, the problems they faced, and the policies they adopted,

The struggle for freedom in India was a difficult one. It required fully thirty years of agitation, organization, protests, demonstrations, personal deprivation, physical suffering, frequent arrests, and long terms of imprisonment. A forceful, influential, and respected leader, Motilal Nehru served two terms as president of the chief organization through which the Indian nationalists worked together, the Indian National Congress. In 1929, when his second term came to an end, it was his son who was elected to succeed him.

Indira was only four when her father and grandfather first served terms in prison for their nationalist activities. Left behind, a lonely indignant child but apparently already an organizer at heart, she lined up her dolls with firm resolve and played a game in which they worked for freedom, too. Throughout her childhood, the nationalist movement was at the very center of her life. Her grandfather had a second term of imprisonment before he died in 1931. Her father had eight more terms, a total of nine years in prison. When Indira was thirteen, even her mother was imprisoned. Later she herself spent more than a year in jail. She had reached the age of twenty-nine by the time independence was finally won, and she and her family were at last able to plan a future without serious danger of further intermittent interruptions by the police.

The Nehrus strongly believed that India was entitled to a place of its own on the world stage. Far from being a narrow nationalist, Jawaharlal especially was an ardent internationalist. Long before independence was won, he had come to think of nationalism as a necessary first step toward playing a constructive role in international relations.

Another reason the Nehrus cared so much about independence was that they wanted to build a better India. So long as decisions on educational policy, economic matters, and social reform rested in the hands of foreign rulers, they saw little likelihood of progress in India.

Jawaharlal, especially, was emphatic that it was British rule that had caused Indian poverty. He knew that India had once been wealthy. In the Middle Ages the few European travelers who reached India took home with them eyewitness reports of Indian wealth. It was because Europeans were so eager and determined to find a short sea route to wealthy India, then spoken of as "the Indies," that the Western hemisphere was discovered. Jawaharlal also knew that the British themselves were dazzled by the wealth they found in Bengal, the first large province they conquered. He knew, as history in fact tells us, that the British at first had plundered Bengal unscrupulously for personal profit. Although he acknowledged that they later reformed their ways, he considered that various of their policies had ruined the once prosperous Indian handicraft industry on which the economy had largely depended, and had tended to prevent the development of new mechanized industries to take its place. To British policies, he ascribed India's failure to keep pace with the industrial revolution then taking place in the West—out of which finally emerged the marked rise in Western standards of living.

In contrast to the wealth of the past, Jawaharlal saw abysmal poverty around him. The vast majority of Indians had to go without things which would seem absolute necessities to the average Westerner. The great majority had no access to electricity and could not afford oil for their little oil lamps except in emergencies such as birth or death. From dusk on, they normally had no choice but to remain in darkness until morning. Most of them dressed in rags and had no shoes. In the countryside, all but a privileged few lived in small mud huts, or huts of woven leaves or bark, with floors of bare earth. Running water was unknown. In the cities, housing conditions for the masses tended to be fully as miserable and far more congested. Then too, many people could not even afford the food the body needs and were painfully thin.

Jawaharlal was also concerned about the high rate of illiteracy. In the 1920's, when he became involved in the nationalist movement, only about 8.3 per cent of the people of India could read. Even as late as the 1940's so few schools had been opened under British rule that almost two-thirds of all Indian children under eleven had no chance to be educated, and 81 per cent of those over eleven were not in school. He was particularly disturbed by the backwardness of the 85 per cent of the Indian population who lived in the country. They knew nothing about modern scientific agriculture and they still used age-old techniques. The resulting low yields per acre were, of course, the cause of their poverty.

When the battle for freedom was finally won, Jawaharlal and his daughter both began to work for a better India, he as prime minister, she at first by organizing many much-needed social welfare projects.

Under Jawaharlal Nehru's leadership, the Indian government made a determined effort to combat poverty, to build new industries, to increase the efficiency of the rural people, to educate them, to pull them out of the Middle Ages into the twentieth century, as it were. The United States, the United Kingdom, the Soviet Union, and other nations have advanced aid to help India in her efforts, some of it in the form of outright grants, most of it in the form of loans.

Among the persuasive arguments made in the United States and the United Kingdom for foreign aid has been that modern high-speed transportation has in effect shrunk the world to a fraction of the size it was in the horse and buggy days, and that just as it is both heartless and unwise for affluent nations to ignore pockets of poverty existing within their own territory, it is also unwise and heartless for them to ignore the poverty of an entire nation as important as India. Although Indians have been remarkably patient in their poverty, this patience cannot be expected to last indefinitely. In other countries in the past, discontent over poverty has proved a fertile seed bed for dangerous political movements. Nazism, for example, assumed major proportions in Germany only when a serious economic depression followed a too brief period of prosperity, which in turn followed a disastrous inflation in which all savings were wiped out. Also, continuing abysmal poverty in India might have unfortunate results of a kind impossible to predict.

With the help of foreign aid, but also through great efforts on India's own part, progress was made along several lines during Nehru's term of office as prime minister. A great expansion of educational opportunities was achieved. Many new industries were developed. Some progress was made in improving agricultural yields. Only a slight rise in the standard of living occurred, however. Poverty and hunger as they exist in India are not easily conquered.

During Nehru's lifetime, many had expected his daughter,

Mrs. Indira Gandhi, to succeed him as prime minister. When he died in May, 1964, however, she showed no interest in the position. Lal Bahadur Shastri was chosen instead. On the latter's sudden death in January, 1966, after only twenty months as prime minister, Mrs. Gandhi no longer indicated a reluctance to be a candidate. Voted into office, she announced that she would carry on her father's policies. When she thus stepped into the post which her father had filled for seventeen years, many found this even more dramatic than Jawaharlal's succession to his father's position in 1929, as indeed it was. In monarchies, succession by heredity is usually expected, but in the case of a people free to choose their own leaders, there is no other case where three generations of the same family filled, each in his turn, such important positions in national leadership.

Each of the three Nehrus stands out as a strong personality in his or her own right. Jawaharlal did not always agree with his father, nor did Indira always agree with Jawaharlal. In each case, the parent seemed to the younger Nehru too moderate, too willing to content himself with only gradual progress. Their personalities were in many ways dissimilar. Even so, their mutual devotion was greater than one usually expects to find among three generations. They were bound together not merely by family ties, but also by their common interest in freedom and a better India.

Because of the continuity of their work and their dedication to a common cause, the story of the three generations of Nehrus forms a single story and is far more dramatic than the story of any one of them alone.

# 1.

# Motilal and His India

MOTILAL NEHRU was born in 1861, four years after a bloody struggle had broken out between the British and Indians, which was to have a lasting impact on Indian history.

By 1857, when the struggle erupted, the British, who had won their first significant military victory in India exactly one hundred years earlier, thought they were in complete control of the Indian subcontinent. From the seaports—Madras, Bombay, and Calcutta—which they had acquired by treaties in the seventeenth century and had used initially for trading purposes only, they had gradually, and almost accidentally, extended their power inland. The record seems to show that they never definitely resolved to conquer India. Instead they were almost inescapably drawn into the confused politics that existed in India at the time. First they fought wars that were clearly necessary for self-defense, but progressively their concept of self-defense led them into wars of expansion.

In the early eighteenth century, the central authority of a powerful dynasty, the Moguls, who had ruled large parts of

India since the sixteenth century, had grown weak. Their provincial governors, or Nawabs, had asserted virtual independence. Likewise, other ambitious men—a few with princely pedigrees but most of them mere adventurers—had carved out of the old Mogul Empire whatever large or small states they could. Even if they nominally still recognized the Mogul Emperor as their overlord, in practice they obeyed no orders from Delhi. Thus India had come to be fragmented politically, divided among a large number of miscellaneous rulers. Each took whatever title caught his fancy. Many chose the title Raja, or Prince, while those with larger territories usually preferred the title Maharaja, or Great Prince. There were other titles also. The ruler of the largest state, Hyderabad, assumed the elaborate title of Nizam-ul-Mulk, Regulator of the Realm.

Among these various rulers there was acute rivalry. It was into this chaotic situation that the British had stepped. As they moved inland from their three chief seaports, they gained more territory in war after war, playing off one rival ruler against another. They left many Indian princes as nominal heads of their princely states, provided that those princes entered into "alliances" with them—of a kind which in effect placed the princes under British control.

The map of India came to be a queer patchwork quilt in which the areas governed directly by the British were interspersed with areas still governed by more than five hundred subservient Indian princes. As the British grew in power, they took over territory from these "allies" whenever it suited them. They came to believe that they were the masters of the whole land.

Suddenly in 1857, the British were forced to realize that their hold over India was by no means as secure as they had believed it to be. On a Sunday in May of that year, Indian soldiers hired by the British for their Indian army mutinied in the city of Meerut in northern India near Delhi. They killed every British man, woman, and child they could find, then raced on to Delhi and continued their slaughter there. It was a time of horror and terror long remembered.

Many other Indians dissatisfied with British rule joined the uprising. Only with great difficulty and after a year of hard fighting did the British succeed in putting it down. A new policy was then proclaimed: the British would not annex any more princely states providing the princes recognized British overlordship or "paramountcy."

This uprising, which the British call the Great Mutiny and some Indians call their First War of Independence, implanted in many British minds the idea that Indians could not be trusted, that they might again at any moment join in a new, equally bloody conspiracy. Some sixty-two years later, this smoldering distrust led to a horrible British massacre of Indians which so stirred the indignation of both Motilal and Jawaharlal that they changed their entire way of life in order to work for Indian independence.

At the time of the uprising of 1857, the Nehrus were living in Delhi. Their ancestors had come from the northernmost state of Kashmir almost one hundred and fifty years before, at the invitation of the Mogul emperor of the time and under his patronage. The Nehru family was and is one of the most aristocratic in India. They are Brahmans, who are generally regarded as the highest caste or social group in India. Originally the Brahmans were teachers or priests. In recent times they have followed other occupations as well. Many Brahman families, and perhaps especially those who trace their origin to Kashmir, place a high value on being learned in the ancient writings of India. It was the exceptional learning of the Nehrus which brought this family to the attention of the Mogul emperor, who then granted them landed estates near his capital city. The Nehrus were well versed not only in the Sanskrit classics, but in Arabic and Persian writings as well.

Thus, although they were Hindus by birth, they were familiar with the culture of the chief minority religious group of India, the Muslims, whose literature was written in these languages.

As the Mogul Empire declined in strength, the Nehru family fortune declined also. They lost their landed estates, but they remained cultured, proud of their tradition of learning, and members of the impoverished Mogul court.

It was not safe to stay in Delhi during the Mutiny, since the old capital city was a main center of the fighting. As refugees flee from any war, Motilal's father, Ganga Dhar Nehru, and his family fled hastily, leaving their library and fine possessions behind them. They went first to Agra, some 120 miles to the south of Delhi. Ganga Dhar died in 1861, just before his wife gave birth to their third son, Motilal. Her two older boys, Bansi Dhar and Nand Lal, had to support their mother, their two sisters, and their baby brother.

Fortunately Bansi Dhar secured a small government job, in which he was moved frequently from one city to another. Nand Lal, who took charge of Motilal, first secured a series of jobs in a small princely state in what is now Rajasthan, then moved back to Agra, where he took up the practice of law. He then moved on to Allahabad, a few hundred miles to the east, which had become a more important city and where the practice of law therefore seemed likely to be more profitable.

Allahabad was now the capital of one of the provinces or main subdivisions of the part of India ruled directly by the British. At that time this province was known as the United Provinces, because the province of Agra had been united with the province of Oudh. When India became independent, the United Provinces became the state of Uttar Pradesh, "northern province." Thus it still retains the same initials, the "U.P."

It is generally known by these initials. It occupies the very heart of the Ganges Valley in North India.

While in Rajasthan, Motilal had been tutored by a Muslim scholar who taught him Persian, which had been the court language of the Mogul emperors, and Arabic, in which the Muslim holy book, the Koran, is written. Until the age of twelve, Motilal could not read English, but he had begun picking up a few phrases from his brothers who had some knowledge of the language.

His own mother tongue was Urdu, a language that had grown up around the court of the Mogul emperors. It was a combination of Brijbhasha, an early form of the North Indian language, Hindi, and of borrowings from the official Persian.

Young Motilal proved bright enough to gain admittance to an English high school in the city of Kanpur, also in the U.P., where his brother, Bansi Dhar, was then working. In those days few Indian boys had such an opportunity. The British had only recently adopted a plan for a coordinated system of education at all levels. In 1854, the committee to which this task had been assigned recommended that schools be set up "not to train highly a few youths, but to provide more opportunities than now exist for the acquisition of" education.[1] Unfortunately progress in carrying out the committee's recommendation for educational opportunities for the many instead of the few was slow. As late as 1882, when Motilal was twenty-one, another government commission would report that there were less than 4,000 schools above primary level in all of India and only 214,000 students enrolled in them.[2] Yet a student had to gain admittance to such a school if he was to prepare himself for higher education. Only through education in a high school and then in a college or university, where the instruction was in English, could a young man hope for the mastery of English essential for a successful career during British rule.

In 1837, the British had made English the official language

of their government in India. Previously the official language had been Persian. Since Motilal wanted to become a lawyer, English was essential to him. It was the language of the higher law courts, and he could not hope to argue cases in a high court unless he knew English thoroughly.

Because Allahabad was the capital of the U.P., it contained such a court, which in American terminology would be called a court of appeals. The cases argued in this court often involved conflicting claims to enormous holdings of land. Each claimant was usually willing to pay a high fee to a good lawyer to argue on his behalf. Motilal soon became one of the most successful and highly paid lawyers in Allahabad, indeed in all of India. He worked hard, and had great ability, forcefulness, energy, and personal charm. The chief judge of the court once wrote that no lawyer appearing before him handled a case better than Motilal.

Motilal was good-looking, with a squarish, well-chiseled face, a determined chin, and penetrating dark eyes under heavy brows. He wore a bristling moustache. Under it, his mouth, though firm, was good-humored. He always seemed ready to smile. He stood straight, had a fine build and muscles made strong by the wrestling and outdoor sports he had enjoyed as a boy.

It was fortunate that he did well as a lawyer. His older brother, Nand Lal, who had previously sacrificed much to give Motilal an education, died, leaving a wife and seven children, so that by the age of twenty-five Motilal had many people to support. He took the entire responsibility for the family. Indians usually have a strong sense of family ties, a willingness to share their home with relatives in distress. In their minds, the ideal family is the large "joint family." Traditionally the head of the family is a grandfather or even a great-grandfather, under whose roof live all his sons and their wives, and their children, and the wives of any of the grandsons who are married, and again their children. Daughters or granddaughters, when they marry, traditionally leave the joint family, while daughters-in-law and granddaughters-in-law join it. Motilal's family was like that of the ideal joint family, except that he was an uncle of many of its members, rather than a father or grandfather.

Motilal himself had married and had a son before he was twenty. Early marriage was customary among Kashmiri Brahmans. Both wife and child soon died, however. Then he married again and had another son, who also died.

Because of these deaths, he was especially happy when on November 14, 1889, his second wife, Swarup Rani, gave birth to another son, Jawaharlal. The name means "Beloved Jewel" or "Jewel-like Son." The boy hated it. When an admirer later wanted to name a child after him, Jawaharlal protested that the child would certainly not like it anymore than he.

In India, perhaps even more than in most countries, the birth of a son and heir is a great event. To Motilal, who had already lost two sons, Jawaharlal was especially precious, the more so when it became apparent that he would remain the only son.

Jawaharlal was an only child for eleven years before the older of his two sisters was born. Named Swarup after her mother but known in the family as Nan, his first sister has since become famous under her married name, Madame Vijaya Lakshmi Pandit. For a number of years she served as Indian Ambassador first to the Soviet Union and then to the United States. She was elected, in 1953, President of the General Assembly of the United Nations, the only woman who has held that position.

His second sister, now Mrs. Krishna Hutheesingh, is a well-known author, who has written about her memories of the family.

For a very few years after Jawaharlal was born, the family

lived in the center of the old "Indian" section of Allahabad. Here the houses were tightly packed together. The ground floor of many of them contained Indian-style open-front shops, or bazaars. Above the shops there were flats where the people of the city lived. In many of these, the rooms were tiny and dark. The rooms and the houses were so crowded that there was little privacy. Although Motilal had an entire house rather than a flat or apartment, and although his neighborhood was a residential one with no shops on the street, he thought his home there far too crowded for his enlarged family.

Then, too, the streets of the old city of Allahabad were noisy and full of traffic all day and late into the evening. The hoofs of donkeys and of horses pulling high, two-wheeled buggies and other carriages clattered over the cobbles. Creaking two-wheeled bullock carts lumbered along. Crowds of people walked back and forth chattering endlessly. Peddlers cried their wares.

When Jawaharlal was three or four years old, Motilal moved out of the old city. He was not only able to move into a larger house, but also into one in Allahabad's most select residential area, the "Civil Lines," where the British officials and other Europeans lived, plus Eurasians of mixed blood. In the Civil Lines, the houses were set apart from one another, with grounds and gardens around them. The streets were wide, quiet, and tree-lined. The entire atmosphere was quite different from the noisy, crowded "Indian" section of the city.

Many Indians would not have chosen to move to the Civil Lines even if they could have afforded to do so. They would have preferred to stay closer to fellow Indians. But Motilal had become increasingly Westernized. Probably one of his reasons for making the move was that he was interested in Europeans and he felt drawn by Western thought, techniques, and attitudes of mind.

It is hard to summarize briefly the contrasts between Western ways of living and thinking on the one hand, and Hindu ways on the other. The variations in attitudes and customs among Westerners are great; those among Hindus are still greater. One point that can be noted, however, is that many, perhaps most Hindus tended and still tend to be religious and intuitive in their thinking. Among Westerners, on the other hand, a scientific, logical, pragmatic approach to problems had become more and more common as the nineteenth century progressed. Certainly this was Motilal's approach. His was a fine, clear, rational legal mind. Although he did not argue against religious beliefs, he was not religious. He was an agnostic far more interested in the enjoyable real world around him than in the unseen other world.

Then, too, Motilal was an independent-minded individualist. Individualism, which is often taken for granted in the West, was not and still is not the norm in Hindu society. There the emphasis is placed on the family and on the larger social group or caste to which the family belongs. All his life an individual remains a member of the caste into which he was born. To the natural Western question, "What if he wants to leave it?", the answer is that for Indians caste membership seems so natural and inevitable that the idea of "leaving" one's caste is almost unthinkable. Obviously one cannot change the family into which one was born; how then could one possibly change one's caste!

Each caste has rules of its own which few of its members would think of challenging. Motilal's caste of Kashmiri Brahmans had a rule against undertaking ocean trips—crossing "black water." If a man did such a thing, his caste members traditionally punished him by never speaking to him again or having anything to do with him. Especially in Motilal's time, such a social boycott could be very painful in India, since social contacts among people of different castes were then usually limited and the average man might have no other friends to turn to when the members of his caste turned their backs on him.

Times were changing, however. While Motilal was a young man, one member of the caste who had traveled abroad was reaccepted by some of his fellow members, but only after he had performed religious penance.

In 1899, Motilal wanted to make a trip to Europe. He thought the rule against foreign travel was silly. He went abroad and refused to do penance on his return. As was to be expected, some members of his caste did boycott him. Others rallied around him and offered to form a Motilal Sabha, a Motilal Association—to protest the punishment he had received. He suggested, however, that if they wanted to form such a group they should not name it after him, since the principle involved was more important than the fate of any particular individual. He urged them to call their group the Satya Sabha, or Truth Association.

In any case, it did not matter to him that some of his caste fellows boycotted him since he had many friends outside his caste and was always making new ones, including high-placed British officials and other Europeans.

In 1900, he bought a new home in the Civil Lines, still larger than the first. It had huge rooms, long verandas, wide terraces, large gardens, ample grounds, and—wonder of wonders in those days—an indoor swimming pool, the first in Allahabad. The house was run-down and dilapidated. No matter. He spent freely to rebuild and redecorate it, ordering for it all the very latest improvements, including electricity and running water. He insisted on having the best and the most up-to-date luxuries that money could buy, and he had a tennis court built.

Although he worked hard, he still found time and energy to entertain crowds of guests. In the late afternoons, he often gave great tea parties in his gardens, on his lawns, or in the enormous halls of his house. While servants passed tempting plates of *pakoras,* hot, fried Indian tidbits, bands played gaily in the background. Sure of his earning power, Motilal spared no expense. The luxury in which he lived, the lavishness with which he entertained, made him very well known. His fabulous, princely way of living was remembered long after he had made great changes in it for the sake of the nationalist movement.

He called his new home in the Civil Lines the Abode of Happiness—Anand Bhawan. For twenty years he kept on adding improvements to it: more tennis courts for the use of his guests, fruit gardens, fountains, buildings for his many horses, his fine carriages, and later for his automobiles.

Motilal followed up his first European trip with several others in succeeding years. After each trip, he taught his family new Western customs and ideas. Instead of eating with the fingers of their right hands, as most Indians still strongly believe in doing, the Nehru family began using knives, forks, and spoons. Western tutors and governesses were employed for the children. Western appliances, knickknacks, furniture, china, and glass were bought for the great house. In 1904, Motilal imported an automobile, the first in Allahabad and perhaps in the whole province. He filled his library with a wide range of Western books. He required everyone in the house to speak English instead of an Indian language and the members of the family who did not know English had to stay silent until they learned it. Motilal dressed in European fashion at this time and had his suits tailored in London. It was even rumored that he sent his laundry to Paris to be washed. Later Jawaharlal indignantly denied this, but the fact that people had believed such a story shows how fabulous Motilal had come to seem.

# 2.

# Three Influences

MOTILAL was influenced by three quite different cultural traditions: the Hindu, the Muslim, and the British or Western traditions. In some ways the three influenced one another in India. But the differences between them also led to conflicts.

The tradition native to India was, of course, the Hindu tradition in which Motilal had been born. Although he himself was not much interested in religion, the women of his family were very religious, and he had Hindu religious ceremonies performed in his home.

Hinduism is really a wide variety of religions, rather than a single definable creed. The term was used to refer to almost all of the religious beliefs of India before the coming of the Muslims. Over the centuries certain bonds have developed which tend to bind together Hindus of all faiths, but if Hinduism is considered as a single religion, which it often is, then it must be said emphatically that it is highly variegated, unorganized, and formless. It has nothing which corresponds to a church organization, let alone a central leader such as a pope. It has no single sacred book; it has many quite different ones.

18

According to their different backgrounds or levels of education, Hindus may hold a wide variety of beliefs. They may believe in an all-pervading divine spirit or godhead that is present to some extent in all living things but that cannot possibly be described. Or they may believe in one or more personal gods with quite human attributes who are depicted in pictures and statues. If they are uneducated, Indians usually believe in the existence of numerous demons who must be propitiated rather than worshiped, persuaded through offerings or magical practices not to harm the people.

One of the more developed personal gods is Vishnu the Preserver, who is believed to have had a number of incarnations. Another is Shiva, the creator and destroyer, who is often depicted dancing within a circle of flames and is considered the master of the great rhythms of the universe, of birth and death, of growth and decay.

Every Hindu family is supposed to set aside a spot in the home for worship, or *puja*. Here on a shelf they place small figures of one or more gods of their choice. Interestingly enough, a *puja* place may contain figures or pictures which belong to religious traditions other than Hinduism itself, such as a crucifix or a figure of the Buddha.

Besides worshiping at home, Hindus go to temples where priests serve and take care of figures of the gods all through the day, as though these figures were alive. They clothe them, "feed" them, take them out for rides on palanquins which the priests support on their shoulders, or in huge elaborately carved wooden chariots pulled by hundreds of eager devotees.

In the different regions of India, these temples are of varying styles of architecture, but they all contrast sharply with Muslim architecture. Before the coming of the Muslims, Indians seldom used the arch, the vault, or the dome. Instead they roofed their buildings with successive overlapping horizontal stones, topped at the apex by single large stones, or they used simple post-and-lintel construction, in which a single long stone or beam spans the space between two uprights.

Temple exteriors, including the towers, are usually profusely ornamented with carving, mostly of human or divine figures in high relief. Some of the famous old temples are so densely covered with sculpture that the entire temple seems from the outside to have been sculptured rather than designed by an architect.

One belief shared by large numbers of Hindus is in the importance of making pilgrimages whenever possible to special sacred places. One of the most important pilgrimage points in India is in Allahabad, not far from Anand Bhawan. Here the great Jumna River, on which Delhi is situated farther upstream, joins with the still greater Ganges. Hindus consider the Ganges sacred throughout its entire course, but regard this confluence of the two rivers as especially sacred.

As in the case of old customs everywhere, the origins of Hindu customs are lost in history. Present-day Hindus are the inheritors of a complex and many-sided tradition that comes to them out of the far distant past. A wealth of fables, fairy tales, legends, myths, and heroic stories is part of this tradition. Many of the animal fables which were later included in European collections originated in India, though their details were often changed before they were introduced to Europe. Many of the wise fox stories known to Western children were originally stories about a clever Indian jackal.

Although the rich assortment of stories that are part of the Hindu tradition are of all levels of seriousness, some of them contain moral messages which Hindus tend to look upon as the proper guides to right conduct. Often they pass them down from generation to generation by constant retelling. Even people who are illiterate tend to be educated in the sense that their parents have taught them much of the great oral Hindu tradition. Two of the longest and most revered stories are those contained in the Hindu epic poems, the *Mahabharata* and the *Ramayana*.

Among the many Sanskrit texts, the earliest and most sacred are the *Vedas*. Their oral composition probably began around 1500 B.C., although they were not written down until much later. Verses from the *Vedas* are still used in marriage services, funerals, and other ceremonies. Another group of sacred texts, the *Upanishads,* composed somewhat later, stress especially the essential unity of the human soul and the Divine. The breadth, simplicity, and beauty of the *Upanishads* have attracted many Westerners who are searching for answers to fundamental questions which they have not found within their own religious tradition.

In spite of their wide gamut of religious faiths and the number of differing sacred texts from which they can draw inspiration, most Hindus tend to share certain common ideas about human destiny and the final purpose of man's life. They believe in reincarnation. One's soul will come back to earth again and again. What one's future life will be like will depend on whether one has done one's duty in this life, just as one's status and good or bad fortune in this life depends on whether one did one's duty in one's previous life or lives. One's own actions determine one's fate. This is called the law of *karma.*

Throughout successive incarnations, the great purpose in life should be to free one's soul from impurities through prayer, meditation, and worship, so that finally it will be able to realize its essential oneness with the Divine.

In the course of the soul's long pilgrimage to its ultimate goal of perfect oneness with the Divine, it inhabits in succession many widely different types of bodies, animal as well as human. Hence, the Hindu feeling of unity with the animal world, of which the special symbol is the cow. Because of the milk that she gives, the cow is regarded also in some sense as the mother of mankind.

Many Westerners and some Hindus themselves speak of their feeling that the cow is "sacred." Other observers consider the word misleading. Hindus do not "worship" cows; they simply would not kill them any more than they would kill another person. The phrase "cattle protection," which most Hindus use, expresses their feeling better than does any word connoting sanctity. Although special emphasis is placed on the cow, all cattle regardless of sex benefit by her position. Killing cattle in general is considered wrong by most Hindus.

The strength of Hindu feeling on the subject was vividly illustrated in the autumn of 1966 when a Hindu holy man fasted to death to put moral pressure on the Indian Parliament to pass a bill banning on a nationwide scale the slaughter of cattle—a matter which had previously been left to the discretion of the individual states. That autumn also, large and sometimes violent demonstrations took place in New Delhi for the same purpose.

Just how it happened that cattle protection came to seem so important to many Hindus is not altogether clear. It is known that in ancient times Hindus ate beef and also slaughtered cattle for sacrificial purposes. One possible explanation of the change is that when their priests saw that the supply of cattle was diminishing dangerously, they realized that it was of utmost importance to make a rule banning cow slaughter. To ensure that it would be obeyed, they made it a religious commandment.

Once any rule becomes a religious commandment it is likely to remain surrounded in orthodox minds by strong emotions, even when external conditions change and the rule no longer serves a useful practical purpose.

The law of *karma* not only determines whether one will be born as an animal or as a human being; in those cases when one is to be born as a human being, it also determines one's social status and caste. Mention has already been made of how inherent in the very nature of social life most Indians consider caste to be. The inner sense of identification with caste was and usually still is so strong that the idea of "leaving" it makes no sense.

Formerly the barriers separating castes were rigid; today they are becoming less so. In many cases, any association with people of other castes was thought to be polluting. Eating together—"interdining" is the Indian term—was generally prohibited, and one had to be careful as to the caste membership of the persons who cooked one's food or even handed one water. To some extent and among some people, old ideas of pollution have dropped away. Both Motilal and Jawaharlal combatted the caste system.

Some Westerners have the mistaken impression that independent India has abolished caste. This is by no means the case. Even though certain of the old caste rigidities may be decreasing, castes are assuming an important new role in politics. It is largely from caste leaders that illiterate people learn how to use their votes.

What has been abolished, theoretically, is "untouchability": discrimination against those persons who had been considered so low socially that they were below the lowest castes, and were called "outcastes," "untouchables," or "pariahs." In Motilal's time, the discrimination against them was extreme. In villages, they had to live apart, they were not allowed to pull up water from the same well used by other villagers, and they were not allowed to enter Hindu temples. They were regarded as so unclean that even to touch them made a caste Hindu unclean also. In certain parts of the country, even close sight of them was thought to be polluting and they were required to keep at least certain stated distances between themselves and caste Hindus. We shall see how this situation came to be changed.

While considering the broad outlines of Hinduism and of the caste system, it is necessary to remember that Motilal, while a Hindu by birth, stood somewhat apart from Hinduism and the caste system, partly because of his temperament and partly because of his close contacts with the other two important cultural traditions in the India of his time: the Muslim tradition and the Western or European tradition. Motilal had many Muslim friends. He had been taught Muslim literature before he learned English. But although Hindus such as Motilal had absorbed Muslim culture, the relations between Hindus and Muslims as separate religious groups within India grew increasingly strained during Motilal's lifetime and thereafter.

In marked contrast to Hinduism, which developed gradually over the centuries and had its roots in the remote past, the Muslim religion was created by a single man, Muhammad, in the seventh century A.D. Westerners often call it Mohammedanism after the name of its founder, but Muslims object. This name sounds to them as though it implies that they include Muhammad in their worship, as Christians include Christ. Actually the very essence of Muhammad's teaching was that God is single and indivisible. The basic formula of the religion he founded is: "There is no God but Allah, and Muhammad is his Prophet." Although Muhammad regarded himself as the last and greatest of the prophets, he included Adam, Noah, Abraham, Moses, and even Jesus among the prophets who had preceded him. He himself chose the word *Islam* as the name of the faith he preached. It means "submitting oneself to God." Muslim, sometimes also spelled moslem or mussulman, is the corresponding adjective.

Muhammad was born in the city of Mecca in what is now Saudi Arabia. This city was an important trading center halfway down the Arabian Peninsula near the Red Sea coast. Mecca was also a pilgrimage point to which the uneducated nomad Arabs from the desert came to do reverence to a curious stone, a large black meteorite which was regarded as sacred. Muhammad was concerned over the ignorance, the intertribal feuds, the superstitions, and the crude polytheism of these Arabs. As a successful merchant who sometimes traveled with his caravans, Muhammad had come in contact with Christian and Jewish communities in Arabia. Their respective religions both seemed to him better than the idol-worshiping Arabian religion of his time. He greatly preferred the strict monotheism of Judaism to the Christian doctrine of the Trinity. On the other hand, he was struck by the Christian doctrines of the Last Judgment, the resurrection of the body, hell, and paradise. And he was also drawn to Christian ethics.

When Muhammad was about forty, he began having trances in which it seemed to him that God spoke to him directly. At first he told only his wife and his closest friends what he claimed God had said. They wrote these sayings down; he himself was probably illiterate. Gradually he began preaching more and more openly, urging the Meccans to give up polytheism and worship the one God only.

After Muhammad's death in 632 A.D., his followers began assembling the various messages from God which they had written down at his dictation. Altogether this compilation, the Muslim holy book or Koran, is about three hundred pages long. Muslims consider that every word in it is the word of God, and not to be questioned. Those who know the Arabic language, Muslims or not, regard it as the most outstanding book ever written in that language. They say that the style of this illiterate man is amazingly rich, sonorous, and poetical. Although many non-Muslims find the Koran confusing and sometimes self-contradictory, much of its teaching is comparable with the best in other great religions. It emphasizes equality and brotherhood among men without regard to race—a great advance over the narrow, hostile tribalism of the Arabia into which Muhammad was born.

The God who speaks through the Koran is clearly omnipotent, wrathful, and jealous. The believer must live in constant fear of him, must serve him by good works, almsgiving, and prayer, and by a pilgrimage to Mecca at least once in a lifetime. Through God's grace he may be forgiven his sins and allowed to enter paradise.

Before his death, the Prophet had become the temporal as well as the spiritual ruler of a Muslim state centered in Mecca. His armies had conquered all of Arabia and he had converted most of the Arabs to his faith.

When Muhammad died, control over the ever-expanding Muslim state passed into the hands of a long series of Caliphs, a word which means "successors." Conversions to the new faith were rapid, and larger and larger armies were formed. Inspired by certain verses of the Koran that can be interpreted to mean that wars against nonbelievers are holy wars, and also activated by more worldly motivations, these armies rapidly achieved an astonishing series of victories. Soon they had defeated the armies of the two giant empires of the day, the Eastern Roman Empire and the Persian Empire, and had conquered all of Syria, Mesopotamia, and Egypt. In less than a century, they had overrun all of North Africa and Spain to the west. To the east they conquered the entire Persian Empire and pushed on into Central Asia, taking famous old cities on the caravan trails to China such as Balkh, Bukhara, and Samarkand. They also established a foothold on the Indian subcontinent in the lower Indus Valley, an area known as Sind, now part of West Pakistan.

Arab conquests had brought Islam only to the periphery of India. The later Muslim conquerors, who made a far greater impact, were central Asians who had been converted to Islam after their lands had been conquered. Over a period of years around 1000 A.D., a Muslim Afghan chief, Mahmud of Ghazni, made annual raids in India from his kingdom in Afghanistan. Far more ruthless than the Arabs, he destroyed certain celebrated Hindu temples and carried off the immense collections of precious gems which he had found in them. Hindus still remember him with hatred. Then in the late twelfth century, another Afghan chief, Muhammad Ghori, sent an army into India for permanent conquest. The result was the establishment of the Sultanate of Delhi, a kingdom under the power of a Sultan, which is the Arab word meaning "person with power."

The Sultanate expanded by conquest until in the fourteenth century it had succeeded briefly in bringing almost all of the Indian subcontinent under its sway. After a few decades, it split into several parts, but much of India remained under the control of Muslim dynasties. Certain areas, however, came again under Hindu control.

More and more central Asians, Turks, and Afghans, who had been converted to Islam, entered India to join the armies or administrative services of the Sultanate or of the independent Muslim states which split from it. The number of Muslims increased even more through conversions. The lower, underprivileged Hindu castes and untouchables welcomed the Muslim message of equality and the brotherhood of man. In some cases, entire castes became converted together, without giving up their caste customs or, ironically, their sense of caste distinctions. In the parts of the Indian subcontinent which now form Pakistan, there finally came to be more Muslims than Hindus. In no other area of India did Muslims come to exceed 50 per cent of the population. In the U.P., a little over 15 per cent were Muslims before independence. In the subcontinent as a whole, before partition in 1947, one out of every four Indians was a Muslim.

The reason for Muslim influence especially in North India was not solely the large number of Muslims. It was also due to the appeal of Muslim culture which reached its height in India under the Mogul dynasty which was founded in 1526 and became far better organized, more tolerant toward Hindus, and more interested in architecture and other arts than had been the earlier Sultanate.

The founder of the dynasty, Babur, was half Turk and half Mongol, a descendant of the two famous central Asian conquerors, Genghis Khan and Tamerlane. A well-educated man, a talented writer and poet, an admirer of the culture of Muslim Persia, he was not proud of his descent from wild, dirty, uncultured Mongol nomads. Yet, the name Mogul, by which the dynasty is known, is an Indianized form of the word Mongol.

While inviting Persian scholars and artists to his court, Babur's grandson, Akbar (1558–1605), one of the greatest, most tolerant, and enlightened rulers of history, also welcomed Hindus, gave high office to many of them, studied Hinduism and attempted to bridge the gap between Hindu and Islamic-Persian-Mogul culture. Akbar made Allahabad one of his principal outposts and built a fort and a palace near where the Nehrus later would live. Many of the Muslims who were Motilal's friends were doubtless descended from Mogul officers.

From Akbar's time on, the well-educated Hindu minority living near Mogul headquarters came to be drawn into the orbit of Islamic-Persian-Mogul influence. It was natural to learn Persian, and once having learned it, to admire Persian lyric poetry, thought by many to be among the finest in world literature. The poetry that came to be written in Motilal's mother tongue, Urdu, was strongly influenced by it. The body of prose works in the Persian language at the time was also rich and stimulating.

Persian manuscripts were often illustrated by small, clear, bright-colored, glowing paintings, done with love of fine detail. Various schools of Indian miniature painting grew up under marked Persian influence but with somewhat freer styles.

Fully as impressive as Persian literature were the mosques, tombs, and palaces of the two chief Mogul capital cities, Agra and Delhi, both within easy traveling distance from Allahabad where the Nehrus lived. In contrast to Hindu temples, Muslim mosques in India (but not in all other countries) typically consist of open arcades much wider than they are deep. On one side the line of arches opens onto a large courtyard where Muslims gather in congregation for simultaneous worship on Fridays. Mosques are always carefully aligned so that the worshipers will face Mecca. They are usually surmounted by domes which tend to be bulbous and to be topped with a slender pointed ornamental detail or finial. At each end of the building stands a tall minaret from the top of which a *muezzin,* or crier, can cry out the call to prayer. Because Muhammad condemned idolatry, no mosque can contain sculpture. Indian mosques are typically decorated with great restraint.

The finest Mogul palaces at Agra and Delhi are exquisite open-arcaded white marble pavilions where privacy was achieved not by walls, but by rich hangings of silk and embroidery. In the decoration of these palaces, the Moguls used more varied and fanciful designs than those in their mosques, and created them by inlays of semiprecious stones.

The most famous of all Mogul buildings is the Taj Mahal, built by the fifth Mogul emperor, Shah Jahan, who ruled from 1628 to 1658, as the tomb for his much-beloved wife, Mumtaz Mahal. Its loveliness is not only due to its fine proportions, the graceful curve of its onion dome, the majesty of its great arched portals, and the beauty of its exceptionally fine marble, but also to the delicate tasteful way in which several contrasting designs are worked into its surfaces, breaking the solidity of the white stone and giving the building a fairy lightness fitting for the tomb of a woman.

Although Hindus found much to admire in Muslim culture, there was friction between the two religious groups on other matters, perhaps especially in the first half of the twentieth century. Because of Muhammad's teaching about idolatry, Muslims were shocked, as were Christian missionaries, by Hindu "idols." Another point of disagreement was regarding cattle.

Whereas Hindus believe it is wrong to kill cattle, no matter how old they may be, traditionally Muslims were accustomed to sacrificing a cow on their festival of *Bakr-id*. They also liked to eat beef and regarded cattle preservation as a superstition to be ignored. Muslims feel it is wrong for any music to be played while they worship; it might distract their attention. The Hindus have many songs about their gods and they often deliberately played their music near a Muslim mosque while a worship service was going on. Especially in the decades before partition, each group tended to offend the religious feelings of the other as though determined to irritate.

If the differences between the Hindu and the Islamic traditions were great, the differences between both of these and the Western tradition brought to India by the British were perhaps even greater. This tradition did not come to have an impact on any significant number of Indians, however, for well over two hundred years after the first British traders settled in Indian ports early in the seventeenth century. Especially during that time the British were few in number. They kept to themselves and had few contacts except with the Indians with whom they traded and the servants who waited on them.

Although slightly more numerous in Motilal's time, the British remained aloof from most Indians, and they had made only a small beginning in enabling Indians even to learn their language.

Until 1858, all British interests and activities in India, including conquest, treaty-making, and the administration of conquered territory, were under the direction of a private company, generally spoken of as the East India Company. Interested primarily in profits for its shareholders, the Company was reluctant to undertake the expense of an educational program.

The Company was not only reluctant to introduce English education; it also tried deliberately not to influence Indian customs or religious beliefs since it felt that to do so might upset the Indians and interfere with profits. Until 1833, it prohibited Christian missionaries from entering the territory it controlled. That year, Parliament, under pressure from the Evangelical Movement in England, required the Company thereafter to permit the entry of missionaries.

The missionaries started schools and colleges which taught English, and used English as the medium of instruction at high school and college level. The teaching was so good that even Hindus who were opposed to missionary activity and had no intention of becoming Christians sent their children to the schools if they could do so. Relative to the population, however, these schools were never numerous. As late as 1853, there were only twenty-two missionary schools and colleges in the vast area then known as the Presidency of Bengal, which included modern Orissa, Bihar, and East Pakistan, as well as West Bengal.[1]

Far greater impetus toward Western learning came from a dynamic pioneering Indian, Ram Mohun Roy (1772–1833) of Bengal, who studied English privately before there were any English schools or colleges in Company territory. Like the Nehrus, he was an upper-class Brahman and a product of the mixed Hindu-Muslim culture dominant among the cultured classes of North India. A brilliant man and a great scholar, he had learned Persian, Arabic, and Sanskrit when he was young and was well versed in their literatures. His intellectual curiosity led him to wonder what manner of people were the British who had recently taken over Bengal.

As a first step, he managed to learn English and worked for a while as a clerk for the East India Company in Calcutta. After learning English, he studied Greek, Latin, and Hebrew so that he could read the Bible in the original and understand the cultural roots of the West. His studies led him to the conviction that the ethics of Christianity were superior to those of

Islam or Hinduism, but he was critical of Christian theology. He emphasized the oneness of God and argued that monotheism was the essential teaching of the ancient Sanskrit texts, that the popular polytheism of the time had no foundation in them.

He urged all manner of reforms which he had learned from the West: trial by jury, freedom of the press, the right of widows to remarry, and monogamy.

Above all, he was impressed by the body of knowledge he found to be available in the West, including the new sciences which had begun to develop. He strongly advocated the substitution of English for Persian as the official language and he pressed for the introduction of schools and colleges where English and Western knowledge and culture would be taught. He himself took part in the founding in Calcutta of the first such college in 1819.

In 1813, the British Parliament had directed the reluctant Company to spend a certain small sum of money per year on education, scarcely more than enough to operate a single institution. When a majority of the Company's Committee of Public Instruction proposed to use this money to establish a Sanskrit college in Calcutta, Roy threw his weight strongly on the side of the minority who favored English education instead. He said that Sanskrit education conveyed only what had been known for two thousand years and that it would keep the country in darkness. It was largely due to his advocacy that English was made the official language and that whatever sums the government spent on education after 1834 were spent on English education. Because those who could afford an education for their children preferred to give them an English education, Hindu and Muslim educational institutions almost died out, though scholars passed on the traditional learning by tutoring a few chosen pupils.

Although never large, the Brahmo Samaj ("Society of God") which Roy organized exerted considerable influence throughout the nineteenth century. Attempting to reform Hinduism from within, its various branches pressed for social changes reflecting Western influence: the emancipation and education of women, and the reduction of caste barriers. It helped spread the best of Western liberal thought among the educated classes of India.

During the nineteenth century, English schools, colleges, and universities gradually increased in number. Even as late as the time of independence, however, only 300,000 students were enrolled in colleges or universities,[2] probably no more than 1 per cent of the young people of college age.

In sum, the impact of Western influence was uneven. The vast majority living in the countryside or in the princely states were untouched by it. Western influence was confined largely to the few cities which the British used as the centers of their rule, and it was especially felt by the small minority who had had higher education. Especially in the nineteenth century, many of these, like Motilal, were anxious to be more British than the British. Some were scornful of things Indian and sure that the West had the best answers to all problems.

After the uprising of 1857, the British government decided to take India out of the hands of the East India Company and rule it directly through an appointed viceroy in whose hands all powers were concentrated. The successive viceroys not only ran the administration, but also made the laws themselves. Under them, British governors were placed in charge of the provinces which became the main subdivisions of British India. Under them, in turn, were district officers in charge of smaller areas. Each official in the entire pyramid of British power took his orders from the official above him.

In the second half of the nineteenth century, the British Parliament passed acts creating a council to advise the viceroy and other councils to advise the governors. At first these were entirely British in membership but gradually a few Indians were added to them also. Until 1919 the councils were purely advisory and the entire system was basically authoritarian.

The Indians who had studied British history in school, however, had learned about self-government, elections, and representative institutions. Moved and inspired by the long struggle of the British themselves to win democracy in their own land, they would not long remain content under an all-powerful foreign viceroy.

# 3.

# Jawaharlal's Youth

WHILE HIS FATHER Motilal grew richer and richer, the boy Jawaharlal was given everything he could possibly want. He had ponies to ride and the most expensive tricycles and later bicycles. Every book that he could possibly want to read was ordered for him. He was taught how to play a good game of tennis on the Nehrus' fine private court and how to swim in their private pool. He loved swimming, tennis, and running. Later he also became a vigorous mountain climber. But he had much less practice with team sports than most boys.

He did not go to school until he was fifteen. Until then he was taught by tutors who came to him at his home. If Jawaharlal did not want to learn what the tutors tried to teach him, he simply did not learn it. Later when he wrote his autobiography, he admitted frankly what a spoiled child he had been.

At the same time he was a very lonely child. The Civil Lines was not a place where boys romped together in the streets in the same way they did in the older part of the city. The great house was full of cousins and other relatives, but

35

they were all older than Jawaharlal. He grew used to being very much alone.

One of his chief occupations was listening to the conversation of people older than he. His cousins talked often about the discriminatory practices of the British and how furious it made them to see again and again the hated sign "For Europeans Only" posted in railway cars, on park benches, and in other public places. Worse than that, if an Englishman happened to want a seat which Indians were entitled to use and which an Indian was actually occupying, he would make the Indian give it up. Little Jawaharlal, like his cousins, was filled with resentment against the foreign rulers who, in his words, "misbehaved in this fashion." Still he liked the English people he knew, his governesses and the friends of his father.

In the evening, when people came to visit his father, Jawaharlal would peep at them from behind a curtain and try to make out what the adults were saying. The men would have a drink together, and the great house would resound with Motilal's tremendous laughter. Sometimes Jawaharlal was discovered behind the curtain and brought into the room with the men. His father sat him on his knee.

The boy admired his father greatly, thought him the strongest, bravest, cleverest man in the world and the most determined. He wanted to be like him when he grew up, but at the same time he was frightened of him. Motilal sometimes lost his temper and punished his son severely. Yet he was very fond of his children, especially his son.

While Motilal was so Western in many ways, he clung to tradition in others. He celebrated his son's birthday according to the custom of the Mogul emperors who had ruled India before the British gained control. Early in the morning of his birthday, the boy was dressed in his best new clothes and placed on one side of a huge balance scale. On the other side were placed bags of wheat until the scale balanced. Then the wheat was distributed to the poor. The Mogul emperors had had themselves weighed in this way, but they had placed gold or silver or even precious stones on the other side of the balance.

From adolescence onward, high-caste Hindu Brahmans must always wear next to their bodies a long loop of string called "the sacred thread." It is worn over the left shoulder across the chest to the right side of the waist. When the sacred thread is put on for the first time, a religious ceremony is performed which corresponds to the Christian ceremony of confirmation. This is one of the many old traditions, the exact origin of which is lost in history.

There is a picture of thirteen-year-old Jawaharlal dressed for this ceremony in traditional fashion. In it he does not look at all like the Western boy of his other early pictures. Around his hips and legs is wrapped an unsewn cloth or *dhoti*. His chest is bare. His head is shaved except for a tiny topknot of hair left at the very top—a high-caste Hindu custom of great antiquity.

Throughout his life, however, Jawaharlal was to seem so very Western that many Westerners expected his ideas to be even more Western than they were. That early photograph is a useful reminder that a long tradition quite different from that of the West was part of his makeup also. He later wrote, "I have become a queer mixture of East and West."

Motilal had hired a Hindu Brahman to tutor his boy in Sanskrit, the classical language of Hinduism, and to teach him ancient Sanskrit literature. Jawaharlal later admitted he made no progress in it.

The boy was much more influenced by another tutor, Ferdinand T. Brooks, half-Irish, half-French, who introduced him to all the best boys' books of the West and to adult books and gave him a love of reading which lasted all his life. Together, tutor and student fixed up a small science laboratory in Anand Bhawan and worked on scientific experiments. Jawaharlal became so interested in science that when he later went to the university he specialized in it.

In religion Mr. Brooks was a theosophist. This was a religion started in the nineteenth century by a Russian woman, Madame Elena Petrovna Blavatsky (1831–91), who claimed she had been in communication with the spirits of certain Hindu religious teachers of past centuries who had revealed to her esoteric truths, always to be withheld from all but the chosen few deemed sufficiently developed spiritually for initiation into this hidden wisdom. Theosophists carried on "scientific" research regarding the possibility of mental telepathy and also of communication with higher spirits inhabiting an "astral" or supersensible plane. At the same time, they had a high regard for the sacred texts of Hinduism and helped restore the confidence of educated Hindus in their Hindu heritage—a confidence that had faltered under the first impact of Western thought.

Through Mr. Brooks, not through his Hindu Brahman teacher, Jawaharlal learned a little about the ancient religions of his country. The center of theosophy was in India and one of its great leaders was a dynamic Irish woman, Mrs. Annie Besant, a close friend of the Nehru family. She had adopted India as her home and plunged vigorously into various movements to improve Indian education and social conditions.

Under the influence of his tutor and Mrs. Besant, Jawaharlal became a theosophist for a short time. But after the tutor left, he gradually lost interest in theosophy and he never again adopted any religion. Throughout his life his attitude toward religion was very much that of his father. Although he had a high regard for some of the great religious leaders of history, especially for the Buddha, he himself was an agnostic.

In 1904, when Jawaharlal was fifteen, Motilal took him, his mother, and his baby sister, then age four, to England. Jawaharlal was put in one of the best English schools, Harrow, where he spent two years. His father went back to India with the rest of the family and wrote his son long letters full of love and pride in him. He urged the boy to try to be a general favorite, to make as many friends as possible, and to spend as much money as he needed for the purpose.

Jawaharlal took up cricket, the most important sport of the school, but by nature he was not the outgoing type that his father was. He read more books and newspapers than his fellow students and he often found these boys dull. They could talk about nothing but games, while he had already become interested in politics and world events.

Especially interesting to him was the fact that little Japan in 1905 defeated the great nation of Russia in a war that had begun in February, 1904. Asians had been so impressed by the tremendous colonial expansion of European nations in the eighteenth and nineteenth centuries and by their growing industrialization that they had come to believe that an Asian nation could never defeat a European one. The news of the Japanese victory delighted Jawaharlal. Years later, in a letter to his daughter, he wrote that the victory of Japan had a far-reaching effect on all the countries of Asia, that every boy, girl, and adult in Asia was excited that a great European power could be defeated by a small Asian nation. From then on nationalism spread more rapidly and the slogan "Asia for Asiatics" was frequently used.[1]

The years 1905–7 were full of activity in the Indian nationalist movement partly for this reason and partly because the British viceroy, Lord Curzon, had taken the unpopular step of dividing in two the important province of Bengal, where nationalist feeling was especially strong. The viceroy claimed he did so to promote administrative efficiency, since the undivided province had been large and unwieldy. Nationalists, however, saw the step as an attempt somehow to weaken their strength.

The chief nationalist organization was the Indian National

Congress which had been formed in 1885. Thereafter, it had held a session annually in one city or another, usually in December. Year after year it had adopted dignified moderate resolutions, professing loyalty to the British throne, but asking for certain reforms: the spread of education, wider employment of Indians and at higher levels in the government services, and the transformation of the Viceroy's Council and the provincial councils into bodies representative of Indians.

As it gradually became clear that the British government would not act on these politely worded resolutions, there developed within the Congress an extremist wing convinced that more vigorous action was needed if reforms were ever to be won. The leader of the Extremists was Bal Gangadhar Tilak, a Maharashtrian from western India. Tilak tried to heighten nationalist feelings by an appeal to Hindu religious sentiment and by recalling the glories of the past. He popularized an annual religious festival to celebrate the Hindu god of good beginnings, the elephant-headed Ganesh, and a new festival to celebrate the deeds of Shivaji, a Maratha hero of the seventeenth century who had laid the foundations for their political power in western India which had been ended by the British only in 1818.

Tilak's religious revivalism, his glorification of the Indian past, and his lack of interest in social reform or the reform of Hinduism from within was in marked contrast to the current of thought which had derived from Ram Mohun Roy and which was in the ascendancy among educated Indians until Tilak reacted against it.

To believe that one's own people are inferior to another people is never comfortable. Yet this had seemed implicit in the teaching of Ram Mohun Roy. Therefore, Indians listened eagerly when Tilak told them they were not inferior to the British and should have *swaraj,* or self-rule, as soon as they could win it, without waiting to learn more from their foreign rulers. Tilak urged Indians to fight hard for *swaraj* and have courage even if they were repressed, as they certainly would be.

Tilak made such vigorous anti-British speeches that several of his followers assassinated British officials. He was imprisoned in 1897 for eighteen months for advocating violence against the government.

In 1905, after the partition of Bengal, political excitement was sufficiently great to induce Motilal again to attend the Congress sessions. Up until that time, he had been so busy with his legal practice that he had attended only one session, that held in Allahabad in 1891 when he had been the Secretary of the Reception Committee. In 1905, the Extremists within Congress demanded not only *swaraj,* but also *swadeshi,* the purchase of goods made in India only. The resolutions they sponsored were not adopted, however.

All over the country, outside of the Indian National Congress, secret societies were formed which believed in revolution. British officials were murdered, bombs were thrown, and other acts of violence were committed. The British retaliated by jailing or deporting agitators without court trial, suspending freedom of the press, and placing severe restrictions on the holding of public meetings.

The British essayist, Thomas Babington Macaulay, who had served the East India Company for four years in India during the 1830's, had predicted that a time would come "when the public mind of India may expand till it has outgrown our system."[2] Now that the public mind of India was reaching that point of development, the British were by no means ready for the change.

In the Congress session of 1906, the Extremists succeeded in pushing through for the first time a motion endorsing *swaraj,* but the next year they were definitely outvoted and driven out of the Congress. Shortly afterward, the government imprisoned Tilak again, this time for six years. So many

other Extremist leaders were also imprisoned that their movement seemed permanently crushed. But they had greatly stirred
young Jawaharlal, far away in England. Writing later of those
years, he said: "Nationalist ideas filled my mind. I mused of
Indian freedom and Asiatic freedom from the thralldom of
Europe. I dreamed of brave deeds, of how, sword in hand, I
would fight for India and help in freeing her."[3] In 1907, as a
result of the Indian unrest of the past three years, the British
promised soon to announce reforms in their way of governing
India.

That year in July, Jawaharlal left Harrow where he had
done reasonably well in his studies, and entered Trinity College, Cambridge, in the autumn just before his eighteenth
birthday. There he spent three pleasant, quiet years, studying
science, reading widely in many other fields, and discussing
many subjects with all sorts of people late into the night. He
usually spent his vacations touring Europe.

The details of the reforms which the British had promised
the Indians were made public in August, 1909. The changes
were disappointingly small. For the first time one Indian representative was added to the Council that advised the viceroy,
and Indian representation on the provincial councils was increased. These councils still remained only advisory, however. All true authority, both to make laws and to administer
the country, was carefully retained in British hands. The
British viceroy could still rule as autocratically as he pleased,
ignoring what the councils might say.

Now even Motilal wondered if the British would ever give
Indians much power over the government of India, unless
forced to do so. But how, on the other hand, could Indians
win power in their own country by force? The British had the
police, the army, the jails. They would punish anyone who
even spoke of using force. This realization kept Motilal a

Moderate. Jawaharlal, likewise, did not see how force could succeed in the face of British repression, but he was so angry at British policy that he remained an Extremist.

In the next elections, Motilal was elected to the Provincial Council of the U.P., where he criticized government policies eloquently and fearlessly. Unfortunately words could have no effect.

After a trip to Ireland in 1910 to see the Irish independence movement, Jawaharlal wrote his father that the policy of the Irish was not to beg for favors, but to "wrest them" from the British. He criticized his father for not doing the same in India, for being "immoderately Moderate." Motilal was not the person to accept such talk from a son. He wrote back icily, "I do not approve of opinions expressed by you, but boys must be boys."[4]

That autumn Jawaharlal began studying law in London, having finished his three years in Cambridge. In his autobiography, he implies that this was his father's decision. Previously there had been some thought of his taking the examination for entrance into the Indian Civil Service, the I.C.S., the elite corps which filled the top offices of the Indian government. Until recently the I.C.S. had been the monopoly of the British, but now a few Indians were admitted to it if they did well in the competitive examination. Jawaharlal felt there was glamour about the I.C.S.[5] His father, however, did not want him to join the government since this would probably have meant that he would be stationed in places far from Allahabad. It seems to have been for this reason that Jawaharlal studied law instead. If he had joined the I.C.S., he would have been expected to help suppress Indian nationalism. This does not seem to have occurred to Jawaharlal at the time.

In London, Jawaharlal came in contact with various political movements of the day, and he was especially influenced by the British socialists who believed that government ownership of the means of production, especially of factories, would raise the living conditions of the poorer people. The socialists expected the profits of industry to go to the government, hence to the people. And they believed that the government could be counted on not to "exploit" workers as they believed private industry did.

Since then, of course, it has become clear that the poorer people do not always benefit by government ownership. Often government-controlled factories are far less efficient than private enterprise and when there are no profits, obviously nobody benefits.

Whatever the practical advantages or disadvantages of socialism, Jawaharlal was definitely influenced by it. He had not had a chance to see its practical effects. He passionately wanted the standard of living in India to be raised, and he saw that socialists showed more concern about the welfare of the poor than did their critics. Unlike some socialists, however, he thought socialism ought to come by gradual change rather than by revolution.

Jawaharlal was "called to the bar" in 1912; he had passed his law examinations and finished all the training needed to become a lawyer. And so at age twenty-three, he went back to India. That year he attended the Congress session but disliked the atmosphere of the meeting. He found it chiefly a social gathering of upper-class Westernized Indians, dressed in the most formal British morning coats and well-pressed trousers. There was no tension or excitement. With the Extremist leaders in jail and the Moderates discouraged, Indian nationalism at the time was in a quiet state.

Violence had not come to an end, however. In the previous two years, many English or pro-English officials had been killed, but the more often these murders occurred, the more the government restricted freedom of speech and assembly and arrested agitators.

Disappointed by what he saw of the Indian National Congress, Jawaharlal went back to Allahabad and began practicing law. At this time, he was not happy with his life. He had no interest in legal matters and felt he was being swallowed up in dull routine.

Besides practicing law, Jawaharlal did something in 1913 which, without his knowledge then, was oddly prophetic. He raised money to help the work being done by a man twenty years older than he whom he had not yet met, but who was later to play a decisive role in his life. This was Mohandas K. Gandhi, later called the "Mahatma," or "great soul."

In 1913, Gandhi was leading a movement for the improvement of the conditions of Indians living in South Africa, where many had migrated in the nineteenth century. A few were in business there, but the majority worked as laborers on sugar, tea, or coffee plantations. For most of them, South Africa was their permanent home, yet they suffered great discrimination.

Gandhi had first gone to South Africa in 1893 as a lawyer, to work on one particular law case only. He had expected to stay briefly. But when he saw the discrimination against Indians, he decided to remain longer. He began holding meetings of Indians to urge them to work together and to correct any bad habits, such as lack of cleanliness, that might give the white people even the smallest excuse for treating them badly. He called on them to forget the religious and caste differences that separated them into many little groups incapable of uniting for common action. Together they must be willing to suffer great sacrifices in order to protest discriminatory laws. These laws differed in the various parts of South Africa. Some cities even forbade Indians walking on the sidewalk. In most places they were not allowed to own land and were denied voting rights. By his organizing and speech-making, Gandhi prepared the Indians for a struggle against discrimination. He persuaded his followers to disobey laws which discriminated against them, and not to resist when the police arrested them.

The South African government passed legislation requiring Indians to go to a government office to register. The law also required them to keep their registration certificates with them wherever they went, in order that the government might keep close track of all Indians. It was a highly discriminatory measure. Gandhi persuaded his followers not to register, and he urged those who had already done so to throw away their registration certificates. He and many other Indians were imprisoned for violation of the registration law.

While in prison, Gandhi read the famous essay on "Civil Disobedience" by Henry David Thoreau. Thoreau, a resident of Massachusetts, had published this essay in 1849 in protest against Negro slavery in the United States. In it, he said he was convinced that if even a single honest man disobeyed laws and refused to pay taxes in protest against slavery, this would lead to the abolition of slavery in America. He wrote, "It matters not how small the beginning may seem to be: what is once done well is done forever."[6] Thoreau himself was imprisoned for nonpayment of taxes. This essay strengthened Gandhi's own belief in nonviolent civil disobedience.

Another South African law forbade Indians from outside the province of the Transvaal to enter it. Gandhi gathered two thousand people to march into the Transvaal from the adjoining province of Natal. Most of the marchers were so poor that they had no shoes. They included many women carrying babies on their hips or backs. Barefoot though they were, they walked 160 miles in eight days. On November 6, 1913, they arrived at the boundary which the law forbade them to cross.

Faced with this large yet peaceful crowd, the frontier guards were perplexed. Not knowing what to do, they let them pass. Gandhi was soon jailed but the march went on without him. The civil rights marches of modern times in the United States trace back to this famous march. A number of civil rights leaders, especially Dr. Martin Luther King, have acknowledged how greatly they were influenced by Gandhi's ideas.

While Gandhi was in South Africa, Motilal and Jawaharlal had followed in the papers the stories of his campaign. It was to help this work that Jawaharlal raised money. But neither father nor son yet knew the kind of a man that Gandhi was, nor the new ideas of utter self-discipline that he had brought to Thoreau's old idea of civil disobedience. They could not foresee how closely they would later work with him.

# 4.

# A Marriage and a New Slogan

IN 1916 Jawaharlal was married. A young Indian of the time was expected to marry a person chosen by his parents after agreement with the parents of the other marriage partner. Jawaharlal's marriage was an "arranged" marriage of this kind.

The girl chosen was Kamala Kaul, a Kashmiri Brahman like the Nehrus. She was tall, slender, fair-skinned, and lovely. But she came of a far less Westernized family than did Nehru and was not so well educated. At first, he did not feel he had much in common with her, and the differences in their backgrounds bothered him. Later they grew much closer to each other; he came to love her deeply and felt guilty regarding his earlier attitude toward her. He wrote that she gave him strength but that he had probably treated her far too casually in their earlier years and that this had perhaps been harder for her to bear than a deliberate unkindness would have been.[1]

The bride and groom went to Kashmir for their honeymoon, a place he had always loved. He was drunk with its beauty,

48

intoxicated by the loveliness of "river and valley and lake and graceful trees." He also liked its other features, "of hard mountains and precipices, and snow-capped peaks and glaciers, and cruel and fierce torrents rushing down to the valleys below."[2]

On this trip he went with other young men to climb one of the high snow-covered mountains. During the climb, he fell down a deep crevass, but fortunately he was tied by a rope to the other men of the party. They pulled him back to safety.

The first child of Jawaharlal and Kamala and the only one to survive, a daughter whom they named Indira, was born in the autumn of 1917. The well-known Indian poetess, Sarojini Naidu, who first saw the child when she was six months old, said, "She was the proudest looking baby I have ever seen."[3] Perhaps already Indira was a determined character.

She was born at a time of great nationalist agitation in India. The atmosphere had once more become electric and would remain so for many years to come.

During 1916, Motilal had tried to make peace between the Hindus and the Muslims who had different ideas about the political goals for India. Motilal saw clearly that if progress toward self-government was to be made, these differences would have to be bridged. Indians of all religions would have to work together for the nationalist cause.

Although a quarter of the population of India were Muslims and thus formed a large, very powerful minority, they feared that if India were allowed to govern herself, Hindu rule was likely to take the place of British rule, since Hindus formed the majority. Some Muslims were afraid the Hindu majority would not treat the Muslims fairly. The Indian National Congress, on the other hand, did not believe that religion had anything to do with politics. While most of its members were Hindus, many Muslims had also joined it.

With encouragement from the British, a separate political organization for Muslims alone had been formed in 1906, the Muslim League. Some British rulers said quite frankly they felt they had a better chance of holding India if they stirred up feeling between the two religious groups, playing them off against each other. Theirs was the idea of "divide and rule."

In the reforms of 1909, furthermore, the British government had made special arrangements to ensure Muslims of representation on the newly enlarged government councils. It directed that a certain number of seats be set aside for Muslims; otherwise Muslims, as a permanent minority in much of the Indian subcontinent, would probably have been outvoted in so many districts that fewer Muslims would be elected to the councils than their proportion in the total Indian population would seem to justify. The British government also arranged for Muslims alone to vote in the elections to choose their representatives, so that Hindus would not have the chance to elect "tame Muslims" to fill the Muslim seats.

This system of "separate electorates" had angered members of the Indian National Congress. They felt that it undermined their efforts to keep religion out of politics and that Muslims should trust the Congress itself to elect Muslims and to protect the Muslim point of view.

Content with their privileged position under the British, various Muslim leaders frankly wanted Great Britain to rule India permanently.

It was this difference of approach that Motilal wanted to bridge. In 1916, he invited leaders of the Muslim League to meet with leaders of the Congress at his home. The great house was becoming a regular meeting place for political leaders. One of the men who came was Muhammad Ali Jinnah. Thirty years later, when Jawaharlal struggled in vain to prevent the partition of the subcontinent of India into two nations, Jinnah was his successful opponent and the father of Pakistan.

In 1916, Jinnah was both president of the Muslim League and a member of the Indian National Congress. At this time it was he who did most to patch up differences between the two organizations. An agreement was reached that the Muslim League would urge more self-government if the Congress, in return, would agree that there should always be separate electorates for Muslims. The agreement, known as the Lucknow Pact, also covered the form of government that both organizations would ask for, which was essentially a cabinet form of government like that of Great Britain, but with the provinces in a federal relationship to the central government.

While Motilal was concerning himself with the important problem of Hindu-Muslim unity, other exciting events had been taking place. In 1914 and 1915 a number of the Extremists finished their jail sentences. In 1916, Home Rule leagues were formed to urge that India be granted the degree of self-government that Canada and Australia already enjoyed. Many of their members were Hindus who had not bothered to join the Congress because they did not consider it sufficiently active; others were Muslims. Home Rule would mean a very great change: virtual independence within the British Empire. "Home Rule" was a new, exciting slogan. Jawaharlal joined the Home Rule Movement, as did many middle-class Indians previously inactive politically.

Motilal did not join at first, although his close friend, Mrs. Annie Besant, threw herself heart and soul into the new movement. Mrs. Besant was an elderly Irish woman who had made India her home. She was the kind of person who is always ready for a fight, always glad of a new cause. She toured India making rousing speeches for more self-confidence on the part of Indians. She urged them to remember the greatness of India's past and realize the possibility of an equally great future. She brought to the cause such energy, such eloquence, such drive and persuasion that it changed the entire atmosphere. She had such an impact on her audiences that the

British authorities decided to keep her from speaking. In June, 1917, they interned her. Internment is a mild form of imprisonment, providing the interned person with better surroundings and more comforts than a person in prison receives. Nevertheless, the internment of this gallant, elderly, white-haired Irish lady stirred Indians as nothing else had.

Many people believed that the British had been right in jailing the Extremists, since they had advocated violence. But Mrs. Besant had not done this. She had merely urged Indians to be more insistent in asking for self-government. All over the country people signed mammoth petitions demanding her release.

Like the members of the Home Rule leagues and many other Indians, Motilal was indignant. He announced that he would join the Home Rule Movement in protest against the arbitrary action of the government. He presided over a huge protest meeting in his own city and was elected president of the Allahabad branch of the Home Rule league. He also cabled the British Prime Minister, Lloyd George, pointing out that England, which had a high regard for law and order at home, was using illegal methods in the repression of India.

So great was the agitation resulting from Mrs. Besant's internment that she was soon released. In August, 1917, the British government also felt it necessary to announce a new policy. The British Secretary of State for India, Edwin S. Montagu, made a ringing declaration that the British purpose would be "the gradual development of self-governing institutions" in India. This sounded like what the Indians wanted.

But just as the earlier reforms of 1909 had proved disappointing when their details were announced, so did Montagu's promise when spelled out in 1918 in the proposed Montagu-Chelmsford Reforms. The Reforms increased the proportion of elected Indian members of the provincial legislatures so that Indians would now for the first time be in the majority, and they increased the degree of provincial self-government through a two-sided system known as dyarchy. On the one hand, the provincial legislatures were to be given the right to enact laws in such areas as education, agriculture, and health. On the other hand, more pivotal provincial matters such as finance, taxation, and control over the police were to remain in the control of the appointed British provincial governors and out of the reach of the Indian ministries or cabinets responsible to the legislatures. Few changes were to be made in the central government. More Indians were to be added to the central legislative Council, but the viceroy, who at the moment was Lord Chelmsford, was to remain supreme.

The authors of the Montagu-Chelmsford report, like most Englishmen of the time, believed that Indians were an inferior race who still needed long training before they could hope to master so high an art as self-government.

Disappointing as the Montagu-Chelmsford report was, an Indian member of the U.P. Council introduced a motion welcoming it. Motilal, who was also still a member of the Council, vigorously opposed this motion. He inquired why Indians should express gratitude when there was nothing to be grateful for. The tendency to do so, he said, showed how much like slaves Indians had become during the centuries of bureaucratic rule. He ridiculed those who said that India would have to learn very slowly how to govern itself. He said, "We cannot learn to walk unless you give us the opportunity to exercise the function. If we keep lying down all the time, then good-bye to all the benefits of the exercise."[4]

Not agreeing with him, of course, his old friends, the Moderates, welcomed the moderate reforms. That summer, they left the Indian National Congress and formed an organization of their own, the National Liberal Federation. After the departure of the Moderates, the Congress passed into the control of people who wanted Home Rule immediately, not in the far future.

The new reforms were not made into law by the British Parliament until December, 1919. Before then, events occurred that greatly changed the atmosphere in India and also the personal life of all three generations of Nehrus. In the first place, a new political leader, Mohandas K. Gandhi, entered the Indian scene with a completely new program and approach to life. Secondly, the British made several blunders. These enraged Indian nationalists so much that the reforms, when they came into operation, seemed insignificant in comparison.

# 5.

# New Leader, New Way of Life

MOHANDAS K. GANDHI had won a partial victory in his South African struggle in 1914. The government of South Africa offered to correct some of the wrongs that Indians had suffered, if he would call off his civil disobedience campaign. He agreed to do so. He left South Africa in 1914, took a brief trip to England, and arrived back in India in 1915. He had been away for over twenty-one years.

Although he was well known for his South African campaign, he did not immediately find a place for himself in Indian politics. He seemed odd to many Congress members. In South Africa, he had developed ideas of his own about simple living and self-discipline. He would eat only the simplest food, chiefly boiled, unseasoned vegetables and milk. Although he had once worn Western suits and high starched collars like other educated Indians, he soon adopted the kind of unsewn yardages of cloth worn by most of the Indian poor. He often wore nothing but a loincloth, though he might wrap a white shawl around his upper body if it were cold. A person dressed in this way must

55

have seemed an eccentric to the Congress politicians of the time. They still considered Western clothes the mark of an educated man and a leader.

Then, too, Gandhi was not impressive to look at. His body was skinny and bony, his legs were spindly, his ears stuck out and his mouth appeared crumpled-in because of loss of teeth. He had a warm and winning smile, but it revealed the great gaps between his few teeth. The loss of those teeth had been part of the price of his belief in nonviolence. He had met violence with nonviolence when it meant loss of teeth. He was ready to do so always, even if it meant loss of life itself.

Gandhi emphasized that nonviolence must not be of a passive type. He felt that people unjustly treated must not sit back and be resigned. They must constantly find ways of protesting injustice. Yet they must do so without allowing themselves to feel hate. He was convinced that hate even if controlled cannot help but damage a person's cause, and indeed inevitably hurts one's very self, one's soul.

He had been strongly influenced not only by Thoreau, but also by the Christian Sermon on the Mount and the Hindu *Bhagavad Gita,* or "Song of the Lord." He took seriously the Christian message of love. He believed that one's whole life must be based on love, that one must love even one's enemies. He was convinced that if one remained firm, patient, and at the same time understanding of the difficulties and point of view of one's adversary, that adversary could not fail to realize sooner or later his mistake and correct his ways.

Every day Gandhi read aloud from the *Bhagavad Gita,* which is often referred to simply as the *Gita,* or "Song." Over the course of time, so many people heard him read from it that it is worth saying more about it.

The *Gita* consists of a conversation supposedly held on the eve of battle between a warrior and the god Krishna, an incarnation of Vishnu. In it, Krishna explains that whatever is done must be done not for one's self, but as a duty, in a spirit of sacrifice to God, with detachment and without a feeling of personal stake in the results.

*Treating alike pleasure and pain, gain and loss, victory and defeat, then get ready for battle. Thus thou shalt not incur sin. . . .*

*He who abandons all desires and acts free from longing without any sense of mineness or egotism—he attains the peace.*[1]

Gandhi blended this emphasis on personal detachment with the emphasis on love which he took from the Sermon on the Mount.

In South Africa, Gandhi had discovered how hard it was to live a life of true love, how difficult it was to remain quietly, serenely detached and without fear or hate in the face of great provocation. He saw it was necessary to discipline himself constantly. This is why he had changed to the simplest way of life. He found it helpful never to touch alcohol or rich, highly seasoned food. He also found it helpful to go without meals altogether, from time to time, to fast for several days or even weeks at a stretch. He prayed constantly, not specifically to any of the personal Hindu gods but to a god of his own conception.

There were many other steps he took as part of his program of self-purification. He adopted handspinning as an aid to self-discipline. He made elaborate experiments to find which diet seemed most cleansing to his spirit and came to believe that goat's milk was of special value. He believed in the use of mud packs on his legs. He regularly set aside days for total silence, during which he would say nothing even if there were urgent matters requiring his attention. When Jawaharlal wrote that Gandhi had fads, it was doubtless practices such as these that he had in mind.[2] He was not the only one among Gandhi's followers who thought his fads were extreme, unnecessary, and even ridiculous.

As Gandhi saw it, religion and politics were not separate. To him, a political fight had to start with a moral victory within oneself. One must first achieve the love and detachment without which, he believed, nothing real could ever be accomplished. He called his entire system *satyagraha*. *Satya* is the Sanskrit word meaning truth, and *agraha* means firmness, or force. Sometimes *satyagraha* is translated "soul force." Gandhi himself once translated it as the "force of love."

It took a number of years before Indian politicians came to understand Gandhi's message. Meanwhile, they were puzzled by many things about him in addition to his odd clothing and odd ideas about nonviolence. As long as World War I lasted, Gandhi believed that Indians should not take advantage of England's difficulty by pressing the Home Rule Movement. Most other nationalists, on the other hand, thought that especially during the war, they would do well to make things as difficult as possible for the British.

After the end of the war, Indians hoped that the British would now become more liberal toward them. Because of the large role which the Indian army had played in France, Egypt, and on other battlefields during the war, the Indians had expected to be rewarded at its end. Instead, the British announced they would adopt new measures, known as the Rowlatt Bills. These would perpetuate the extraordinary repressive powers which the government had conferred on itself during the war, supposedly only as temporary measures to meet the war emergency. The Defence of India Act, during the war, had provided that people could be imprisoned without trial and without any of the ordinary legal procedures which English law in England had developed for the protection of accused persons. Under the Rowlatt Bills persons could be imprisoned on the mere suspicion that they might in the future act subversively, and again they would have no benefit of trials in ordinary courts of law, merely one-sided inquiries by official tribunals. Severe restriction on freedom of speech and of the press was to continue. This was to be the permanent, normal state of affairs. From London, the British Secretary of State for India, Edwin Montagu, tried to reassure Indians by telling them that these extreme measures would be used only in extreme cases—of anarchical or revolutionary movements. But of course the interpretation of when an extreme case existed was left in British hands alone.

Up until then, Gandhi had been merely watching Indian politics. Now he leaped into the struggle. He immediately urged everybody to join in a nonviolent *satyagraha* campaign against the Rowlatt Bills. People should not obey these laws, he said. They should print and publish and say whatever they wanted to, and go to jail gladly if this was the result. He argued that widespread nonviolent non-cooperation with the government would be the most effective form of protest.

As soon as Jawaharlal read about Gandhi's proposal, he felt afire with enthusiasm. Nonviolent non-cooperation seemed to him a way out of the impasse that India had been in: the dilemma between moderation which gained nothing and extremism which resulted only in more repression. He wanted to join the nonviolence movement immediately.

His father, however, was strongly opposed to the idea. Tension between father and son mounted, as did tension and conflict in Jawaharlal's own mind. He loved his father and did not want to defy him, yet he very much wanted to join Gandhi's movement. Motilal invited Gandhi to Allahabad to discuss the matter with him. After their talk, Gandhi advised Jawaharlal not to join the movement yet, while his father was so opposed to it. The son waited.

Soon Gandhi decided to ask for a nationwide *hartal,* or day of mourning, to protest the Rowlatt Bills. On April 6, 1919, the day which he set for the *hartal,* people all over the country stopped work. They held meetings and peaceful demonstrations against the hated laws.

Three days later, however, trouble occurred in Amritsar in the Punjab, the province lying north of New Delhi. The name "Punjab" means the "land of the five rivers." The rivers are tributaries of the southwestward-flowing Indus which is the second most important river of the Indian subcontinent, the first being the eastward-flowing Ganges. Most of the Punjab is a flat fertile plain, the chief wheat-growing area in India. The people of the Punjab are of stronger, sturdier build than most other Indians and tend to be fiery in temperament. The city of Amritsar is the holy city of the Sikh religion, a religion founded in the fifteenth century by a religious leader named Nanak, who wanted to bring together the best of Hinduism with the best of the Muslim religion.

On April 9, 1919, news spread through Amritsar that the police had arrested two prominent Congress leaders and were not permitting them even to communicate with their relatives. At this news, an angry crowd began to march toward the European quarter of the city, the Civil Lines, with the intention of demanding the release of their leaders. The police barred their way. In the scuffle that followed a few demonstrators were killed. Now more angry than ever, the crowd became a mob and took to violence and arson. Five Europeans were killed.

To repress what he considered likely to be a major uprising against British authority, Brigadier General E. H. Dyer, the British commander at Amritsar, proclaimed martial law and forbade processions and meetings. The official commission which later investigated his actions concluded that he did not give sufficient publicity to the order prohibiting meetings. He announced it orally in a few places to whatever groups surrounded him, and he distributed leaflets which illiterate Indians could not read. The inquiry commission estimated the order was probably unknown to about nine out of ten people in the city. On April 13, twenty thousand unarmed people gathered for a meeting in a vacant lot, many of them apparently without any realization that this was in violation of an order.

Then came the greatest British blunder. General Dyer marched an army detachment of about 150 men and two armored cars with machine guns to the scene. Without giving the crowd even a warning, he ordered the soldiers to fire at point-blank range. The people had no chance to escape. The lot was surrounded on three sides by the walls of neighboring houses, and the soldiers occupied the only opening. Even that opening was so narrow that the armored cars carrying Dyer's machine guns had not been able to pass through it. If they had done so, the slaughter would have been even worse. As it was, Dyer's Indian and Nepalese soldiers kept on firing until they ran out of ammunition, even though the crowd had done its best to disperse as soon as the first shot was fired. Some tried to scale the high surrounding walls. Some flattened themselves on the ground. But there was no cover. Even the official report finally admitted that the soldiers killed 379 people and wounded at least 1,500 more. Eight months later in the inquiry into this event, General Dyer frankly said that on his way to the place of meeting: "I had made up my mind that I would do all the men to death if they were going to continue the meeting. . . . I was going to punish them. My idea from the military point of view was to make a wide impression. . . . I wanted to reduce their morale. . . . The morale of the rebels."[3]

General Dyer followed up this terrible blood bath with further brutality. Convinced that he was faced with the danger of an uprising as serious as the one of 1857, he extended martial law to a number of other districts. He ordered villages to be machine-gunned and bombed from the air. He arrested and imprisoned hundreds of nationalist leaders and had many other Indians publicly flogged. He made it a crime for two Indians to walk abreast, and he even stopped a marriage ceremony, put the bridegroom in prison and ordered that the priest and the guests be flogged. He also issued a most degrading order: all Indians passing through a particular lane where one English woman had been killed should be required to crawl on all fours.

It is hard to believe that the British would act in this brutal, inhuman manner, so unlike the way they would have behaved in their own country. The explanation seems to be that they were overcome by fear, obsessed with the terrible memories of 1857, and furthermore, that their autocratic power in India had seriously affected them for the worse. It was with situations such as this in mind that the prominent British essayist and publicist, Lord Acton, wrote in a much quoted phrase, "All power corrupts, but absolute power corrupts absolutely."

It was some time before the press in England showed any awareness of what had happened at Amritsar. There was no correspondent of an English newspaper there and in any case the English papers tended to rely heavily on the version of events supplied to them by the British officials in India. These stressed the killing of the five Europeans on April 9–10, the continued threat to European lives and government property, and the seriousness of the "riots." The viceroy, Lord Chelmsford, said that India was in "open rebellion" against British rule and that he would continue to use the army to put down demonstrations wherever they occurred.[4] In an editorial on April 15, the *London Times* stated that the "passive resistance movement continues to lose its passive character." On April 22, the *Times* took the position that a "sinister organization" was plotting revolution.

Finally, more than a month after the terrible massacre, rumors of what had actually happened began to filter into Great Britain. By May 23 it was known that several hundred Indians had been killed at Amritsar. Opposition members of Parliament demanded an inquiry. On the floor of Parliament, Edwin

Montagu, as Secretary of State for India, resisted this demand at first, saying, "Let us talk of an inquiry when we have put the fire out."[5]

Then in July, the Indian poet Rabindranath Tagore, who had received the Nobel Prize for his poetry in 1913, and had been subsequently knighted by King George V, wrote a letter to the viceroy, Lord Chelmsford, which made headlines around the world. In his letter he said, "The enormity of the measures taken in the Punjab . . . [are] without parallel in the history of civilized governments." He explained that he was writing this letter to "give voice to the protests of the millions of my countrymen, surprised into a dumb anguish of terror. . . . Badges of honor make our shame glaring in their incongruous context of humiliation." Consequently he asked to be relieved of his knighthood.[6]

That such a distinguished Indian of world renown should thus support the "rioters" led many in Great Britain to suspect that the whole truth had not come through to them. Demands for an inquiry increased. Finally, in October, 1919, an inquiry commission was appointed, headed by Lord William Hunter, who had been solicitor general for Scotland. It was composed of five British members and three Indians.

This Amritsar massacre, the repression that followed it, and particularly the immediate callousness of the viceroy and other British officials in India regarding it, formed a major turning point in the nationalist movement. The effect all over India was electric. Many who had believed the British would grant them self-government in the course of time, now no longer trusted their rulers. Many Moderates urged more vigorous action. Motilal and Jawaharlal were both profoundly affected.

Motilal's wife had come from Lahore, the capital of the Punjab, and he had many friends there including some who had been imprisoned on the charge of "waging war against the King." Motilal especially wanted to defend in court one of his close friends so charged but was not allowed to enter the Punjab because it was under martial law. He protested vigorously by telegram to the British government of India, and to the British government in London.

This time Motilal's pressure on the government brought results. Martial law was withdrawn and he was allowed to go to Lahore. Without charging a fee, he defended not only his friend, but also many of the other accused persons. This made him both well known and popular, and brought him into the very thick of Congress politics.

Although the Hunter Commission was taking testimony in Delhi and in the Punjab in the autumn of 1919, the Congress decided that it would conduct a parallel inquiry of its own. So prominent had Motilal now become that he was appointed a member of it. Gandhi also was a member, and young Jawaharlal was assigned to help.

This marked the end of Jawaharlal's comfortable, purposeless life. He plunged into the Congress movement heart and soul. Seldom again did he have an idle moment. The three men went to the vacant lot where the shooting had taken place, examined it carefully, and listened to what the people of Amritsar had to say about the horrible incident. When the official Hunter Report was published in the spring of 1920, Indian nationalists were indignant at it. Although the report recited the facts of the massacre and criticized Dyer for not giving the crowd warning before he opened fire and for continuing to fire so long even though the crowd was trying to disperse, it took the position that he had acted out of a sense of duty. It condoned the brutal use of planes to bomb or machine-gun even small groups of peasants in their fields, on the ground that a dangerous conspiracy was afoot and that in the cases where planes were used, no other means were available to disperse conspirators and protect European lives.

The members of the Congress Inquiry Committee knew that

there was no conspiracy and that the actions taken by the British in the Punjab were completely unjustified. The Hunter Report led to one development, however, of which the Congress leaders heartily approved. The British army relieved General Dyer of his command, and stated that he should never again serve in India. A broken man, he retired from the army, was paralyzed by a stroke the next year, and died in 1927 after more than two thousand long motionless days in which to brood over what he had done.

Serving on the Congress Inquiry Committee, Motilal had a chance to see Gandhi at work day after day. He gained a great admiration for the Mahatma's clear-cut mind, his determined will, his moral earnestness and love of justice. He and others discovered that the religious turn in Gandhi's thinking did not cloud his sense of what was practical and of how best to get publicity for the movement. Like his son, Motilal became fond of Gandhi, and Gandhi of him.

Gandhi was eight years younger than Motilal and twenty years older than Jawaharlal. The three men formed an odd trio. Each was so different from each of the others that one might have expected their differences to split them apart.

Gandhi lived as simply as the poorest villager and seemed the very symbol of traditional India. Motilal, on the other hand, was a rich man, fond of luxury, and the very symbol of Westernization. He was an aristocrat not only by birth, but also by belief. It would never have occurred to him to copy the way of living of poor villagers, as Gandhi had done. For Gandhi, religion was so much the essence of life that it permeated all his thinking. Motilal, with his practical legal mind, considered many of Gandhi's politico-religious notions absurd.

Disagreeing with Gandhi in a different way, Jawaharlal believed that traditional India should be completely transformed and modernized in order to combat poverty. He thought religion tended to make people resigned and was therefore an obstacle to progress. He was also impatient with his father's relative conservatism. To the two older men, Jawaharlal seemed an impractical young idealist, often too much in a hurry. Especially after 1927, he was a radical whom both his father and Gandhi tried in vain to restrain.

These basic differences in point of view and temperament led to innumerable differences about tactics. The three men argued out the issues between them in private and debated them in public. Unable to convince the others, each sometimes went his separate way. Often they seemed on the verge of a definite break.

Still they remained bound to one another by the closest bonds of affection. It was soon well known that Jawaharlal was Gandhi's favorite disciple; this remained the case even when the disciple would not follow the master. All the while Jawaharlal continued to regard Gandhi as his teacher, even as his second father. He called him Bapu, father. Whenever he heard that Gandhi was ill or that his life was in danger he was in an agony of grief and worry.

The many descriptions of Gandhi which Jawaharlal later wrote convey clearly how strongly he was drawn by Gandhi's unique quality. He wrote: "This little man of poor physique had something of steel in him, something rocklike which did not yield to physical powers however great they might be."[7]

He said that although Gandhi was unimpressive looking, "there was a royalty and a kingliness in him which compelled a willing obeisance from others." He knew how to issue commands which had to be obeyed. Jawaharlal was caught by the spell of Gandhi's "calm deep eyes," and "his clear limpid voice" which "would purr its way into the heart and evoke an emotional response." He was impressed by the "utter sincerity of the man" and the impression he gave of tremendous inner reserves of power.[8]

The emotional bonds between Motilal and Jawaharlal, and

between Motilal and Gandhi, were equally strong. The letters between them which are full of arguments, are also full of love.

From 1919 on, in spite of their differences of opinion, these three men together were the chief leaders of the independence movement until Motilal's death. Thereafter the same disagreements, tension, and love continued between Gandhi and Jawaharlal. The struggle for independence was not simply a struggle against the British, but often at the same time a struggle within the team.

# 6.

# Jail for the First Time

IN DECEMBER, 1919, the annual session of the Congress was held in Amritsar as a tribute to those who had lost their lives there earlier in the year. Because of Motilal's work for the Punjab, he was quite naturally elected Congress president for the year. It was customary for Congress to rotate the presidency among those of its leaders who were most active.

Considering the events that had recently taken place in the Punjab, the tone of the meeting was mild. This was partly due to a gesture of conciliation made by the King of England just before the session started. It was also due to Gandhi's growing influence. He said to the members of the Congress that they should not return madness with madness, that if they returned madness with sanity, the whole situation would be theirs.

Gandhi urged the meeting to endorse his ideas of non-cooperation and *satyagraha*. But Congress was not yet ready to do so. Many members still found his program strange.

At the next meeting of Congress in September, 1920, Gandhi again pressed for the acceptance of his ideas. For the time being he asked that Congress adopt only a few specific forms of non-cooperation. The member should not use imported cloth or other imported items, he said. They should not vote in the elections which were to be held under the new Government of India Act, nor serve in the new legislative assemblies resulting from the Reforms of 1919. They should have nothing to do with government schools or colleges or with the British-controlled Indian law courts. He urged everyone to take up handspinning partly for self-discipline and partly to make India more independent of imported cloth. Indira has written that her very first memory is of the day when all over the country foreign clothes were burned in response to Gandhi's appeal:

> *I can still feel the excitement of the day and see the large terrace covered with piles of clothes—what rich materials, what lovely colours! What fun for a toddler to jump on, play hide and seek in the heaps of velvets and satins, silks and chiffons! That was the day too when I discovered my power over my parents. Everybody was going to the bonfire but I was considered too small and was being put to bed. I appealed to my grandfather, who then as always later, took my side. However I fell asleep almost as soon as we arrived, seeing only the burning wood being thrown on the mountain of clothes and the fire putting forth its first flickering testing tongue of flame.*[1]

In September, 1920, the Congress gave Gandhi's program its approval. A number of Congress leaders, including the head of the Muslim League, Muhammad Ali Jinnah, strongly objected. Jinnah resigned from the Congress at this time and never returned to it. Motilal, on the other hand, acquiesced in the decision, although it meant changing his entire way of life, a difficult thing to do for a man of his age. Although he was almost sixty at the time, he immediately resigned from the

U.P. Council, gave up his money-making legal practice, made his second daughter, Krishna, give up her job at the government school, sold his horses, carriages, dogs, valuable china and Venetian glass, his fine cellar of wines, champagne, and whiskey, and dismissed most of his servants. He laid aside his London-made suits. Over close-fitting white homespun trousers, he now wore a knee-length white homespun shirt. Jawaharlal, of course, also gave up his practice as a lawyer and wore homespun, too.

In the autumn of 1920, Motilal became a member of the Working Committee of the Congress, the small group of the Congress leaders who spent practically full time directing its affairs between the annual sessions. Motilal was also elected General Secretary of the Congress. The office of the Congress Committee was located in his own house and most of the Congress work fell on his shoulders. He had become such a public figure that it was difficult for him or his family any longer to have a private life. The great house was always full of Congress workers.

The entire atmosphere at the Congress meetings began to change. The delegates came dressed in homespun, and they were no longer only from the upper-middle classes. Gandhi had traveled widely throughout the country speaking to large crowds and as a consequence Congress was becoming a mass movement.

Throughout 1920 and 1921, Jawaharlal worked as hard as he could for the cause. He was completely absorbed in it. He formed new local branches of the Congress. He rounded up volunteers to picket shops that sold foreign cloth. He was so engrossed in his work that he later admitted he had almost forgotten even his family, his wife, and his daughter.

Even before the Congress adopted Gandhi's program of non-cooperation, Jawaharlal had been regarded by the police as a person to be watched. They were very worried, therefore, when May 10, 1920, was chosen as the date for the wedding of his sister, Swarup. May 10 was the anniversary of the outbreak of the great uprising of 1857. The British suspected that the wedding was being used as an excuse for assembling together on that significant date a large number of conspirators from all over India. Their fears seemed confirmed when Gandhi and the entire Congress Working Committee, who had quite naturally been invited to the wedding, began arriving in Allahabad. They were even more worried when thousands of peasants poured into the city in the hope of seeing Gandhi.

Many of the British left the city in fear for their lives, or sent their women and children away. The police ordered those who remained to carry their rifles with them whenever they went out. While the wedding and the wedding festivities went on, Anand Bhawan remained surrounded by the police and secret service men. Little did they understand Gandhi and his ideas!

Swarup was married to Ranjit Pandit, a handsome lawyer from the area in western India that is now the state of Gujarat. On marrying, she changed not only her last name, but also her own personal first name, becoming Mrs. Vijaya Lakshmi Pandit. Vijaya Lakshmi means victorious goddess. It was the name by which her husband's family chose to call her. Since she liked it also, she decided to adopt it herself.

Shortly after the wedding, an event took place which influenced Jawaharlal greatly. A group of peasants from a village fifty miles away from Allahabad walked to the city in order to protest their miserable conditions. Hearing about them, Jawaharlal went to see them. The peasants told him how badly they were being treated by their landlords. They were made to pay more than the law allowed, and if they did not pay, they were beaten and even ejected from their mud huts and their land.

The peasants begged Jawaharlal to go with them and see

their living conditions. He agreed to do so. No car could travel over the rough land which had to be crossed in order to reach their village. He had to go much of the way on foot. It was the hottest time of the year, but Jawaharlal was so interested in what the peasants showed him and told him that he scarcely noticed the scorching sun. Because the police already considered him a possible conspirator, several policemen trailed him. With impish delight, he discovered he could out-walk them.

For three days, he went from village to village, eating with the peasants, living in their mud huts, and talking to them for hours. Wherever he went peasants poured out across the fields from the neighboring villages to hear him. Until then he had been afraid of speaking in public, but with these peasants he suddenly found that he could talk. He simply told them whatever he had in his mind, in a conversational and personal way. They responded with gratitude that he had taken this interest in them.

On this, the first of his many trips to the Indian countryside, he realized acutely how cut off he had been from the vast mass of his fellow Indians. On this occasion, he had a chance to see at first hand both how the peasants lived and the nature of the land system of India under which they suffered. He saw the skimpy meals that were all they could afford to eat. He saw how hard the village women worked to carry home on their heads jar upon jar of water from the village well. He came to understand that a large part of Indian agricultural land was held in enormous parcels by relatively few *zamindars,* who were a cross between landlords and tax-collectors.

Jawaharlal saw that the peasants whom he visited in the U.P. were being made to pay as much as could be squeezed out of them. Thus those who did the actual plowing, sowing, and reaping always faced the danger of eviction, and had, therefore, no incentive to improve the land they cultivated. What was perhaps worse, there were often many "intermediaries" between the peasant and the *zamindar*. The *zamindar* might rent land to a person who had no intention to cultivate, who in turn might rent it to another such person, and so on down, until finally someone would rent it either to an actual cultivator or to a person who at least supervised its cultivation by hired landless laborers. The result of this was that several people tended to make their living idly off the work done by the cultivator, and the latter's income was correspondingly decreased.

Jawaharlal also learned at this time how heavily the peasants were burdened with debt, how desperately they needed more credit which they could not secure except by the payment of interest rates that might range as high as 40 per cent per year.

This first encounter with village India made a profound impact on young Nehru. Seeing the misery, poverty, and hunger of the villagers, he felt ashamed of his own easygoing, comfortable life, and he realized with a shock to what an extent the politics in which he had been involved in the cities ignored the vast multitudes of rural India. At the same time, he was deeply moved by the gratitude of the peasants that he had been willing to come and by their childlike faith that he could do something about their plight. It filled him with a new and frightening sense of responsibility.[2]

He went back to the villages for more and more visits. From his contacts with the peasants, Nehru saw that economic and social improvement was fully as important as political freedom. He was one of the first nationalists to stress this point.

Toward the end of 1921, the Prince of Wales, heir to the British throne, went to India on what was intended as a goodwill tour. On Gandhi's urging, the Congress decided to organize demonstrations against British rule wherever the Prince went. The government was worried and afraid. It decided to strike hard at the Indian National Congress. In the next few months thirty thousand members of the Congress were arrested. The total membership of the Congress at the time seems to have been several hundred thousand. On the evening of December 7, 1921, an Indian police officer came to arrest the two Nehrus. The officer was nervous: it must have seemed to him odd to be arresting such a distinguished, well-known man as Motilal who was known to be a personal friend even of the exalted governor of the U.P. himself. It took the policeman some while to screw up courage to say that he was going to arrest them. First he only said he had orders to search the house. Motilal's great laugh boomed out. "To search this house well would take you six months," he said. [3]

While Motilal's trial took place, he held his four-year-old granddaughter, Indira, on his lap. It does not seem to have occurred to him that it might be hard on a child to see her grandfather condemned to a jail sentence. Because of the non-cooperation pledge, neither he nor his son made any attempt to defend themselves, and each was sentenced to six months in prison.

When they were gone, little Indira must have found it difficult to understand why her grandfather and father could no longer be at home. She must have worried to see how distressed were her mother and grandmother. As Krishna Nehru later wrote, for the women in the family "this was the beginning of a new life, a life of uncertainty, of sacrifice, of heartache and of sorrow." [4] To make matters worse, the police soon came and took away furniture and rugs and other valuables in place of fines which the Nehrus had not paid. Small Indira protested violently.

She was an exceptionally lonely child. One writer has said that "loneliness colored her future views even more than anything the police did. . . . She herself has no recollection of playing with children, although she later married one boy who sometimes came to Anand Bhawan." [5]

Shortly after the two men had gone to jail, Gandhi invited the women of the family to visit him at his *ashram* or religious center at Sabarmati, across the river from the important city of Ahmedabad. The annual Congress session was to be held that December in Ahmedabad, and Gandhi thought that Swarup Rani, Kamala, and Jawaharlal's younger sister, Krishna, might like to attend. Taking with them Indira and some female cousins whose husbands were also in jail, they started out, traveling for the first time in a third-class railway compartment which was far less comfortable than the first-class compartments which the Nehrus had used as a matter of course during their affluent days. At Sabarmati they stayed in a "sort of hostel for students, very bare and unadorned and not too comfortable."[6] Only Motilal's wife had a room to herself; the other women and the child had to sleep on the floor in one room all together. Gandhi required them to get up at 4 A.M., in the December cold, to attend morning prayers. After prayers they had to wash their own clothes, which was hard to do since the handwoven cloth they now wore was coarse and thick. They stayed at the *ashram* for two weeks.

In the speeches she has made as an adult, Indira has referred repeatedly to the Mahatma, his leadership and the sense of mission which he instilled. Clearly, she was both influenced by him and deeply fond of him. She has written, "As a very small child, I regarded him not as a great leader but more as an elder of the family to whom I went with difficulties and problems, which he treated with the grave seriousness which was due to the large-eyed and solemn child I was."[7]

While her grandfather and father were in prison, a relative brought Indira a dress from Paris. She liked it very much. Her mother reminded her that the members of Congress had pledged themselves not to wear or use anything imported, but told Indira that she could decide for herself whether to wear the dress. She decided not to. Her mother remarked that her favorite doll had also come from abroad. The choice was

harder. Writing of the incident many years later, she said:
"I was passionately fond of the doll. I could not think of it,
or indeed of anything, as lifeless. Everything was given a name
and immediately developed its own personality. The doll was
my friend, my child."[8]

She brooded over the problem for days, lost her appetite,
and could not sleep. Her mother thought she was sick. Finally
she reached her decision. Quivering with tension, she took the
doll to the roof-terrace of the house and set fire to it, then cried
as though the tears would never stop.

After that she worked even harder for the *satyagraha* movement, organizing her remaining dolls into anti-British demonstrations and giving the servants of Anand Bhawan lectures in
which she strung together the various phrases about the
movement that she had learned from her elders.

One day, when Jawaharlal was allowed visitors, his wife
brought Indira to see him. With a shock, he saw immediately
that the child was pale and weak. Small wonder. She had been
through experiences which few young children have to face.
Although she herself could not yet read, he wrote her a little
letter: "To dear Indu, love from her Bapu. You must get well
quickly, learn to write letters and come and see me in gaol.
I am longing to see you. Have you tried the new spinning
wheel which Dadu [grandfather] has brought for you? Send
me some of your yarn. Do you join your mother in prayers
every day?"[9] "Indu," which means "moon," was his pet name
for her. Her middle name, Priyardarshini, means "dear to
the sight." In another letter to her from prison some years
later, her father said that she was indeed "dear to the sight,"
that he felt this especially when the sight of her was denied
him.

On their first trip to jail, Motilal and his son were treated
fairly well. They and two cousins were housed in a small shed
about twenty feet by sixteen. They had freedom to move about

from one prison building to another and to talk to the other prisoners.

Jawaharlal was released in March, 1922, but arrested again six weeks later on the charge of picketing stores that sold foreign cloth. This time jail rules were much stricter. His letters to people at home and his visits from them were now restricted to once a month. He could receive a few books from outside but he had to return them before he could receive others.

Motilal was to go to jail once more before his death; Jawaharlal seven more times. This meant nine imprisonments for the son altogether, totaling about nine years in the very prime of his life.[10] Such confinement would have broken the spirits of many men, but Jawaharlal managed to turn his years in jail to good purpose.

Neither he nor his father, however, found jail life easy. Their cells were tiny and damp, their food was so poor they could hardly swallow it, and they were bothered by insects of various kinds. Also they were homesick and missed their families very much. Jawaharlal later wrote: "One misses many things in prison, but perhaps most of all, one misses the sound of women's voices and children's laughter."[11] Prison life made him nervous and tended to undermine his health. Sometimes he ran a temperature for months at a time. Usually he lost weight.

To try to keep his body, mind, and spirits in good condition, he worked out a regular schedule in which exercise, manual work, reading, writing, and relaxation each had its place. When he was allowed to do so, he ran every day around the prison courtyard. The distance he covered per day often added up to as much as two miles. He also did a few exercises of the Indian system of body training known as *yoga*. One of these was to stand on his head for a few minutes every day. Even after he was out of jail he kept doing this until the last years of his life.

Jawaharlal liked doing the manual chores that had to be done in prison, such as washing his own clothes and cleaning his cell. Until recently he had been waited upon by an army of servants, but in prison he found these simple chores helpful for his morale. He also took good care of any fellow prisoner who was sick. Several have written how gentle, thoughtful, and patient he was as a nurse.

Jawaharlal made careful plans for keeping his mind occupied also. He read systematically and he wrote abundantly and well. He read the history of many peoples intensively, and the great literature not of one country but of many. From all this reading, he gathered so much information and so many ideas that he finally had to pour out his accumulated inner wealth through writing books. In his fifth, sixth, seventh, and ninth jail sentences, he wrote three of the greatest books of twentieth-century Indian literature. His style was always vivid and lively. He had a fresh new viewpoint on any subject he touched. In every way, he towered over contemporary Indian writers of nonfiction. If he had not become famous as a prime minister, he would still be remembered as a distinguished author.

In February, 1922, while father and son were in jail together, they heard with delight that Gandhi had decided to enlarge the *satyagraha* campaign by calling for mass civil disobedience. But soon after the campaign started, they heard very different news—Gandhi had called it off. The peasants in a remote little village had grown excited and attacked and burned a police station. Gandhi took this as a sign that the country was not yet ready to use mass civil disobedience, that the people must first be disciplined—by more handspinning.

When Motilal heard about this, he was furious. Handspinning of all things! This struck him as ridiculous. Jawaharlal was plunged in despair. If civil disobedience had to be ended just because there was violence in one small area, how could it ever succeed? Surely the British authorities would always be able to provoke violence somewhere. He wrote Gandhi an angry letter. Gandhi wrote back in soothing tones that the cause would certainly prosper by this temporary retreat. Jawaharlal was not convinced.

Beside the Nehrus, many members of Congress were angry and discouraged when they heard that the struggle had been stopped at a time when it seemed to be moving ahead so well. The British, of course, were relieved. The writings of British officials show how worried many of them had been that Gandhi could really force the British to give the nationalists major concessions. Up to this point, the police had not arrested Gandhi. They had felt it might be dangerous to do so, but now that civil disobedience was ended, they arrested him and sentenced him to six years in prison.

When Jawaharlal's second term in prison ended in January, 1923, he found that the old spirit of excitement had completely gone. Gandhi was still in jail. He himself felt none of the enthusiasm for the non-cooperation movement that he had felt in 1920–21.

Motilal meanwhile had begun practicing law again on a part-time basis to pay the family bills, although he spent most of his time on politics. His son talked to him about his earning money, too, but Motilal would not hear of it.

With Gandhi in jail and the *satyagraha* movement called off, Congress began to split into factions. New friction soon broke out between Hindus and Muslims also. It was a most discouraging period. Now that no active program was afoot, Motilal and a few others decided it was time to join the legislatures. Since the Congress was opposed to this, they formed a new party which they called the Swaraj (Self-Rule) party. Motilal was its chief organizer. Elections were held in 1923. The Swaraj party did well at the polls. It won 42 out of 101 elective seats in the Central Legislative Assembly which had taken the place of the old Viceroy's Council, and it won many seats in the provincial legislatures also. Motilal was elected to the Central Legislative Assembly and was chosen as the Swaraj party leader there.

About this time, parenthetically, Jawaharlal had his third experience of jail. It was brief, but in some ways it was the most unpleasant of all. His cell was small and damp. He had to sleep on the floor, and now and then he woke up realizing with horror that a rat or a mouse had just run over his face. Although he was soon released, he had contracted typhoid fever from the unsanitary conditions of his cell. He was quite sick for a number of weeks.

At the end of 1923, Jawaharlal was elected general secretary of the Congress. He was later re-elected for several more terms. His father had held this position before him. This was the first of the many occasions when a younger Nehru followed in the father's footsteps.

From 1923 to 1929, Motilal continued to serve as a member of the Central Legislative Assembly. Even high British officials regarded him as an outstanding member of it. One of them commented on his "impressive face, deeply-lined and careworn on which character and intellect were so deeply imprinted." This British official also said of Motilal that he had a most dynamic personality, that he was outstanding whether as a lawyer, a speaker, or a political leader, and that he could not fail to make a profound impact on people around him wherever he was.[12] In 1924, ten days after the Central Legislative Assembly met for the first time, Motilal introduced in it a resolution asking that a Round Table Conference be called together, composed of representative Indians. This Conference, he said, should draw up a new constitution for India. The Legislative Assembly approved Motilal's resolution by a vote of 66 to 48, but the British did not consider such a resolution binding on them. A government spokesman said that, instead, the British government would send out a Royal Commission to India in 1929 to decide for itself what new changes should be made.

In 1924, Gandhi, who was still in prison, had an emergency operation for appendicitis. Then the government quickly released him for fear that he might die on their hands. When he was well enough to talk again with his friends, Motilal went to see him. The two men argued hard about Motilal's membership in the Legislative Assembly. Gandhi regarded it as spiritually wrong to have anything to do with the Assembly. Motilal could not agree.

Gandhi was due to be President of the Congress session to be held in December, 1924. He found that so many people shared Motilal's point of view, rather than his own, that he wrote Motilal that he thought he should not accept the presidency, that he should retire from the Congress. But Motilal wrote back, "I for one will be no party to an agreement which is based upon your retirement from the Congress. . . . Your retirement goes against my very soul."[13] The two men reached an agreement to prevent an open clash on the conference floor between those who believed in serving on the government councils and those who did not.

That year, Indira, age six, went to a real school for the first time, to St. Cecilia's School in Allahabad, a private school, therefore not included among those which Gandhi had asked his followers to boycott. Soon after she learned to read, she tried to teach the illiterate gardener of Anand Bhawan how to read also but with no success.

Indira never had a chance to stay long in any single school. Prison terms, foreign travel, and illness at home led to frequent shifts. She has said she finds it difficult to keep straight all the schools she attended. But if her schooling was jumpy and disjointed, she nevertheless had one great advantage—a father who always regarded himself as her personal tutor. If he was in jail or away from her for some other reason, he wrote her long letters telling her in a warm personal way of the many things he wanted her to know and the many ideas he wanted to share with her.

# 7.

# European Interlude

TOWARD THE END OF 1925, Jawaharlal's wife, Kamala, fell ill. Finding that she had tuberculosis, the doctor suggested she be taken to Switzerland, where the climate would help her. She and Jawaharlal sailed for Europe in March, 1926, taking eight-year-old Indira with them.

They went first to Geneva, Switzerland, where they rented a three-room apartment and put Indira in a Swiss school. Jawaharlal's younger sister, Krishna, came from India to help keep house.

At that time, Geneva seemed to many the capital of the world. The League of Nations had its headquarters there. In 1926, it was still a new organization, from which people expected far more than it was able to perform. The leading statesmen of many nations attended the sessions at the League and prominent people of Europe and the Americas went to Geneva to see the League in action.

Many of these distinguished people—authors, professors, and scientists, as well as statesmen—gave a lecture or two at the Geneva School for International Studies, an unusual school held there in the summers. With such lecturers, the school quite naturally attracted students from all over the world. Jawaharlal and Krishna attended the lectures in the summer of 1926.

From then on, Jawaharlal saw clearly that nationalism by itself was a "narrow and insufficient creed," that all the nations of the world are interdependent and must try to understand one another and work together in peace and harmony. His experience in Geneva aroused in him a keen interest in international relations. His understanding of world affairs came to be far greater than that of most Indians. Hence, it was natural that he soon came to be recognized by the Indian nationalists as their great authority on world affairs and that he should later shape the foreign policy of independent India almost single-handedly.

This visit of the Nehrus to Europe occurred at a time when many people were hopeful about the peace of the world. Germany was still governed by the conciliatory Weimar Republic. Even France seemed almost reconciled at last with her former enemy. In 1925, a group of security treaties, the Locarno Pacts, had been drawn up and ratified. They were designed to prevent future aggression by guaranteeing common action against it. Germany was then admitted to the League of Nations.

Hopeful as these developments seemed to many people, Nehru regarded the international situation as dangerous. He was particularly struck by the way in which England and all the other great powers except Germany, which was still disarmed, were building up their armed forces, and how impossible it apparently was for them to reach an agreement to end this arms race. He blamed England for this. In his autobiography there is no indication that at this time he had even heard of the man who, as it turned out, would destroy the peace of Europe in the next decade.

Hitler had already, in 1923, attempted to seize control of the government of Germany. He had failed, was taken prisoner, and put on trial for treason. For this offense the penalty was supposedly life imprisonment. At his trial, however, Hitler boldly argued that there was "no such thing as treason against the traitors of 1918" who had signed the armistice ending the First World War, leaving the way open for the humiliating Treaty of Versailles which the Allies then imposed on Germany. His eloquence saved him from a long imprisonment; he was jailed for only nine months. He spent these nine months writing his famous book, *Mein Kampf* ("My Struggle"), in which he openly urged a militant, aggressive policy for Germany and stated his own determination to shape it.

While the Nehru family were in Europe in 1926 and 1927, this book was still selling only at the rate of a few thousand copies a year. Hitler, though free again, was still largely unknown. The German people, prosperous for the time being, were not yet flocking to join his small band of supporters. No one yet foresaw the disastrous world economic depression of the early 1930's which was to give Hitler his chance and cause his book to become a fabulous best seller.

When Kamala was well enough for him to leave her, Jawaharlal went off on trips through Europe—visiting Italy, France, Germany, England, Belgium, and the Netherlands. He often took his sister Krishna with him. In February, 1927, he attended an anti-imperialist conference in Brussels. Known as the Congress of Oppressed Nationalities, it had been organized by a group of revolutionaries from lands which, like India, were then under foreign rule. Representatives had come to it from Asia, the Near East, and Africa.

At the conference, Jawaharlal made a vigorous speech telling of the ways in which he believed that British rule had harmed India. The British had overtaxed and impoverished

India, he said. They had uprooted India's traditional educational system. Above all, he charged that they had stirred up "communal" discord, between Hindus and Muslims. In India, "communalism" means an appeal to a religious group to consider itself a "community" inevitably opposed to other religious groups.

Just as his talks with the peasants in 1920 had given him new confidence, so too did this his first speech before an important international conference. He made such an impression on the conference that it paid him the honor of electing him to membership in the small executive committee of the new organization it established, the League Against Imperialism. He served on this committee briefly, but soon found that many of its members were communists too rigid in their doctrine for his liking. Friction resulted and he resigned.

He himself at the time was drawn to the ideas of Karl Marx, but he never became a communist and he was always critical of communist methods. He liked, however, the goal the communists theoretically worked for: greater equality among people and especially the improvement of the conditions of peasants and workers.

In India, while Jawaharlal was away, new elections to the legislative assemblies were held. To gain votes, many of the candidates used the crude appeal of religious communalism, and tensions between the Hindus and the Muslims reached a new peak. Motilal tried in vain to take religion out of politics. It was a lonely, thankless task. People accused him of being anti-Hindu, of plotting to legalize cow slaughter. He was shocked by the unscrupulous hatred-stirring slogans used by both Hindu and Muslim communalists.

After the elections, Motilal wanted to join his son in Europe. He was tired of his work in the Legislative Assembly, which seemed to bring no results, and disillusioned with Indian politics. But he stayed in Allahabad for a few months longer because he was building a new smaller house on the grounds of Anand Bhawan. Since the nephews had left and set up homes of their own, the old house had seemed too large, especially now that he no longer had his old enormous income. When the Nehrus later moved into the new house, Motilal gave it the same name as the old house, Anand Bhawan. He changed the name of the old house to Swaraj Bhawan, "House of Self-Rule." The office of the Congress movement continued to be in it. Motilal later gave the old house to the Congress.

It was September, 1927, when Motilal finally joined his son in Europe. Leaving Indira behind in her Swiss school, the family traveled through Italy, France, Britain, Germany, and finally visited Russia. They had been invited to attend the tenth anniversary of the founding of the Soviet Union, held in Moscow that November. They stayed in Moscow only three or four days. Jawaharlal was impressed by what they were shown, Motilal less so.

When Jawaharlal returned to India, he wrote a series of articles about the Soviet Union for one of India's leading newspapers, the *Hindu* of Madras. Later these were collected and published as a book entitled *Soviet Russia*. As he pointed out in this book, in these early years of the Soviet experiment, "all the world" was watching to see how the experiment would turn out. It was hard, he said, to feel indifferent toward Russia and harder still to judge her impartially. "She is today too much of a live wire to be touched without a violent reaction, and those who write about her can seldom avoid superlatives of praise or denunciation. . . . No one can deny the fascination of this strange Eurasian country of the hammer and sickle, where workers and peasants sit on the thrones of the mighty and upset the best-laid schemes of mice and men."[1]

Quite naturally he saw the Soviet experiment in the light of the bearing it might have on India's problems. He pointed out that India could not rely on her past glories to solve the problems of today. Indians would have to "venture forth along new avenues of thought and search for new methods." It seemed to him that Russia might help Indians find a solution for their own problems, particularly because conditions there were not "very dissimilar to conditions in India. Both are vast agricultural countries with only the beginning of industrialization, and both have to face poverty and illiteracy. If Russia finds a satisfactory solution for these our work in India is made easier. Russia again cannot be ignored by us, because she is our neighbor, a powerful neighbor, which may be friendly to us and cooperate with us, or may be a thorn in our side. In either event, we have to know her and understand her and shape our policy accordingly."[2]

The desire to learn from the best features of the Soviet experiment remained with him. The attitude toward the Soviet Union which he expressed in this book helps explain features of his later foreign policy which puzzled many Westerners.

Right after their trip to Moscow, Jawaharlal, Kamala, and Indira went back to India. Motilal stayed on in Europe a few months longer.

Jawaharlal went home refreshed and stimulated by his European experiences. His point of view had been broadened. He had acquired a new understanding of world events. He also had a new sense of urgency about the social and economic changes he believed should be made in India. He spoke with new conviction and maturity. He was no longer merely Gandhi's bright young follower. Now thirty-eight years old, he emerged as a leader in his own right.

# 8.

# Forward Again

IMMEDIATELY AFTER returning from Europe, Jawaharlal plunged straight into politics with new vigor and sureness. He had hardly had a chance to unpack his baggage when the annual session of Congress was held in December, 1927, in Madras. He not only attended it, but also spoke in such a way that the younger members of the Congress quickly recognized him as their natural leader.

He introduced a resolution asking for complete independence. This was the first time that the Congress had considered so drastic a change. The lesser change of Home Rule within the British Empire had seemed revolutionary only ten years before, but now the Congress approved Jawaharlal's resolution by a wide margin.

It also approved other resolutions which he introduced. One urged cooperation with the League Against Imperialism, another dealt with the danger of war which, as the resolution argued, was being increased by the war preparations carried out by the British government in India and the "Eastern seas," and by the war preparations of other countries as well. Jawaharlal strongly believed then, and was to continue to believe, that any war nowadays is an international disaster. He later wrote that he thought the members of Congress had not understood the full meaning of his resolutions. Certainly, as the following year was to indicate, many had not taken seriously his resolution on independence.

In addition to becoming Secretary of the Congress again, Jawaharlal at that time became President of the All-India Trade Union Congress. Before meetings of this organization he pressed his socialist ideas, for which he realized the Congress was not yet ready. He urged that not only imperialism should be abolished, but also capitalism and what he called "feudalism." He demanded "equality between man and man"[1] and said that the future of India lay with the peasantry.

At the time, Gandhi was concentrating chiefly on promoting handspinning and handweaving and on protesting the practice of untouchability. He traveled all over India to make his views known. Sometimes he went by rail, sometimes by motor car, but often on foot. Millions came to know him. A single meeting might draw a crowd of more than one hundred thousand. Many could not hear what he said. The crowds seemed satisfied, however, just to see the Mahatma. Since 1924, when Gandhi had seen clearly that most of the members of the Congress favored working with the government councils, he had kept out of politics so far as he could. Congress leaders still often consulted him, however.

Now Gandhi wrote to Jawaharlal, "You are going too fast."[2] For his part, Jawaharlal resented Gandhi's preoccupation with handspinning, which he regarded as a minor side issue. When Gandhi said that the poor were God's chosen people, Jawaharlal did not like it. He thought this was a glorification of poverty which would serve as an excuse for doing nothing about it. He could not persuade the Mahatma to favor socialism, which he thought of as the best way to attack the system which produced poverty. More than ever he disliked the way Gandhi mixed religion with politics. He thought there should be land reforms and other measures to equalize wealth. When he talked about this with Gandhi, the latter would only answer that the rich ought to regard their wealth as a trust held for the benefit of the poor. Jawaharlal felt this was completely unrealistic. He did not believe that rich people could ever be counted on to protect and help the poor. Gandhi considered that Jawaharlal was now in open warfare against his ideas, but that even this would not affect their personal relations.

Jawaharlal had done much to stir the Congress to new life. Unintentionally the British government helped him. When it sent to India in February, 1928 (a year earlier than had been originally planned), the promised Royal Commission to study whether changes should be made in the form of the Indian government, it made the blunder of including no Indians in the membership of the Commission which was composed of seven members of the British Parliament. Its chairman was Sir John Simon, described by the *New York Times* as "probably the most authoritative lawyer in the British Empire."[3]

Indian nationalists were infuriated that they themselves should still have no voice in deciding on their own constitution. Congress decided to boycott the Commission as did the moderate Liberal Federation. The Muslim League split over the issue; half of it, still following Jinnah's leadership, boycotted the Commission, the other half decided to cooperate with it.

As the Commission traveled around India, it was pursued by hostile crowds waving black flags and shouting "Simon, go back." The Congress helped organize demonstrations against it.

At this time the police began to assault demonstrators with heavy clubs. Congress members were not accustomed to this, but they stood their ground and received the damaging blows nonviolently.

When the Simon Commission came to Lucknow in the U.P., Jawaharlal took part in arranging a demonstration. One evening he and the men with him were attacked by the mounted police. Some of his men scattered and took shelter in the little shops nearby. He also wanted to flee. But then something checked him. He stood still in the middle of the street while policemen on horseback beat him on the back of the neck with the long new clubs they were using. Through the extreme pain, he felt a kind of exhilaration that he was strong enough to face and bear these blows.

The next day great crowds gathered in the open square near the station where the Simon Commission was due to arrive. Again a line of galloping cavalry knocked down the unarmed crowd and trampled on them. This time Jawaharlal was hit even harder than the night before. He felt half blinded. When the beating was over, he found himself covered with wounds and bruises, but he was not injured in any vital spot.

Many of his comrades did not come out of these encounters so well. One very popular leader, Lala Lajpat Rai of the Punjab, died, apparently as a result of the police blows on his chest, and several of Jawaharlal's friends suffered permanent injury. There was now no mistaking the risk involved in nonviolence.

Western newspapers failed to understand the reason for the Congress demonstrations and boycott of the Simon Commission. The general attitude in the London papers and also in the *New York Times* was that the Congress was acting with poor judgment, that by not cooperating with the Commission it was throwing away an excellent opportunity, and that it was probably doing so only because its sense of dignity had been hurt. At that time, the Western press took seriously Gandhi's claim that he had retired from politics. It referred to him as "the former leader." Accordingly, it regarded nonviolence as a thing of the past.

As for the demonstrations, Western newspapers referred to

them as "riots" and showed no surprise that numbers of "riot-ers" were hurt when the police tried to "restore law and order." Only after the death of Lala Lajpat Rai was there some con-cern that the police might have acted with undue brutality. An official commission appointed to investigate his death soon reported, however, that in its judgment the death had resulted from causes independent of the man's severe injuries.

The report of the Simon Commission was not published until May, 1930. It said that all members of the provincial cabinets should be responsible to the provincial legislatures. It enlarged the central legislature, but made no change in the central executive which was still to be chosen and headed by the British viceroy. On one important point, it agreed with Congress policy. It noted that the provincial boundaries bore no relation to the location of the different language groups of India, and that Congress in 1921 had reorganized its branches so that on the whole each branch represented people speaking one language. The Commission recognized the popular desire that the provincial boundaries of British India should be similarly redrawn.

Little attention was paid to the Simon report because by the time it was published, the political atmosphere had grown so turbulent that the British government had taken an entirely different approach toward the problem of constitution-making for India, in an attempt to appease popular resentment.

At its Madras conference in 1927, the Congress had decided that one good step to take would be to draw up a constitution for India on which Indians of various shades of thought could agree. To do this it realized it needed to consult other groups such as the National Liberal Federation, the Muslim League, the Hindu Mahasabha which represented the strictly Hindu religious point of view, the Akali Dal which represented the Sikhs (a minority religious group centered in the Punjab), and other organizations.

The Congress invited these various groups to send representatives to an All-Parties Conference in February, 1928. Together the groups agreed that India must have full self-government. They did not cross the bridge as to whether this should be as a dominion within the British Empire or as a completely independent nation. A committee was chosen to draft the proposed constitution. Motilal was made its chairman. Jawaharlal worked with him as his secretary.

That summer as he worked on the "Nehru Report," as the findings of Motilal's committee came to be known, Jawaharlal found time to write an interesting series of letters to his daughter, then age ten, while she was away in Mussoorie. Published in book form as *Letters from a Father to His Daughter,* they form a delightful little primer on how the earth came into being and what it is like now. In it he tells her how the history of the world can be read in the rocks, how the first living things appeared, followed by animals then man. He gives her his ideas on how mankind came to be divided into different races. He also tells her, "In every country people imagine that they are the best and the cleverest, and others are not as good as they. . . . This is all conceit . . . really . . . there is no country which is not partly good and partly bad."[4] He explains that India today is full of poverty. To make it a place where people can be happier, it will be necessary to take some of the good ideas of other countries. Indira herself apparently already was interested in social welfare. Six miles from Anand Bhawan there was a home for lepers. She has recorded that shortly after she was ten, she began bicycling there to work as a volunteer.[5]

The report on which Jawaharlal was working that summer for the Nehru Committee was published in August. It recommended a parliamentary system of government with two houses for the legislature. The cabinet should be responsible to Parliament as in Great Britain, not independent of the legislature as in the United States. The committee also decided on other matters which a constitution would have to cover, such as what the system of the law courts should be like and who should be entitled to vote.

In 1916, Congress had made peace with the Muslim League by agreeing to the League's demand that Muslims should vote separately and that a certain number of seats in the legislature should be reserved for Muslims. Now Motilal was opposed to this system of separate electorates. He had seen how it increased tensions among the Hindus and the Muslims whenever elections took place. In 1916, he had felt that it was important to make peace with the Muslim League. Now the League seemed to him less influential than it had been twelve years before. So many Muslims had joined the Congress after Gandhi had emerged as its leader that the Muslim League no longer seemed to represent Muslim opinion. The Nehru Report did not favor separate electorates for Muslims, and the Muslim League resented this abandonment of a principle explicitly endorsed by the Congress in the Lucknow Pact of 1916.

One issue arose in Motilal's committee on which he and his son disagreed sharply. Jawaharlal strongly favored complete independence, not dominion status. Motilal was not opposed to independence, but he felt that full self-government as a dominion within the British Empire would be enough to ask for. This had been his aim in the Legislative Assembly. The other parties represented on his All-Parties Committee preferred this to complete independence. When the report of his committee was published, it provided for dominion status. It angered him that the younger radical wing of the Congress, led by his son, should suggest that this report should now be altered on this one point. He decided that if the Congress followed his son instead of himself, he would resign.

Father and son also disagreed sharply at this time on the new ideas the son had brought back from Europe. Since coming home, Jawaharlal had argued for radical land reforms. Although he was not always explicit about these, he seemed to imply that land should be taken away from large landowners in return for small compensation, if any, and then given to the peasants. When he spoke of socialism and of greater equality of wealth for everyone, he seemed to suggest expropriation of private property by the government.

Motilal could not share these views. He had a firm belief that private property was almost sacred, certainly not to be taken away from a man by land reform. He believed in capitalism. He felt sure that socialism would not make the poor richer; it would only make the rich poorer. As he put it, socialism might "devour both complete independence and dominion status."[6] He was convinced that socialism would make the country poorer, not richer, and thereby defeat their basic purpose.

Toward the end of 1929, Motilal said to a grandnephew who was staying at Anand Bhawan at the time, "Father and son are atilt, but Jawahar would not be my son if he did not stick to his guns."[7] The son wrote that he did not think that at any previous or subsequent time the tension between him and his father had been so great.[8]

The issue of dominion status versus independence was to be voted on by the annual session of the Congress to be held in Calcutta in December, 1928. Motilal had again been elected president. He was escorted to the opening meeting by a great parade. He himself rode in a carriage drawn by thirty-four white horses ridden by young Congress volunteers. More volunteers followed on horseback. Women volunteers in green and red-bordered saris also marched in the parade which was a splendid turnout.

Meanwhile everyone was asking: Which Nehru would the Congress vote to support, the father or the son? Anxious to prevent a complete break between father and son, Gandhi suggested a compromise. The Congress should adopt the whole of Motilal's report including the clause on dominion status. At the same time, the Congress should announce that if the British did not grant dominion status within two years, the Congress would then demand complete independence instead. It would fight for this with a campaign of mass civil disobedience.

This compromise was not enough for Jawaharlal. He insisted that the British be given only a year of grace, not two. Congress then endorsed Motilal's report, but with an important proviso: they would start to fight for complete independence after a year if they had not received dominion status in the meanwhile.

The British paid no attention to the Nehru Report. It became clear that they had no intention of giving India dominion status within a year. Everyone in the Congress began thinking about the coming fight for independence.

Motilal knew that when the fight began the first person the government would take prisoner would probably be his son. He wrote to Gandhi, "You can understand what this will mean to me, but will it do any good to the country? Perhaps some, but in my opinion out of all proportion to the price."[9]

With the fight for complete independence ahead of them, everyone realized that the Congress president who would take office for the crucial year beginning December, 1929, would have an especially heavy responsibility. During the autumn of 1929, the various provincial Congress committees made their nominations. Most of them wanted Gandhi. But to everyone's surprise, Gandhi refused and put forward the name of Jawaharlal. Motilal had urged him to do so. He had written Gandhi that the youth of the Congress party were now in revolt, that Jawaharlal was their natural leader, that, of course, Gandhi would have to direct the civil disobedience campaign, but that the campaign could not succeed unless "the head of Gandhi and the voice of Jawahar" were combined.

When the son was approached on the matter, he said he

did not like the idea at all. In spite of his protests he was chosen. Motilal was delighted. Although he had so recently been at sword's point with his son, he was not only at peace with him now, but also proud of him.

To persuade the Congress conservatives to vote for Jawaharlal, however, Gandhi had to make a special plea that he be elected. Gandhi said of him: "He is pure as crystal. He is truthful beyond suspicion. . . . The nation is safe in his hands."[10]

Before Jawaharlal took office as Congress president, the viceroy, Lord Irwin, had realized that the Congress meant business by its threat to start a fight for independence if dominion status were not granted by December, 1929. He tried hard to persuade the British government to make major concessions in order to avoid a struggle with the Congress. He secured permission to announce that Great Britain agreed to dominion status for India and proposed that a Round Table Conference be held in London in 1930 to which representative Indians should go. Although he did not actually say so, the viceroy implied that the Round Table would have the authority to frame a new constitution. Taking it to mean that, the Indians welcomed the announcement.

But the British did not intend to let the Conference have any such power. They wanted it only to express the ideas of Indians, leaving the British Parliament free to frame the Indian constitution as it saw fit. When this became clear, Motilal and Gandhi decided that the Congress should not be represented at the Round Table Conference.

In the end, as it turned out, three separate Round Table Conferences were held, one after the other. The first began its meetings in November, 1930, and was attended by representatives of the Indian Liberal Party, the Muslim League, and other organizations, and also by representatives of the Indian princes. The Congress sent no one to it. Indeed, before the

Conference began, the Congress was well launched in a massive civil disobedience campaign.

Jawaharlal had taken office as Congress president on Christmas Day, 1929, at the annual session held that year in Lahore, the capital of the Punjab. The city was decorated with bunting and flags and colored lights sparkled at night. Unlike his father, Jawaharlal rode to the meeting not in a carriage but on the back of a fine white horse. He was followed by a detachment of Congress cavalry, as great crowds lined the streets to watch the procession pass.

At the meeting, Motilal, who had been the president of the Congress for the preceding year, handed over the presidency to his son after making a little speech. In it, he quoted a Persian saying, "What the father is unable to accomplish, the son achieves."[11] It was a very moving scene. No son had ever before succeeded his father as president of the Indian National Congress. Up until this point the name Nehru had meant Motilal. Now the second leader in the family came to the fore.

When the American Colonies declared their independence from Great Britain on July 4, 1776, they did not yet see much chance of winning actual independence. Just so, under Jawaharlal's presidency, the Indian National Congress declared India's independence, before they knew how they could win it. It was decided that Independence Day would be January 26, 1930.

All over the country on that day great gatherings of people met and solemnly recited the Indian declaration of independence. After a full summary of the harm which Indians believed British rule had done, it announced that "we hold it to be a crime against man and God to submit any longer to a rule that has caused . . . disaster to our country."[12]

So many people joined the Independence Day celebration that it was clear that the country was ready for another campaign of *satyagraha,* another movement of mass civil disobedience and mass arrest. Everybody looked to Gandhi as the person to plan how the campaign should be waged, but he could not decide at first. There was a lull.

Jawaharlal went back to his home. There he found out, "almost accidentally," as he later said, how popular he had become with the masses. It was the time of the great annual pilgrimage to Allahabad, and hundreds of thousands of pilgrims streamed into the city for the huge festival. They came from every corner of India to bathe in the holy Ganges. But this year their pilgrimage included also the home of the Nehrus, Anand Bhawan. They went there in a steady stream. Many asked questions. What had Congress decided to do? What was going to happen? At first Jawaharlal gave a speech once a day to the group around the house. Then more and more people came, and he had to go outdoors more and more often to answer their questions and quiet them. The crowd outside kept shouting slogans or calling his name. The wide verandas of the house were constantly full. There was no longer any privacy, with prying eyes looking through each door and window. Jawaharlal found it "annoying and irritating." Yet, at the same time, he was moved by the "shining eyes full of affection, with generations of poverty and suffering behind them and still pouring out their gratitude and love and asking for little in return except fellow-feeling and sympathy."[13]

In some ways Jawaharlal found his new prominence a strain. At the various meetings over which he had to preside, he recorded that such pompous language was used to praise him that it gave him an almost uncontrollable desire to laugh or to stick out his tongue or to stand on his head just for the pleasure of shocking and watching the reactions on the faces.[14]

Later, in his autobiography, he asked himself many questions about the effect his extraordinary popularity had had on him. He admitted frankly that it had gone to his head, even intoxicated him, but he also thought it had given him confidence and strength. Fortunately, his family teased him about the flowery language used to praise him. His daughter Indira joined in the game of thinking up fancy new words of praise to apply to him.

Presently Gandhi announced the plans for the new civil disobedience campaign. At first his program seemed strange to the others. Gandhi said, "We shall not pay the tax on salt, we shall make salt ourselves instead." Jawaharlal was bewildered. He could not see any relation between the nationalist struggle and common salt. Gandhi, with his sure sense of how the people of India would react, knew better. Salt was something that everybody needed. On the poor, the salt tax was a real burden; yet it was against the law to make salt oneself. Gandhi saw that a campaign based on disobedience of this law could have a wide appeal.

Before taking action, Gandhi courteously wrote to the viceroy informing him of what he intended to do. He would walk to the sea to make salt. After he had done so, others would follow his example. He told the viceroy that, of course, the latter could stop all of this by arresting him. The viceroy did not reply.

The sea was two hundred and fifty miles away from Gandhi's *ashram* (religious center) near Ahmedabad. On March 11, he started toward it on foot along the hot dusty roads. At first only a few followers walked with him. Then every day more people joined his "Salt March." By the time he reached the sea, his band of followers had swelled to several thousand.

While Gandhi walked toward the sea, it was Jawaharlal's job to plan how the campaign was to be directed. He knew that he would probably soon be arrested and that other leaders would be also. It was decided that each should have the power to decide who should act in his place when he went to jail. Jawaharlal directed that if he himself should be jailed, the Congress presidency should pass either to his father or to Gandhi.

On April 6, Gandhi reached the shore, scooped up some sea water, and began to make tax-free salt. All over the country Indians followed his example. The Congress issued leaflets telling people how to make salt. They were to collect sea water in pots and pans, and let the water evaporate. In this way they finally collected a little salt of poor quality. Yet the idea spread like wildfire. When the other leaders saw this, they wondered at Gandhi's extraordinary knack of catching the imagination of the masses.

As part of this new forward movement that year, in one city or another, all traffic had to come to a halt from time to time because masses of people lay down in the streets to show their unwillingness to cooperate with the authorities even on traffic regulations.

So many Congress sympathizers were hurt by the police in 1930 that the hospitals could not accommodate them all. Kamala Nehru converted one large room of Anand Bhawan into an emergency ward. One boy was brought there with such a serious stomach wound that the doctor said that the only thing that could be done for him was to make him as comfortable as possible until he died. Twelve-year-old Indira was given the responsibility of nursing him. "He was my first patient," she later said. "I almost staked my faith in God on his pulling through."[15] He did.

Eight days after the civil disobedience campaign began, Jawaharlal was arrested as he had expected. In his absence, the Congress presidency passed back to his father. Motilal's health had begun to fail, but he was ready to work as hard as he could so long as any strength remained in him.

While the salt campaign continued, the boycott of foreign cloth and all British goods became more complete. Women who had never before done anything outside of their homes joined the Congress volunteers. They stood for hours in the hot summer sun picketing foreign cloth shops. In jail, Jawaharlal heard that his wife, Kamala, had been especially skillful in organizing this work. He was proud of her, yet also worried. She had recently been very ill and was still far from strong.

Indira was even more impressed by her mother's activities. She not only admired how her mother ran the Congress party branch in Allahabad while the men were in jail, she was also struck by her mother's determination to do something about women's education at a time when few seemed disturbed that only one Indian woman in a hundred could read. She has since said that her mother influenced her even more than did her father and that she thinks she is more like her mother than anyone else.[16] According to her father, she resembled her mother so much in appearance that the two could have been mistaken for sisters.

On this, his fourth term in jail, Jawaharlal was at first confined by himself in an isolated little building designed for especially dangerous criminals. He had worked so hard in the Congress cause throughout the two and one-half years since his return from Europe that he was tired out. He felt lonely and depressed. At first he was not even allowed to go into the main prison courtyard where there was room to exercise. Later he was allowed to go there a half hour in the early mornings while it was still dark, to ensure that he would have no contact with the other prisoners. In June, his father and a friend were imprisoned and joined him in his solitary barracks. Now each had a tiny cell to himself but the three were allowed to see one another.

The annual rains burst from the clouds. The roof leaked. It was hard to find a place where their beds could be dry. Motilal had been far from well when he was arrested; the dampness of jail made him worse. In September, the authorities decided that he was too sick to keep in prison any longer and released him.

A month later, Jawaharlal was also released. Accompanied by Kamala, he traveled to Mussoorie, a lovely cool place in the foothills of the mountains, for a few days of vacation. His father was already there, recuperating. Indira was there, also, as were the three daughters of his sister, Madame Pandit. Jawaharlal always loved playing with children. Together they marched around the house in stately procession, carrying Congress flags. The youngest niece, age three, led the procession. Jawaharlal's vacations had always been rare and this one was especially precious. As it turned out, it was the last vacation he was to have with his father, and the next to last with his wife.

All too soon Jawaharlal felt he had to go back to work. On leaving jail he had decided to launch a campaign to persuade landlords and peasants alike not to pay taxes on their land. Nehru called a mass meeting to get the campaign underway. For the "seditious" speech he made at this meeting, he was imprisoned for the fifth time—after only eight days of freedom.

With his son again unable to function as Congress president, the ailing father took over once more. Although he was coughing blood he worked with his old energy, stimulating the civil disobedience movement all over India. He arranged that Jawaharlal's birthday, November 14, should be set aside for an all-India celebration. On that day, meetings would be held in which passages from Jawaharlal's speeches would be read. When the day arrived many of the crowds attending the meeting were charged and beaten by policemen on horseback. Five thousand arrests were made. As Jawaharlal wryly commented, "It was a unique birthday celebration."

At Allahabad's celebration of that birthday, Jawaharlal's wife, Kamala, read aloud the entire "seditious" speech for which her husband had been arrested. For this and her other activities for the Congress, she, too, was arrested on January 1, 1931. In jail, her husband heard that she had said at the time when the police came for her, "I am happy beyond measure to follow in the footsteps of my husband. I hope the people will keep the flag flying."[17] He was proud of her, but also worried because of her fragile health. Fortunately, she was released after only a few weeks in jail.

Twelve-year-old Indira was also at her father's birthday celebration in Allahabad. She felt herself to be as much a part of the Congress movement as any of her elders and applied for membership in it. She was told she was too young. Angry at this, she decided to form an organization of her own.

On January 26, 1931, the first anniversary of India's Independence Day, more mass meetings were held. People repeated the Indian declaration of independence to which they had pledged themselves the year before. Since neither newspapers nor the mails could be now used to give notice of the meeting places, Jawaharlal rightly realized these meetings were most remarkable. News of them had had to be spread by word of mouth.

One of the people who had taken an important part in making this possible was Indira. In what she later described as "a fit of temper," she had already taken steps to form her new organization, the "Monkey Brigade." She had passed around word inviting all young people to come to an opening meeting. Several thousand came. There were no loudspeakers. How could she make herself heard? Resourceful always, she decided to ask those near enough to hear her to repeat after her, sentence by sentence, everything she said. Her human loudspeakers bellowed forth her speech so that all could hear. The organization quickly attracted six thousand members in Allahabad alone and branches were formed in a number of other cities. It was no small achievement for a twelve-year-old girl.

She called the organization the Monkey Brigade because of the important role that the monkeys played in the old Hindu epic poem, the *Ramayana*. In that epic, the King of the Monkeys helped the hero, Rama, to reach his wife who had been abducted to Ceylon. He ordered his monkeys to build a bridge from India to Ceylon across which Rama could go to her rescue.

At first her grandfather and the other Congress leaders did not take her Monkey Brigade too seriously. From jail, her grandfather wrote, "I suggest the wearing of a tail by every member in it, the length of which should be in proportion to the rank of the wearer."[18] He came to realize, however, that his granddaughter's organization was not a trifle to be laughed at.

The Monkey Brigade formed the essential bridge between one Congress leader and another. Normal methods of communication between them were impossible. Letters were often intercepted, telephone wires tapped, and houses completely surrounded by police. But as Indira had foreseen, nobody would bother about a child going in and out of a house. The children memorized the messages that they carried so that if the police should grow suspicious, nothing could be found on them.

Beside passing messages, the children also spied on the police. While sitting in front of their police station, the police had a way of talking about what was about to happen, who was to be arrested, and when a raid on some Congress office was to be made. With their ears wide open, members of the Monkey Brigade innocently played hopscotch on the sidewalk in front of police stations, later passing on to the Congress leaders whatever they had heard.

In the evening of the first anniversary of Independence Day, Jawaharlal was released from prison and so were the other members of the Congress Working Committee. Motilal Nehru was seriously ill. Gandhi immediately started out for Allahabad to see him. Other people came also. The dying man saw them in groups of two or three. As his son later described him, "He sat like an old lion mortally wounded and with his physical strength almost gone, but still very leonine and kingly."[19]

The Congress Working Committee held meetings in the house next door. But he took no interest in them. He said to Gandhi, "I am going soon, Mahatmaji,* and I shall not be here to see Swaraj. But I know that you have won it and will soon have it."[20]

The doctors urged that he be taken to Lucknow for special treatment. Jawaharlal stayed close to his father's bedside in the hospital there. One night Motilal had a particularly restless, sleepless spell. Toward morning the son noticed that his father's face had suddenly grown calm. Thinking that his father had at last fallen asleep, Jawaharlal was glad. But his mother, who was also watching, knew that her husband had died.

The funeral service for the great man was held at the sacred meeting point of the Ganges and the Jumna. Many thousands attended it. Religious verses were recited and Gandhi paid a moving tribute to his much-loved associate.

Of her grandfather, Indira has said,

> *I admired my grandfather as a strong person and I loved his tremendous zest for life which he had and which my father also developed later on, but I was tremendously impressed by my grandfather's bigness—I don't mean physically— but you know he seemed to embrace the whole world. I loved the way he laughed.*[21]

---

* In India, the addition of *ji* to a name betokens respect, in somewhat the same way as does our use of Mr., Mrs., or Miss. It is applied indiscriminately to all kinds of people, and to children as well as to adults. Nehru himself explains this in *Toward Freedom* (page 40), and he specifically repudiates the common definition of the suffix as a term of endearment or extreme respect.

# 9.

# In and Out of Jail

ALMOST IMMEDIATELY after Motilal's death, Gandhi made another of those retreats which so discouraged his followers. He made a truce with the viceroy, Lord Irwin. He promised Lord Irwin not only that Congress would attend the second Round Table Conference to be held in the autumn of 1931, but also that he would call off the civil disobedience campaign.

The other Congress leaders were dismayed by this truce. Jawaharlal, especially, argued hard for its rejection. But finally the Congress leaders decided they had to stand back of what Gandhi had pledged them to—such was their regard for his leadership.

Young Nehru felt utterly exhausted. The months in prison, the strain of his father's last illness, the sorrow at his father's death, and finally the discouragement over the truce: all this had been too much for him. The doctors advised him to rest, so he took his wife and daughter on a boat trip to Ceylon. It was a most happy holiday. Later he wrote that on this trip he and his wife had discovered each other anew and entered into a closer relationship than they had ever had before.

107

They spent two weeks in a mountain resort in Ceylon and another two weeks touring the island and seeing its early Buddhist art which Jawaharlal had always especially liked. Then they crossed over to southern India, stopping in various of the princely states: Travancore, Cochin, Mysore, and Hyderabad. This was one of his first opportunities to see the India ruled by the princes, so much more cut off from the modern world than was British India.

That autumn, Gandhi went alone to London for the second Round Table Conference. As Motilal and Jawaharlal had predicted, this Conference, like its predecessor, accomplished nothing. It became involved in lengthy debate about how the various minorities should be represented in the new legislatures. Not only the Muslims, but also the Sikhs, the untouchables, the Parsis, the Indian Christians, and the Anglo-Indians, asked for separate representation in both the federal and provincial legislatures. Gandhi opposed these separate electorates. He was particularly strong in his opposition to separate electorates for the untouchables. He said that the untouchables were part of the Hindu community and should not be considered separate.

When the Conference was over and Gandhi was about to leave London, he told a news reporter that a new civil disobedience campaign was unlikely. He had reckoned without young Nehru. The latter had not liked the truce and thought it time to resume civil disobedience. He persuaded the Congress to go on again with the no-tax campaign he had started in 1930.

Because of his leadership in this campaign, he was back in prison in December, 1931, even before Gandhi's ship had docked in Bombay. At the same time, a large number of other leaders were arrested. The government was so quick and thorough in its repression that the Congress was unprepared. It had not made arrangements, as it had done in 1930, for the passing on of authority from one Congress leader to another as arrests took place. Indeed hardly any active Congress leader remained free. In the first four months of 1932 some 80,000 were arrested.

Nevertheless, Congress volunteers, especially the women, kept fighting back by picketing liquor and foreign cloth shops, violating the salt law, and illegally publishing propaganda. Even Jawaharlal's mother, Swarup Rani Nehru, joined a large demonstration. Not deterred by her age, the police knocked her down, and when the tumult was over, she was found lying seriously injured in the road. She never fully recovered.

In jail, Nehru wrote angrily, "The thought of my frail, old mother lying bleeding on the dusty road obsessed me, and I wondered how I would have behaved if I had been there. How far would my non-violence have carried me? Not very far, I fear, for that sight would have made me forget the long lesson I had tried to learn for more than a dozen years."[1]

While Nehru was in jail, Gandhi became involved in a different struggle of his own with the British government. The government had announced in the autumn of 1932 what it proposed to do about the representation in the new Parliament for the various groups which had asked for separate electorates. This announcement was called the Communal Award. Among other things, the British had decided to grant separate electorates to the untouchables. Gandhi considered this an immoral discrimination against them. Their own leader, the brilliant, well-educated Dr. B. R. Ambedkar, on the contrary, thought it would be an advantage for them to be sure of political representation, as were the Muslims.

Gandhi had often championed the cause of the untouchables. In the community which he had founded in South Africa, he had done much of the dirty work traditionally done by the untouchables. Much to the confusion of his wife, he had even adopted an untouchable child. He called the untouchables *harijans,* or "children of God." His feelings were so strong that he decided to "fast unto death," to take no food unless the British changed the Communal Award in this respect. In opposing separate electorates for the untouchables he believed that he was considering their best interests far more than was their own leader who relied on political strength alone.

Still in prison, Jawaharlal heard about Gandhi's fast. Again, as in the case of handspinning, it seemed to him that Gandhi had gone off on a side issue not essential to the freedom struggle. Also he felt terribly distressed and grieved over the danger to Gandhi's very life. Writing to his daughter about Gandhi, he said:

> *My little world in which [he] has occupied such a big place, shakes and totters, and there seems to be darkness and emptiness everywhere. . . . Shall I not see him again? Whom shall I go to when I am in doubt and require wise counsel? . . . What shall we all do when our beloved chief who inspired us and led us has gone?*[2]

Ambedkar clung to the idea of separate electorates for untouchables until Gandhi had fasted so long that he was on the point of death. Finally the two men reached a compromise; seats would be reserved for the untouchables in the legislatures, but all the voters together would vote on the candidates for those seats. There would be no separate electorates. The British government agreed, and Gandhi called off his fast.

It was ironic that Gandhi, the champion of the untouchables, should thus pit himself against the proclaimed leader of the untouchables. This "epic fast" actually did more, however, to diminish discrimination against untouchables than Dr. Ambedkar could possibly have accomplished by himself. Previously they had not been allowed to enter Hindu temples or use the common wells of the villages. Now, as a tribute to Gandhi, a movement sprang up to give them these and other privileges.

During this, his sixth, prison term Nehru did not feel at all well, and usually ran a temperature every day. Also he found that the treatment he received in prison on this occasion was worse than it had been previously. Then, too, he was depressed and discouraged by the news he received from outside. Not only did Gandhi's fast for the untouchables seem to him a side issue, Nehru also realized from what he heard that the freedom movement as a whole was growing inactive, as the high enthusiasm of 1930 petered out.[3] Again the government had resorted to the policy of whipping Indians publicly. It gave him a feeling of dull pain.

Then he received the dreadful news that Hitler had come to power in Germany. Few people at that time can have been more alert to the full implications of this event. From then on Nehru frequently said that the increasing power of both Hitler and Mussolini would mean that a terrible war would have to be fought if human freedom were to be defended. It never occurred to him, however, that England would be among those who would fight for freedom. What he saw of England's policies had made him cynical. He wrote: "I have always wondered at and admired the astonishing knack of the British people for making their moral standards correspond with their material interests, and for seeing virtue in everything that advances their imperial designs."[4] He pointed out that the British condemned Mussolini and Hitler for attacking liberty and democracy, yet this was just what the British themselves were doing to India.

His depression was deepened by the fact that he felt it necessary to give up for seven months the precious privilege of occasional visits from his family. He did this in protest against the rough treatment that the police used on his mother and wife when they came to see him one day. Thus cut off from the one all too rare pleasure which had made prison life bearable, he sometimes yearned so intensely for the company of friends and family that he could not control his restlessness.

During this period, a friend of his sent him a picture of a famous old statue of the seated Buddha at Anaradhapura in Ceylon. He kept it on the little table in his jail cell, and later wrote that the strong, calm features of Buddha's statue soothed him, gave him strength, and helped him to overcome his depression.[5] He added that he was not interested in Buddhism or any other dogma, that it was Buddha's personality which attracted him, and that he was similarly attracted by the personality of Christ. It is moving to think of this agnostic gaining strength to endure his prison loneliness through contemplation of the Buddha's serenity. Many people who knew him considered that, in spite of his frequent condemnation of formal religion and his explicit disavowal of interest in religions, he was at heart and by temperament a religious man.

During this prison term, he turned to writing as the most effective, positive way of combatting his depression, and he wrote one of his most extraordinary books. Significantly, it consists of a series of letters to Indira like the book which he had written in the summer of 1928. To talk to her, whether face to face or by letter, always seems to have been one of the greatest joys of his life. He had written the first letter included in this book on her thirteenth birthday, during his previous jail sentence. It has become famous. It shows clearly his love for her and also tells much about his own ideals and his dedication to his country.

He says that he cannot send her any tangible birthday present from jail. His presents, therefore, "can only be of the air and the mind and spirit, such as a good fairy might have bestowed on you—things that even the high walls of prison cannot stop."[6]

He will not only send her love and good wishes, he will also write for her a series of letters about world history. Ordinarily, he says, most people are not heroic. But there come times when great leaders inspire people to do more than they normally could have done. He reminds Indira how fascinated she was when she first read the story of Joan of Arc and how her ambition was to be like her. (She herself does not remember this ambition and has said that she never wanted to copy anyone, that so far as she can remember, she always just wanted to be herself.[7])

Then he tells her that not only he, but also she, will have a chance to take part in the making of history in India. It is an extraordinary thing that a political leader of such stature should suggest to his thirteen-year-old daughter that she will have fully as great a role to play as he. But this is precisely what he did. He added, "If we are to be India's soldiers, we have India's honor in our keeping, that honor is a sacred trust." He ended the letter affectionately, "Goodbye, little one, and may you grow up into a brave soldier in India's service."[8]

Thirty-six years later, while prime minister of India, Indira mentioned in an interview how much her father's letters had meant to her when she was a child. She has said she valued them especially because they were her only contact with him. The woman who, as a child, had received this wonderful birthday letter from her father was now in a position to be the kind of leader he had described. There was no doubt that she had learned from him what leadership requires in the way of fearlessness and dedication.

Nehru made good his promise about his birthday present to her. This jail sentence lasted over one and a half years. Throughout the long months, he wrote her a series of letters about world history. Since he was not allowed to send them out of jail at the time, he pinned the pages together and put them neatly in a stack, not knowing when Indira would be able to see them. They were later printed in a great book entitled *Glimpses of World History*. There are few books to compare with this. In it, Nehru looks at the history of the entire world with a fresh eye and gives a balanced view of man's life on many continents. His was truly a world view—not an Asian view any more than it was a European one.

Throughout its thousand tightly packed pages, *Glimpses of World History* is simple and easy to read. It is as though Nehru was sitting face to face with teen-aged Indira, not only telling her the general outline of what happened in the past, but also trying to think with her about the great unanswered questions which history poses.

Why do empires rise and fall? Why, after great periods, does collapse always seem to follow? Were the advances which civilization made in the great periods lost forever when enemies, internal or external, destroyed those civilizations? Or were the advances later taken up and used by others? Has man's history been one of progress, or just a series of ups and downs? Has evil in man increased or decreased over the ages? What should we think about religion?

As Nehru deals with it, history is by no means a long series of happenings that one is supposed to remember and usually cannot. He almost suggests that it is not so important to *remember* history as to *use* it—to go to it again and again always with fresh questions in one's mind, to draw from it more and more understanding of the nature of man, of society, and of civilization.

The last letter of the series contains a fine statement of Nehru's philosophy of life. He says that history teaches of growth and progress and the possibility of an infinite advance for man. Therefore, if one has courage and fellow-feeling for mankind, there is always some great undertaking to be ventured. People sometimes avoid the challenge of such action, he says, because they are afraid of risk and danger. But danger is "not so bad if you have a close look at it. And often it is a pleasant companion, adding to the zest and delight of life."[9] Indeed, he points out, many people who have discovered this, intentionally take great physical risks, as in climbing high mountains. But he suggests that one can also have the same exhilaration by working for a cause. There are low, unhealthy, swampy places in a person's life. But there is also always a chance to climb one's own personal mountain, as it were, and breathe pure air there. He ends the letter by quoting a poem of the leading Indian poet, Rabindranath Tagore—a poem that well expresses the passionate belief in freedom that both men shared.

> *Where the mind is without fear and the head is held high;*
> *Where knowledge is free;*
> *Where the world has not been broken up into fragments*
> *by narrow domestic walls;*
> *Where words come out from the depth of truth;*
> *Where tireless striving stretches its arms towards perfection;*
> *Where the clear stream of reason has not lost its way into*
> *the dreary desert sand of dead habit;*
> *Where the mind is led forward by thee into ever-widening*
> *thought and action—*
> *Into that heaven of freedom, my Father, let my country*
> *awake.*[10]

Toward the end of August, 1933, the government discharged Nehru from prison. His mother had become critically ill. He stayed by her bedside until she was somewhat better, then rushed off to see his beloved Mahatma. They had long talks and afterward exchanged many letters. But they could not agree on the tactics to be adopted. And they disagreed sharply on the economic policy to be followed after independence. Nehru urged socialism and the abolition of landlordism. He did not want a few rich people to be left in a position to exploit the poor. Gandhi argued back that these privileged persons should be won over to the idea of the welfare of the masses by conversion, not coercion. He repeated as always that the rich should be led to see that they should hold their wealth in trust for the poor and give the poor the benefits of that wealth.

Gandhi and Nehru also disagreed on the relative importance of means and ends. Gandhi insisted that *how* one works toward one's goal is more important than whether one reaches it; they must remain nonviolent, he said, even if this did not bring them independence. Jawaharlal retorted, "Although I greatly prefer [nonviolence] to violence, I prefer freedom with violence to subjection with nonviolence."[11]

For Nehru, the next six months were full of personal problems. He was concerned with the education of his daughter who was now sixteen and ready to enter a college or university. When the Nehrus had come back from Europe in 1927, she had gone first to a convent school in New Delhi. This did not prove satisfactory, and she went back to Allahabad to a day school. Then when both parents were in jail she was sent at Gandhi's suggestion to the Pupils Own School in Poona run by Mr. and Mrs. Vakil, two Indian nationalists who were friends of the Nehrus. There she had completed four years' work in three. Mrs. Vakil has said that she was an excellent student and has described her as "very active, very conscientious, accommodating, with a good and peaceful temperament."[12] Among the other students she was a natural leader. Then as always, she had an organizing temperament. She organized games, sports, picnics, excursions, meetings, and debates. Once the students held a mock parliament and Indira was unanimously elected prime minister.[13]

While Indira had been at school in Poona, Gandhi was in jail nearby. It was during this jail sentence that he held his "epic fast" on behalf of the untouchables. Like the rest of the nation, Indira was intensely concerned that he should survive the fast. She received permission to visit him in jail, and she spoke at a meeting held to pray for the Mahatma's life. There she said that what Gandhi needed were not their prayers, but their actions. One thing she herself did was to work in the untouchable neighborhoods of Poona teaching handspinning.

In 1934, after three intensely active years at the school in Poona, Indira passed the matriculation or college entrance examinations. Early that year, Nehru arranged that she should enter Shantiniketan in Bengal. This was an unusual educational center that had been founded by Tagore, whose poem on freedom Nehru loved so much. Tagore had the idea that teaching should be much less rigid than that offered at the typical government-aided university in India. It must also serve as a meeting place for many cultures of the East and the West. Tagore was as strong a believer in internationalism as Nehru. Nehru considered that Tagore had performed the immense service for India of forcing people to some extent out of narrow grooves of thought and making them think of broader issues affecting humanity. He regarded Tagore as the great humanist of India.[14]

Having settled the question of his daughter's education, Nehru turned to his other worries—one of which was money. To pay even the routine family bills he had to sell more of their possessions: silverware, jewelry, and other items.

There were even more serious worries. His mother's health continued to fail. Kamala became increasingly ill. On top of all this, he never knew when he was going to be arrested again. The police came for him in February, 1934. Kamala was so ill that she knew she might never see her husband again. When they went to their room to collect his clothes, she broke down completely, clung to him, then, fainting, collapsed.

To his daughter, he sent a sardonic telegram: "Going to

other home." She was troubled and anxious over his rearrest and over the illness of her mother, but at the same time she was engrossed in her studies and the new fascinating world of art that Tagore opened up for her. Tagore was not only India's leading poet, dramatist, and novelist, he was also a painter and a musician, and he took great interest in the revival of dancing, especially the easy, free-flowing type native to Manipur in the extreme eastern tip of India.

Because Tagore believed in austerity, no servants were employed at the college. The girls themselves had to take turns cooking and serving the meals. They had to clean their rooms, make their beds, and do their own laundry. When the other girls heard that a member of the aristocratic Nehru family was coming to join them, they wondered how she would take to such unaccustomed work. They assumed she would be accorded special privileges. Not at all. She neither asked for privileges, nor was accorded any. She did her share of the work cheerfully, energetically, and without comment.

Again, as at Poona, she did well in her studies and was regarded by her teachers as a remarkable pupil. She dressed simply, behaved with quiet seriousness, never failed to do her homework or classwork, and always received high marks. Her handwriting was neat, precise, and small. Some thought it resembled that of her father.[15]

A fellow student remembers her as "shy, sober but lively, and interested in everything," with an enormous appetite for learning and also a desire to study painting, singing, and dancing. Though she was shy, she entered into the fun and games of the other girls, and even participated in a number of pranks directed against a visitor who the students thought took herself too seriously.[16]

She has said that at first she felt "rather overawed by Gurudev ('teacher-god')," which was what the students called Tagore. In traditional Hindu education, it had been the cus-

tom for a student to sit at the feet of a teacher or *guru* chosen
for his saintliness and wisdom rather than for his knowledge
alone. A student was supposed to try to absorb that wisdom
as well as learn everything his *guru* knew. The relationship
between student and *guru* tended to be a close one, with the
student almost worshiping the *guru* and serving his every need.
Tagore was critical of the impersonality of English education
and the frequent lack of any meaningful personal relationship
between student and teacher. At the institution he had developed at Shantiniketan, he tried to make teaching more personal and apparently succeeded. He put the shy, young girl at
ease with him. She later wrote her father that she was happy
at Shantiniketan chiefly because of Gurudev and that his spirit
had greatly influenced her life and thought.[17] She also wrote:
"Many were the evenings when a small group of us sat at his
feet and talked on diverse subjects, or silently watched him
paint. Often he would recite or read aloud. These were moments of serene joy, memories to cherish."[18]

She spent only a year at Shantiniketan, but it seems to have
been an especially rich one for her. The peaceful meditative
atmosphere of the place apparently was just what she needed.

In this, her sixteenth year, she found herself changing "almost overnight" from a "long-legged tomboy" who wore Western dresses to a young lady desiring, like all Indian women, to
clothe herself in a graceful sari. She later wrote, "I had wanted
to be a boy, but at sixteen the delight of being a woman began
to unfold itself."[19] She let her hair grow long and wore it in
a pigtail down her back. Curiously, she had not grown to the
height the lanky legs of her childhood had suggested that she
would someday reach. In adulthood she is only five feet two.

That year, her grandmother tried to arrange a marriage and
several proposals of marriage were received, including one
from a young man six years older than she named Feroze
Gandhi. Feroze was no relation of the Mahatma. He was a

Zoroastrian, a member of the Parsi community which had fled from Persia in the seventh and eighth centuries to escape persecution by the conquering Muslim Arabs. (The word Parsi is derived from the word Persian.)

Since their arrival in India, the Parsis had lived chiefly in Bombay. Feroze had been born in Bombay, but his family home was in Allahabad and, though older than Indira, he had seen her occasionally since childhood. He had come to Anand Bhawan while Motilal was still alive and had come under the old man's influence.

Although sixteen was a normal age for a girl to be married off in India, Indira herself did not want to be married yet, and her mother staunchly helped her oppose her grandmother's desires that a match should be arranged before she felt ready for it.

Meanwhile Jawaharlal was in a particularly unpleasant jail within the city limits at Calcutta. Near him, the chimneys of the jail kitchen poured smoke in his direction all day. On at least one occasion Indira left Shantiniketan to go with her mother to Calcutta for the brief twenty-minute interview with her father in prison, which was permitted once or twice a month. Afterward she and her mother went to the Ramakrishna Math, a religious center started by a saintly nineteenth-century Hindu mystic, Ramakrishna. There mother and daughter sat by the bank of the Hooghli River, moved by the peaceful contemplative atmosphere of the place. Indira wrote of the episode that a new world of thought and experience opened out to her there.[20]

In prison Jawaharlal was again disheartened by the political news outside. In April, 1934, Gandhi called off the civil disobedience movement yet another time. Gandhi wrote that he had done so because a valued companion of long standing had been reluctant to perform the full prison task, preferring instead his private studies. Whoever the man may have been who thus disappointed Gandhi, he was not Nehru; though the latter was also fond of his private studies, he was scrupulous in the performance of prison tasks.

Nehru had more than once been puzzled and irritated by the odd, often metaphysical irrelevancies which seemed to him to turn Gandhi's attention from the main goal: independence. This latest irrelevancy infuriated and discouraged him more than any other. Nehru could not understand why a vast national movement should be thrown out of gear because a single individual had erred. He saw increasingly that a vast gulf separated him from Gandhi. It made him sad and lonely. He wrote: "Of the many hard lessons that I have learned, the hardest and most painful now faced me: that it is not possible in any vital matter to rely on anyone. One must journey through life alone; to rely on others is to invite heartbreak."[21]

In this jail sentence in 1934 and 1935, his depression led him to think back over his entire life—his actions, his motives, and the kind of a person he was. The result was a deeply moving autobiography, which was first published in 1936 under the title *The Autobiography of Jawaharlal Nehru*. The book reveals that although Nehru was immensely dynamic and concerned with making changes in the outside world, he was also an introvert, interested in examining his own character. One passage, already referred to, is worth quoting more fully because of the light it sheds on how he felt about the mixture of traditions in his upbringing and education.

> *I have become a queer mixture of the East and the West, out of place everywhere, at home no where. Perhaps my thoughts and approach to life are more akin to what is called Western than Eastern, but India clings to me as she does to all her children, in innumerable ways. . . . I am a stranger and alien in the West. But in my own country also, sometimes I have an exile's feeling.*[22]

Because the book also told about the freedom struggle in

India, its American edition was published under the title *Toward Freedom*. It immediately became a best seller. From it hundreds of thousands of people in the outside world came to understand the nature of the freedom movement in India and to have some sympathy with it. Nehru's income from this book and from his earlier writings solved the financial problem.

In October, 1934, his wife became so ill that the authorities allowed him out of jail for eleven brief days to see her. It was clear that she might die soon and he might never see her again. The thought appalled him: "Surely she was not going to leave me now when I needed her most? Why, we had just begun to know and understand each other, really; our joint life was only now properly beginning. We relied so much on each other; we had so much to do together."[23]

During these brief days out of prison, Nehru wrote Gandhi a scorching letter, expressing his intense disappointment at the calling off of civil disobedience. Gandhi wrote back serenely, "I fancy that I have the knack for knowing the need of the time."[24] But though they disagreed, Gandhi wrote a letter the very next month in which he spoke of Jawaharlal as the man "who is bound to be the rightful helmsman of the organization in the near future." The odd interplay between the two men continued. Each remained firm in his own convictions. Each was devoted to the other. In spite of Jawaharlal's criticism of him, Gandhi seems always to have been determined that Jawaharlal should be the leader of the Congress when he was gone.

Jawaharlal, back in jail, soon received bad news from home which became increasingly worse as the months passed. In January, 1935, his mother had a paralytic stroke. In May, Kamala became so ill that the doctors said that she should be sent to Europe for treatment. Unable to go to Europe with her himself, Nehru wired to Indira at Shantiniketan to do so. The telegram arrived while she was in the middle of a dress rehearsal for her first solo appearance on the dance stage. Tagore summoned her to his studio to break the news to her. She received it quietly and declined Tagore's offer that one of the professors should accompany her to Allahabad, saying, "My father has trained me to travel alone."[25]

The girl took her sick mother to a sanatorium in Germany and watched by her bedside month after month as her mother grew slowly worse. It was a lonely anxious time. To help her take care of her mother, her friend, Feroze Gandhi, who had gone to the London School of Economics, came to the German sanitorium. This was doubtless chiefly because he was still in love with Indira and not discouraged by her rejection of him the preceding year. It may also have been because he was an intense nationalist and this was the least he could do for Jawaharlal Nehru, who was serving the freedom movement in jail.

Meanwhile, Nehru was in agony about his wife. By August, she had sunk so low that Indira sent off a cablegram to her father which the jail authorities opened first. Taking pity on him at last, they released him and he hurried to Europe by air to join his wife and daughter. He stayed in a boarding house nearby. He visited his wife every day, read aloud to her, and talked about the past. For a little while she improved sufficiently so that he felt able to take Indira for a two-week visit to England. There he arranged for the publication of his autobiography. V. K. Krishna Menon, head of the India League in London, helped him in this, and the two men became close friends.

When the autobiography was published, Nehru received many letters praising it highly, including one from Tagore, whom Indians regarded as the greatest living Indian author. Tagore said that he was very impressed with the book, that through it there ran "a deep current of humanity which overpasses the tangle of facts and leads us to the person who is greater than his deeds, and truer than his surroundings."[26]

Toward the end of 1935, Nehru received word from India that he had been elected Congress president again for the year 1936. It was scarcely kind of his supporters to elect him while he was far away with his sick wife. How could he accept? While Kamala seemed better, he hated to leave her. After consultations with the doctors, however, he decided to go home for a few months. Then, just before he was due to leave, she died. With Nehru and Indira at her bedside was Feroze Gandhi.

Desperately tired and unhappy, Nehru went back to India. His younger sister, Krishna, wrote how aged and lined with sorrow his face had become in the space of a few months, adding: "His sad expressive eyes held a world of agony."[27]

When her father returned home, Indira went to England to continue her studies.

Young Jawaharlal and his parents, Motilal and Swarup Rani Nehru

Jawaharlal, aged 13, after his initiation ceremony of the "sacred thread"

Jawaharlal and Kamala Nehru after their marriage in 1916 (upper left); Mohandas Gandhi working at handspinning (upper right); Indira, wearing the Monkey Brigade uniform, with her parents, 1930 (below)

The Jhelum River, Srinagar, Kashmir;

Anand Bhawan, home of the Nehrus, Allahabad

Indira and Feroze Gandhi after their marriage in 1942 (upper left)

Indira, in 1937, reading her father's autobiography (lower left)

Hindu temple in Mysore State (upper right)

Schoolchildren reciting lessons outdoors (lower right)

The Parliament Building, Delhi (upper left)

Muslim mosque at Lahore in the Punjab (lower left)

A village courtyard in North India (upper right)

An ancient village well, gathering place for women (lower right)

British pomp in its final hours in India—Lord and Lady
Mountbatten with a Maharajah

One of India's problems—starving cattle

# 10.

# Toward Partition

THE SESSION of the Congress at which Nehru was due to take over the presidency again was held in Lucknow in April, 1936. In his speech before it he said: "I am weary and I have come back like a tired child yearning for solace in the bosom of our common mother, India. That solace has come to me in overflowing measure. . . . How can I thank you, men and women of India?"[1] He always had this way of including warm personal human remarks in his speeches.

After the April meeting, he toured the country making many speeches urging socialism. The Congress conservatives, the "Old Guard," were angry. They did not agree with his socialism, and they thought it wrong for a Congress president to express ideas which the Congress itself had not adopted. Because of their criticism, Nehru almost resigned, but Gandhi persuaded him not to do so. Surprisingly, he was even reelected to the presidency for the following year. It was unusual for a man to be given this office two years in a row, but Gandhi most emphatically demanded Nehru's reelection, and the "Old Guard" would not oppose the wishes of the Mahatma.

133

In November, 1937, just before Nehru's reelection, an article appeared in an Indian magazine, criticizing him vigorously. It warned of his dictatorial tendencies. Signed by "Chanakya," it said:

> *Is it his will to power that is driving him from crowd to crowd? . . . He calls himself a democrat and a socialist and no doubt he does so in all earnestness . . . but a little twist and he might become a dictator. . . . He has all the makings of a dictator in him—vast popularity, a strong will, energy, and pride . . . intolerance of others and a certain contempt for the weak and inefficient. . . . His overwhelming desire to get things done and to sweep away what he dislikes and build anew will hardly brook for long the slow processes of democracy.*[2]

Later, it was revealed that Nehru himself had written this article under the Chanakya pseudonym. It may seem curious that he wanted to criticize himself in this way when he was up for reelection, yet he was always most candid about his qualities, good and bad. Probably no other national leader has ever expressed as openly as he what he saw within himself in his introspective moments. The dictatorial tendencies he ascribed to himself in that article were there, but his deep love of democracy overrode them. Doubtless it was this basic love of democracy which led him to caution people against himself. Certainly he was a man of great inner contradictions.

The year 1937, during which he was president of Congress for the third time, was a critical one. New elections were to be held which would be especially important because the British in 1935 had granted to the provincial legislatures greatly increased powers. The new legislatures would have almost complete responsibility for the government in the provinces. They could set up ministries or cabinets of their own choice.

Nehru worked with incredible energy in the election campaign, traveling up and down the country. He went fully fifty thousand miles in less than five months. He himself said that he passed through his vast country like a hurricane. He traveled mostly by automobile, partly by airplane and railway. Now and then, for short distances, he had to use an elephant, a camel, or a horse, or travel by steamer, paddleboat, or canoe, or use a bicycle or go by foot. This was necessary because he went far from the beaten track—to remote places out of contact with roads, railroads, or airports. He took with him microphones with batteries—to places which had never heard of such inventions before.

Everywhere huge numbers of people came out to hear him speak. It has been estimated that he spoke to over ten million people that year. The surging crowds gave him a feeling of exhilaration. He discovered again, and on a much larger scale, what he had first discovered in 1920 when he went to the villages: he could speak easily and simply. Now he came to realize that he could have a hold on the masses very much like that of Gandhi and that he could appeal over the heads of the more conservative Congress "Old Guard" directly to the people.

In this election campaign, he based his appeal chiefly on his demand for land reforms and he became more specific as to the type of land reforms he wanted. There should be reduction of rents and of land taxes for the poorer peasants. Very small land holdings should be totally exempted from taxes. There should be partial forgiveness of rural indebtedness, and credit facilities at low-interest rates should be provided by the government. One of Nehru's biographers has said that in that year Nehru "won the provincial elections almost single-handed by promising land reforms."[3]

Nehru encouraged peasants and workers to join the Congress. Largely as a result of his efforts, the membership of Congress grew from less than half a million in 1936 to almost five million in 1939.

In the 1937 elections, Congress won an absolute majority in five of the eleven provinces of British India and emerged as the leading party in three more. What seemed even more significant, Muslim candidates nominated by Congress won many of the seats in the Muslim separate electorates. The Muslim League, on the other hand, secured less than 5 per cent of the total Muslim vote. It appeared that Muslims themselves did not like the Muslim League.

Here and there, the Muslim League had cooperated with the Congress in the elections on the understanding that some of its members would be included in the Congress ministries or cabinets to be formed if the Congress won. But after the Congress saw how few votes the Muslim League had secured, it did not carry out this promise fully.

This angered Muhammad Ali Jinnah and he decided to fight the Congress. He called upon the Muslim League to strengthen itself for this struggle. He toured the country talking to gatherings of Muslim peasants. Everywhere he said, "Islam is in danger." This simple war cry won many new members for the Muslim League. From then on, the tension between Hindus and Muslims steadily increased. The old irritations over such matters as cow slaughter and the playing of music near mosques at prayer time were nothing compared to the new struggle for political power. Fundamentally religious belief had little to do with this struggle. The basic question was whether or not the Hindu majority would discriminate against the Muslim minority in an independent united India. The majority, of course, would have control over the power to distribute government jobs and government contracts. The chief Muslim fear was that this would put them at an economic disadvantage. Congress leaders considered that Congress could be trusted to distribute economic opportunities fairly to Muslims as well as to Hindus. Muhammad Ali Jinnah disagreed; he emphatically distrusted the Congress. To secure support for his position he did not argue out this point, however. Instead, he used a simple emotional religious appeal when he spoke to the uneducated masses.

When his third term as Congress president came to an end in 1938, Nehru went back to Europe. He wanted to see Indira, who was now a student at Somerville College, Oxford. She had prepared for Oxford by studying for a while in London, where she had joined the British Labour party and met many of its leaders. The British Labour party's brand of socialism appealed to her, as it had appealed to her father. The widow of the prominent socialist, Harold Laski, remembers her as a "mousey, shy little girl who didn't seem to have any political ideas."[4] On the other hand, one of her fellow students remembers an interesting occasion when she attended a debate organized by the Indian Students Union on the subject of whether or not the Congress movement should be more revolutionary. During the debate her father was much criticized. At the end, a vote was taken, and she raised her hand in favor of the proposition that Congress should, indeed, be more revolutionary. Fond as she was of him, she clearly felt capable already of taking a position different from his.

While at Oxford, Indira worked when she could at the office of the India League which had been organized by V. K. Krishna Menon to influence British public opinion in favor of Indian independence. Speaking later of Menon in those days, she said: "I saw a lot of him, or rather a lot of his office, because I worked for the India League in the afternoons and evenings. In the evenings, he was usually away, organizing meetings. He was very good at that. Menon gave you the feeling that there was something worthwhile to do for India. Otherwise, there was no outlet at that time."[5]

The India League undoubtedly had a real impact on British thinking, particularly in the ranks of the British Labour party, which came to be sympathetic to the Indian cause.

Feroze Gandhi was studying in the London School of Economics at the time and also working for the India League when he could. He and Indira saw each other frequently. Since they were in a foreign country, he could court her more openly and more assiduously than he might have been able to do had they both been in India where open courtship is not yet completely accepted. Not discouraged by the fact that she had rejected his offer of marriage a few years earlier, he wrote her many love letters when their respective studies at Oxford and London kept them apart.

During his 1938 trip to Europe, Nehru not only saw his daughter, but also visited Spain, which was in the throes of a civil war. What he saw on this trip to Europe worried him greatly. Fascist Italy had sent troops to Spain to help General Franco's army overthrow the Republic of Spain. No one seemed ready to stop Hitler who had come to power in 1933, had violated the Versailles Treaty by rearming Germany and reoccupying the Rhineland, and in 1938 had just occupied Austria. Nehru realized that all of Europe would lose its freedom unless a great war were fought to check the continued growth of Nazism and Fascism.

When he returned home he made many speeches about this. He said, "The world is in a tragic mess; tragic to those who are sensitive; heartbreaking to those who feel."[6] As early as 1927 he had predicted World War II. Now he did so again, this time correctly judging where the danger lay. The fact that his prophecy soon came true led Indians to have even greater respect for his understanding of international affairs.

In September, 1939, the great war in Europe began. The Germans invaded Poland. Seeing at last that appeasement did not stop the Nazis, England declared war on Germany. Then the viceroy declared that India also was at war against Germany. The Indians did not like this highhanded action. They

felt that they should take part in the war only if they were free
to make a choice in the matter. On Nehru's urging, Congress
passed a resolution that India would associate herself with
other free nations against the dictators but only if the British
granted her freedom.

Nehru's position on this matter brought him again into sharp
conflict with Gandhi, who, of course, still argued that violence
should not be used under any circumstances. Although Gandhi
publicly announced that his sympathies were with Great
Britain, he said he did not believe in aiding her war effort, even
nonviolently. He added that if, contrary to his wishes, Congress
were to offer England some form of cooperation, the offer
should be unconditional.

To gain Congress support, the viceroy promised some concessions but not the much desired independence. So Congress
called for the resignation of its provincial ministries, and
British governors again took over the government of the provinces. In their two and a half years in office, the Congress
ministries had governed well. Before Congress would have a
chance to govern again, there was to be another long, difficult
struggle against the British. For Nehru, it was to involve two
more terms in prison.

In Europe the winter of 1939–40 was the period of the
so-called "phoney war." After the sudden Nazi seizure of Poland, little fighting took place. The war seemed to have come
to a standstill.

That winter, Indira, still at Oxford, became severely ill with
pleurisy and was sent to Switzerland to recover. In December,
1939, a friend of Nehru's, the British author, Edward Thomp-
son, who had spent many years in India as a professor, wrote
Nehru from England: "I have seen Indu. She looks well, and
she *is* well. She is thin of course, and there seems no doubt that
just now she is what used to be called 'delicate' and will have
to go carefully. But she is wiry underneath, and when she is

past these difficult days that end adolescence, she will pull into real strength."[7] He added that "if anything should happen" in the way of a new German attack, he would "see to her." Nehru was not to worry about her.

Suddenly in May, 1940, the German Nazis sent their armored divisions racing through the Netherlands and Belgium. They drove the British forces on the continent to the very edge of the water at Dunkirk, in northern France. Fortunately, a heavy fog hung low over the ground for several days, hiding the British soldiers from the German planes which otherwise would have bombed them from the air. Boats of all sizes came over from England to ferry the troops back home across the English Channel. England then knew the strength of the Nazi army, and how hard it might be even to defend their little island from the Germans.

For this desperate last stand, the British Parliament chose a new prime minister, Winston Churchill, who frankly told the British that if they were to win or even defend themselves successfully, they must be prepared for "blood, sweat, and tears."

With England facing such mortal peril, Jawaharlal became strongly opposed to civil disobedience. He did not want to do anything which might further weaken the British. Many other Congress members shared his point of view.

In June, 1940, the Working Committee of Congress again offered the British complete cooperation in the war effort if the British immediately declared India's independence. This offer was turned down, however, and those who, like Nehru, wanted to give Great Britain positive aid had reluctantly to bow to Gandhi's plan for a new non-cooperation campaign instead. This time, however, the campaign was to be restricted in scope, a token protest which would interfere as little as possible with the British effort. Only a few selected individuals were to offer civil disobedience. Nehru was one of the first whom Gandhi directed to do so. He was arrested in October, 1940. This, his eighth term, lasted a little over a year. He was released on December 3, 1941, just four days before the Japanese attacked the naval base at Pearl Harbor.

This surprise attack made a marked change in Indian thinking. Many became still more eager to cooperate actively with England and her allies. There were rumors that there would now certainly be a final rift between Nehru and Gandhi. Both men, however, emphatically denied that such a thing could occur. Gandhi repeated what he had said many times before: when he died he wanted Jawaharlal to be his successor.

After the attack at Pearl Harbor, the Japanese advanced rapidly through Southeast Asia. Their armies threatened to invade India also. With the Japanese right at the borders of India, the British sent a distinguished leader, Sir Stafford Cripps, to India with the offer of full dominion status after the war and the right of the Indians to draw up their own constitution. The Cripps offer added that any province was to have the right to stay out of the new dominion if it so chose.

This was the first suggestion by the British that India might be partitioned. Two years before, in 1940, the Muslim League had voted for partition. Muhammad Ali Jinnah, who always dominated the League, had decided the Muslims must have a nation of their own on the Indian subcontinent. He called it Pakistan, which means "land of the pure." He argued that all the provinces where the Muslims were in the majority should be included in Pakistan.

When partition was first discussed, few people in India took the idea seriously. Many Muslims emphatically did not want a separate Muslim state. The elections of 1937 had seemed to show that Jinnah and the Muslim League could not command much support. Congress considered Jinnah a crank with an ill-considered idea that few people would ever endorse. Therefore, this first mention of partition in the Cripps offer did not worry them greatly.

Although the Cripps offer did not include the immediate independence that Congress had asked for, it was almost accepted. Nehru and other members of the Congress wanted so much to make peace with the British that they were inclined to seize any opportunity of doing so. Gandhi, however, threw all his weight against acceptance. Congress followed Gandhi.

This was chiefly because many were skeptical that a promise which was not to be carried out until the end of the war would ever be carried out. They remembered that the new British prime minister, Winston Churchill, had said the year before, "I have not become His Majesty's first minister to preside over the liquidation of the British Empire."[8] A prime minister of such an imperialistic viewpoint seemed likely to find a way of not fulfilling the Cripps promise, once the war danger was over.

In 1942, Gandhi invented a new, short, simple slogan— "Quit India." He made it clear that if the British did not leave India completely, he planned a new mass civil disobedience campaign. Nehru was very disturbed. He saw that if the British did leave India, the Japanese would certainly invade it. Indians would not gain freedom, they would merely exchange British rule for Japanese rule. He fought hard to get Gandhi to change his mind. Gandhi later said that Nehru fought him at this time "with a passion I have no words to describe."[9] At first so many members of Congress were opposed to the "Quit India" idea that it seemed certain that Gandhi would be defeated when the matter came to a vote. But Gandhi said that if the Congress defeated his resolution he would form a new movement, bigger than the Congress. They gave in.

The day after the decision was reached, Nehru and all the other Congress leaders were arrested. This time he was imprisoned with the ten other members of the Congress Working Committee. Each of the eleven had a room opening out onto a large courtyard in which there was a neglected garden. Nehru planted seeds in the garden and made it beautiful. His prison mates later reported that in every way he was "the soul of our party." He had such wide interests that he always gave them something new to think about.

This was Nehru's longest prison term. It lasted over a thousand days. During it, he wrote his third great book, *The Discovery of India,* a history of India written from an Indian point of view and for the layman. It is also the story of how he, who had been brought up and educated in such a Western way, came to discover his own Indian heritage through abundant reading of Indian history but more especially through personal contacts with villagers as he traveled throughout the land in his campaigns. He found that even illiterate villagers knew every incident of the great Indian epics, the *Ramayana* and the *Mahabharata,* and that they understood their moral teachings. In spite of their poverty and lack of education, they had a "mellowness and a gentleness, the cultural heritage of thousands of years, which no amount of misfortune had been able to rub off."[10]

He explains that Indian history begins with a surprisingly high civilization which flourished in the Indus Valley in Northwest India as early as 2500 B.C. The people of this civilization were the first to know how to use cotton for textiles. They had well-laid-out streets, well-built houses and baths of baked brick, a wealth of ornaments of all kinds, copper vessels and metal implements, exquisite art which included finely modeled human statuettes, and engraved seals of animals which were remarkably naturalistic. It filled him with pride when he realized that few lands had reached so high a level of civilization as had early India.

He goes on to explore the other periods of high culture in India's past and the many early achievements in technology, mathematics, and other forms of learning of which India could rightly be proud.

Perhaps the chief theme of the book is that Indian culture

is by no means to be identified with Hindu culture alone. It is a composite, to which many different religions and traditions have contributed. While he was critical of the British for their imperialism in India, he recognized fully the value for India of the Western cultural tradition which the conquerors had brought with them. He was glad that this had become part of the culture of educated Indians. He saw that it had widened Indian thinking and had brought to India both new techniques and scientific thought. He points out that this scientific approach contrasts with the reliance on intuition characteristic of traditional Hinduism. Although he was critical of this and certain other aspects of the Hindu tradition, he saw within it positive values as well, especially its tolerance, which he regarded as one of its essential strands from early times. He wrote: "It is not some secret doctrine . . . that has kept India vital and going through these long ages, but a tender humanity, a varied and tolerant culture, and a deep understanding of life and its mysterious ways."[11]

In the spring of 1940, when France fell before the swift Nazi attack, Indira was still in Switzerland. She wanted to go back to India immediately. This was clearly not the time to continue her studies at Oxford. In 1938, when she returned to India briefly with her father at the end of his European trip, she had suddenly realized that being twenty-one she was old enough to join the Congress movement. She did so promptly. Now in 1940 she felt that she should be working for Congress back home. All the frontiers of Switzerland, however, were closed and it was not easy to get out.

Finally, the still faithful Feroze somehow managed to help her do so and secured for them both passages on a British steamer sailing for India. For weeks they followed a zigzag course, dodging German submarines. Instead of taking the short route through the Suez Canal, the ship went around the southern tip of Africa, and made long stops in South African ports.

During their stop in Durban, a series of events occurred which may have been as pivotal in Indira's life as Nehru's first visit to the Indian villages was in his. Many Indians still lived in South Africa, including a group of well-to-do merchants and bankers who fawned on the South African whites in the attempt to escape discrimination themselves. This Indian community organized a reception in honor of the daughter of Jawaharlal Nehru. The people who were organizing the reception asked her ahead of time if she would be willing to say a few words. Feeling too shy to do so, she politely declined. They pressed her, but she was firm. Then, before the meeting took place, she drove around the city with Feroze, saw the living conditions of the African Negroes, and was appalled by South African segregation.

She went to the meeting. It began with the placing of a garland of flowers around her neck, an Indian custom, and by a speech of welcome on the part of the chairman, who went on to say that Miss Nehru would be unable to speak. But Miss Nehru had changed her mind. She spoke. She described the Negro ghettos as she had seen them, she condemned *apartheid* and criticized her Indian audience for their own aloofness from the Africans. Just as her father had discovered in the Indian villages that it is easy to speak if one has something to say, so did she. She spoke well and so forcefully that the Indian community boycotted her for the rest of her stay in Durban.

When she and Feroze finally reached India in 1941, he took a job with a newspaper in Allahabad. They continued to see each other frequently. Like her, he also became deeply involved in the Congress movement. They decided to be married, although her father and the entire Nehru family were strongly opposed to the match. The public seemed even more opposed than was the family. To the average Indian, it was unthinkable that a Brahman girl should marry a Parsi. Every day for some while she received hundreds of letters of protest. But Indira was and is a determined person. She would not be deflected by either her father's opposition or public opinion. As she later said, "I go my way. And once I had made up my mind, there it was." Her father became reconciled, and Gandhi gave her his blessing.

She herself wanted a small wedding, but Gandhi pointed out to her that this would lead people to gossip about her father's opposition to the marriage. So the wedding, held in March, 1942, was a large one. She was then twenty-four. By Indian standards, it was almost shocking for a girl not to be married until such an age.

Indira's aunt, Krishna Hutheesingh, has described the girl as she looked on her wedding day. She wore a pink sari made of thread spun by her father during one of his terms in prison. She was "slightly flushed and a little excited, though pretending to be quite calm. . . . Lovely to look at, on this special occasion she looked lovelier than ever, frail and almost ethereal."[12]

Priests sat cross-legged in a circle. In the center they lit a sacred fire, the symbol of purity. Indira and her father sat next to each other on cushions on one side of the fire. On Indira's other side, there was another cushion on which her mother would have sat if she had still been alive. Feroze Gandhi sat opposite them. When the senior priest asked who was to give the bride away, Jawaharlal took the hand of his daughter and put it in the hand of the groom. With their hands thus clasped across the fire, they repeated their wedding vows after the priest. Then they rose and walked, hand in hand, seven times around the fire, as the priests chanted. Next they sat side by side while the priest chanted the final words of the service: "As Rama was to Sita, so may the husband be to his bride."

The young couple went off to Kashmir for their honeymoon. When it was over, they immediately plunged into the freedom movement.

Both Indira and Feroze went to Bombay for the meeting of the All-India Congress Committee which passed the crucial

Quit India Resolution. Staying at the house of her aunt in Bombay, Indira helped her father pack his bag when the police came for him at five o'clock the next morning. Later she took the train back to Allahabad. The morning after she arrived the police came to arrest her aunt, Madame Vijaya Lakshmi Pandit. A warrant was issued for the arrest of Feroze, but the police did not find him. Instead of quietly surrendering, he believed in going "underground." In an attempt to catch him, the police kept constant watch outside their house, and Indira had no way of knowing where he was.

She decided that it was time that she herself should court arrest in the Gandhian tradition. One day the students of a college decided to hoist the Congress flag. She went there expecting to be arrested. On arriving she found the police beating up the young students. The boy who was hoisting the flag fell to the ground bleeding badly, but still clutching the flagpole. Indira rushed forward and picked it up. The police began raining blows upon her. She fell to the ground and the policemen deliberately stepped on her body. Nonetheless, the students managed to hoist the flag.

A few days later she decided to hold a public meeting contrary to a government order that prohibited such gatherings. Through word of mouth news was spread as to where the meeting would be held and quite a crowd gathered for it. As Indira started speaking, she was surrounded by soldiers with loaded guns. After she had spoken for a few minutes one soldier said, "Stop speaking or I fire."[13] At that moment, someone rushed out of the crowd and crashed into the soldier with the gun. It was Feroze. Probably his unexpected arrival saved her life. For it is doubtful if this courageous and determined young woman would have stopped talking just because a policeman threatened her life if she continued. As it was, she was so surprised to find her husband by her side that she hesitated. After a scuffle, they both were arrested and pushed into a police van.

They were together briefly, then she was put in a female prison and he in a prison for men.

Indira's term in prison was thirteen months. During all this time she was not allowed to receive anything from the outside world: no visitors, no letters, not even the present of luscious ripe mangoes which her father sent her. She was imprisoned in a barracks with twenty-two other women, many with life sentences for such crimes as murder. She took an interest in their lives and problems, and taught those who were illiterate how to read and write.

Like her father, Mrs. Gandhi set for herself a strict routine in prison, but she reacted to the experience of being cut off from the outside world somewhat differently than he. As she has described it:

> *The reaction in me was to seal in my mind so that while I was in prison, I didn't consciously feel that I was missing anything. . . . It was only when I left prison that I suddenly found I had cut off my emotions and intellect and I had been living only at a surface level. It took me some time before my feelings thawed out and I could look at a color without feeling the shock of it, or hear a noise, or even feel a texture.*[14]

In the spring of 1945, the viceroy of India, Lord Wavell, persuaded the British government that it would be wise to offer the Indians new concessions. He released Nehru from prison to attend a conference of leaders of various parties which he was calling.

The conference was held in Simla, the curious mountain city high in the foothills of the Himalayas from which the British had ruled India during the hot months. Some of its streets are horizontal, but the ones which cross these are almost vertical. Often a building which can be entered from one horizontal street at its "ground floor" can also be entered from the next higher horizontal street across a bridge to its top floor. While the British rulers remained cool and aloof in this mountain retreat, the masses they governed had sweltered on the plains.

At this Simla conference the British made it clear that they now really wanted to give India dominion status and self-government. No reason for doubt on this score remained. But a new difficulty had arisen. During the time when the Congress leaders had been in jail during World War II, Muhammad Ali Jinnah had greatly strengthened the Muslim League. He had not forgotten that the Congress in 1928 had gone back on its agreement of 1916 that Muslims should have separate electorates, nor that the Congress ministries which had been formed after the 1937 elections included only what he regarded as "tame" Muslims who would follow the Congress lead. Jinnah now claimed to speak on behalf of all the ninety million Muslims of India. For the next two years he said again and again that the Muslims must have a nation of their own, Pakistan.

From the end of the War until the spring of 1947, there were endless three-cornered negotiations between the British, the Congress leaders, and Jinnah. The Congress worked hard to find some basis of compromise with Jinnah. The British in 1946 suggested an odd three-tiered federation as a form of government which would keep the subcontinent united while giving to the Muslim provinces a large degree of autonomy. No workable form of government for a united India satisfied Jinnah. He would not compromise. He kept on insisting on partition.

No one can be sure why Jinnah set out to destroy the unity of India. He himself was not a religious man. He cannot have believed sincerely that religion alone was a good basis on which to build a modern state. Perhaps his ambition was the reason. He could see no chance of rising to political power in a united India, but he knew he could dominate Pakistan.

The British announced that new elections would be held in the winter of 1946 and that the long desired Constituent Assembly of Indians would be formed right after the elections.

To win votes in the election campaign, the Muslim League used crude scare tactics, saying that Muslims would be in danger in an independent united India. To calm Muslim fears, Congress promised that any government which it formed would be neutral or "secular" in religious matters. Nevertheless, the scare tactics worked. The Muslim League captured 86 per cent of the votes of Muslims, compared to less than 5 per cent of that vote nine years earlier. Jinnah's claim that he spoke for all the Indian Muslims could no longer be treated as absurd. Naturally, however, Congress as the most powerful party in the country won more seats in the legislatures than did the Muslim League.

That summer the British decided to let Indians form an interim government which would govern the country while negotiations over the constitution of independent India continued. The viceroy invited Nehru and Jinnah together to form a cabinet, assuring them that it would have the same powers as the cabinets in the self-governing dominions. Jinnah refused to cooperate. The viceroy then invited Nehru to select a cabinet of his own choosing. Since Nehru had just been elected president of the Congress for the fourth time, and since Congress was the largest political group in the country, Nehru was the logical man for the viceroy to select as the interim prime minister. He took office on September 2, 1946.

That same month Jinnah called for "direct action" to achieve Pakistan. Jinnah did not openly say that this direct action should include violence but that is what resulted. In the city of Calcutta alone, four thousand people were killed within four days' time. The senior British military officer in the area reported that gangs of "homicidal maniacs" went into the slums where Hindus lived and slaughtered Hindus wholesale.

Hindus in other places retaliated and the violence spread. Gandhi went to two of the troubled provinces, Bengal and Bihar, and succeeded in calming the communal passions there. But he could not be everywhere at once. Far to the west in the Punjab, violence kept mounting. Muslims formed the majority in the Punjab, but the minority included not only Hindus but Sikhs, who were also strongly anti-Muslim. The Sikhs emphatically did not want India to be partitioned. They formed a private army to resist partition by force. The Muslims in the Punjab did likewise, and so did the Hindus. The chief minister of the province should have put a stop to this before the three private armies came into being but he did not. Throughout 1946, tension in the Punjab mounted.

The British saw that India was heading fast toward civil war. Quick partition of the country and independence seemed the only way to avoid it. They sent to India a new viceroy, Lord Louis Mountbatten, with orders to arrange for the transfer of power as soon as possible. It was finally agreed that the new nation of Pakistan should include the provinces of Baluchistan, the Northwest Frontier Province, and Sind, where Muslims were in the majority. It was also to contain part of the Punjab and part of Bengal far to the east. Jinnah had claimed all of these two important provinces for Pakistan but the decision was that they, like India as a whole, should be partitioned. The exact boundaries were to be determined by a boundary commission. India and Pakistan were both to become independent dominions on August 15.

Reluctantly Nehru agreed to partition. To the end, Gandhi remained opposed.

# 11.

# Independence, Slaughter, and Survival

JUST BEFORE MIDNIGHT on August 14, 1947, Nehru spoke in the Indian Parliament building to the Constituent Assembly meeting there to celebrate the very moment of the coming of independence. He said:

> Long years ago we made a tryst with destiny, and the time comes when we shall redeem our pledge. . . . At the stroke of the midnight hour, when the world sleeps, India will awake to life and freedom. A moment comes, which comes but rarely in history, when we step out from the old to the new . . . when the soul of a nation, long suppressed finds utterance.[1]

He pled for unity, for combined efforts toward constructive action, and for putting aside recriminations about partition.

> This is no time for petty and destructive criticism, no time for ill-will or blaming others. We have to build the noble mansion of free India where all her children may dwell.[2]

152

Each member of the assembly then recited a pledge of service to India. It was a very moving occasion. Indira watched from the gallery. She later said she was so excited and proud she really thought she would burst.

Indians always love a *tamash* or festival. No *tamash* had ever been celebrated with more ebullient enthusiasm than the one held August 15, 1947. With mass meetings, speeches, parades, and fireworks, people all over India, in every town and village, expressed their joy over their hard-won independence. It was the great moment toward which the entire country had been looking forward for years.

Nehru himself had a busy day. In the morning he and his cabinet were officially sworn in at the mansion of Lord Mountbatten, the viceroy who now, at the invitation of that new cabinet, accepted a new post as the first governor general of free India. Nehru then made a radio broadcast to the nation stressing the importance of increased production. He attended a series of meetings in New Delhi ending with a mammoth flag-raising ceremony at Delhi's historic old Red Fort from which the Mogul emperors had ruled. There a crowd of half a million gathered to watch and roar its applause as the flag of the Congress movement was raised for the first time as the flag of independent India.

But the happiness of the occasion was marred both by partition and by the dreadful communal rioting. By the summer of 1947, the Punjab was in anarchy. Neither the police nor the detachments of the regular army which had been sent there could maintain order. Roving bands of armed Muslims killed every Hindu or Sikh they came upon. Hindus and Sikhs killed Muslims with equal fury. Whichever religious group happened to be in the minority in a particular village was often wiped out completely.

For fear of spoiling the celebration of independence, the boundary commission did not make its report until August 17.

When the exact line between India and Pakistan was announced, terror reached panic proportions. Each minority religious group acted exactly as people do when caught in a burning building—they rushed to get out. Muslims in the Indian part of the Punjab crowded into trains headed for Pakistan. Hindus and Sikhs in Pakistan crowded into trains headed for India. The dusty roads were filled with refugees in bullock carts or on foot, fleeing for their lives. Many of them were killed before they could escape.

During that terrible year of 1947 about twelve million people made their way from one side of the Punjab boundary to the other. It will never be known exactly how many were killed, but some place the figure as high as a million.

On the two sides of the new boundary that divided Bengal, people did not panic in this way. Gandhi was still among them, talking to them quietly about the importance of nonviolence, of love, trust, neighborliness, and forgiveness. Hindus and Muslims listened and remained at peace.

No ruler of a new country ever took office under such difficult conditions as did Nehru. Under the Mountbatten Plan, everything which had been part of British India was to be divided, not only the actual territory but also the civil service, the army, the air force, the navy, even the office equipment and typewriters, and the cash balances of the government. At the very time when Nehru most needed his government services and his armed forces to be in their best operating condition, men were leaving these services to join those in Pakistan.

Meanwhile, Hindu and Sikh refugees poured into the city of Delhi. They settled down to live wherever they could find any open land: in public parks, in mosques and temples, on the grounds of ancient public monuments and tombs, even on the sidewalks themselves. There were no toilets for them to use and no water supply.

Hastily, temporary refugee camps were thrown together, with water lines running to them. Then more careful plans were formed for settling the refugees permanently in new townships. The resettlement of these vast hordes is one of India's very real achievements under Nehru's leadership. No nation in all history has ever had to absorb so many refugees, a total of about nine million over the years. Another six million left India for Pakistan.

Hearing from the refugees their tales of violence done to them or to their slain relatives by Muslims, many people in Delhi grew angry and communal madness spread from the Punjab to the capital city itself. While in many cases individual Hindus, Muslims, or Sikhs risked their lives to save members of the other religions, communal rioting increased. Mobs of Hindus and Sikhs set out to destroy every Muslim shop and kill every Muslim they could find. Nehru himself rushed to place after place where they were on the rampage. Angrily, he ordered them to leave the Muslims alone, telling them that free India would destroy herself if the fighting continued. He risked his life repeatedly. If his words had failed to quiet the mob, the mob would have killed him.

There are countless stories of his personal bravery at that time. Once he rescued two Muslim children who had gone up on a roof while a mob below waited to kill them. On another occasion, he came upon a Hindu mob looting Muslim shops in the middle of New Delhi's most modern and expensive shopping district, Connaught Place. He rushed into the midst of the mob and angrily ordered it to stop. He acted with great political as well as personal courage at the time. He ordered the police to shoot Hindu looters, and he said vigorously and often that India was not a Hindu state and would not become one so long as he was prime minister, that it was a secular state and must be maintained as such, that the lives and possessions of Muslims were entitled to as much respect as those of

Hindus. His uncompromising firmness in taking this stand, unpopular at the time, was an important factor in the gradual decrease of violence.[3] But his campaign to restore peace and sanity was greatly aided by his daughter and by Gandhi.

One day while Indira was riding through the streets of Delhi in an automobile, she saw an old man running as hard as he could. After him ran a mob of perhaps two hundred people, some of them armed. Without stopping to think what she was doing, she immediately jumped out of her car before it had even come to a full stop, and with her back to the running man, faced the mob. A man in the crowd shouted at her, "What are you doing? Who are you?" She answered, "It doesn't matter what my name is, but I want to know what *you* are doing? I know what I am doing. I am saving this man." They answered her, "You cannot save him. We are going to kill him and if you stand there we will kill you too." She replied, "If you want to kill me, you certainly may. But I don't think you have the courage, not one of you." They turned away and dispersed.

When Gandhi, who had returned to Delhi in September, heard what she had done, he praised her for risking her life in this way. She replied that there had been no risk, that "nothing frightens a bully mob more than anybody not being afraid. No weapon is needed and nothing is needed except the fact of genuinely not being afraid."[4] It must have pleased him to see the courage and conviction of this young woman whom he had known from babyhood. He said to her: "I want you to do a job of work. I want you to go into the Muslim *mohallas* [neighborhoods] of Delhi and report and let me know whether they have food, how they are faring, what is the general condition of health and so on." She replied that she had never lived in Delhi before that year, that she did not know her way about, nor which were the Muslim areas and which the Hindu ones. She asked, "Who will go with me?" Gandhi quietly answered,

"If I had one person who could go with you, I would not ask you to do this." So without protesting further, she started out by herself. There was clearly a job to be done and she would do it. She seems always to have been as direct and positive in her response to a challenge as were her grandfather and father.

Not knowing where to go, she went to the town hall. There she saw a girl wearing a white handspun sari, which probably indicated that she too was a member of the Congress. So Indira walked up to her and asked her if she knew her way around Delhi. The girl answered that she did, that she herself had been working in the areas where the laboring classes lived. Indira explained that she wanted to go to Muslim areas and asked if the girl would go with her. She said she would, and they started out before they had even told each other their names.[5]

They went to the Muslim areas not once but many times. They not only found there poverty and want; they also repeatedly came across persons attempting to kill or hurt Muslims. Again and again they called the police, until one day they decided it was more important to do what they could to strengthen the hand of citizens opposed to communal violence than to help the police catch those who practiced it. So they asked each Muslim they spoke to if he knew any Hindus who, throughout this dreadful period, had not done anything to hurt Muslims. Usually a Muslim would concede that he knew one or two such Hindus. The women took down the names and then went to Hindus to ask the same question about Muslims. Next Indira and her companion tried to arrange a meeting between Hindus and Muslims whose names had been given to them in answer to their questions. At first, Hindus and Muslims alike refused to meet each other. The two women went back and forth repeatedly from one house to another. Finally they were able to arrange for a meeting of five members of the one religious group with five of the other. After that the work became easier. Within ten days they organized a meeting of five hundred people. By continuing to remind each group that all members of the other were not evil, they helped decrease communal tension within Delhi.

For months Indira spent over twelve hours a day in the worst trouble spots. Whenever possible she went back to Gandhi to report, for as she said, "These visits gave me fresh strength." Although she had known Gandhi all her life, it was at this time that she came really close to him. When the work for communal harmony took so much of her time that she had no chance to visit Gandhi, he would send her a message of encouragement or sometimes simply a flower.[6]

Finally when the communal tension eased, he decided it was time for her to rest and he sent her off to Lucknow, now the capital of the U.P., where her husband had recently moved to become the editor of a Lucknow newspaper, the *National Herald*. Before she left for Lucknow, Gandhi praised this dauntless young woman whom he had loved since the time when she was a baby, saying to her, "Now I know your education and your years abroad have not been wasted."[7]

Meanwhile, Gandhi too had gone about among the people trying to quiet them. In January, 1948, when complete peace still had not come, he announced that he would begin a new fast, which would last until the Hindu and Sikh communal leaders had promised him they would do everything they could to end the insane killings.

His fast began on January 13. He was now seventy-eight and frail. Fearing for his life, the leaders of the various religious groups hastened to promise him that they would do what they could to bring peace. He ended his fast four days after he had begun it.

Always Gandhi had held prayer meetings in the evenings. At this time the meetings were held in the garden of a prominent businessman, G. D. Birla, Gandhi's host in New Delhi. Troubled by the hatred and violence, thousands of people wanted to hear his message of love. He read from the *Gita,* the New Testament, and also from the Muslim Koran. Day after day he sought in his quiet, loving way to bring the different religious groups together and calm the tension between them.

At his prayer meeting on the evening of January 30, a young man stepped forward toward him and fired three pistol shots straight into his body. Gandhi had time only to say "Ram," one of the Indian words meaning God. Then he fell dead. The whole world was appalled that anyone should want to kill so saintly a man as Gandhi.

The assassin turned out to be a Hindu communalist who said frankly at his trial that he had killed Gandhi because he believed the Mahatma had been too soft toward Pakistan, too loving toward Muslims.

Hindus, Muslims, and Sikhs alike were so shocked by Gandhi's death that at last they stopped fighting completely. So it was that he accomplished by his death what he had not been able to accomplish alive.

Nehru not only felt deep grief over Gandhi's death, he also felt what responsibility he now bore with Gandhi no longer at his side to help and advise him. Nehru's daughter has written: "He left us so suddenly that like the 'babes in the woods' we felt alone and guideless in the forest of problems and difficulties."[8]

She has also painted an unforgettable picture of Gandhi as she saw him the day before he died. He had sent for her and she went to see him taking her three-year-old son, Rajiv, with her. There were garlands of flowers in the room, which visitors had brought to do honor to Gandhi. The little boy took a garland and tried wrapping it around Gandhi's ankles, then draped it over his big toe. Clearly enjoying the little boy's experiments as warmly as did the mother, Gandhi laughed and joked. He was in a remarkably relaxed mood and they talked of many things. Writing of the experience nine years later, she

said, "Little did we guess that we would never see his wide
toothless smile again, nor feel the glow of his protection."[9]

Nehru was fifty-seven at the time of independence. Those
whose image of him was formed by reports of his later years
when his health began to fail, should realize how strong, how
vital, how able, and brilliant a person he was in his full maturity, before the burdens of office tired him out.

Particularly in the early years of independence, the Indian
government under his direction accomplished things which no
one believed possible at the time. One of these many accomplishments had to do with the princely states.

Before the transfer of power to Pakistan and to the new
India, less than two-thirds of the area of the Indian subcontinent was ruled directly by the British. The rest was ruled by
some 562 Indian princes who, at least theoretically, controlled
the internal affairs of their states, under British overlordship
or paramountcy. The British government did not feel that it
could transfer this paramountcy to new India or Pakistan, because, in many cases, it had guaranteed the princes their
thrones. Instead it gave the princes the right to choose for
themselves whether to become independent or to join India or
Pakistan. This could have led to serious results. Many of these
princely states were right in the middle of the subcontinent,
their territories separating the various parts of British India
from one another. Some observers were afraid that because of
this, new India would never be able to remain united.

By clever, patient bargaining, Nehru's deputy prime minister, Vallabhbhai Patel, managed to persuade most of the
princely states that were adjacent to the new India to join it
so far as foreign policy, defense, and communications were
concerned. Next he persuaded the princes to give up their autocratic powers so that democratic institutions like those in the
rest of India could be introduced. He did this by offering them

generous annual allowances for the rest of their lives in return for their renunciation of rule. Quite naturally, many of them did not want to give up their princely powers, but the fact that their territory was often surrounded by the territory of new India made it difficult for them to resist India's pressure on them to comply.

The third step in the process was to join together many of the smaller states or add them to neighboring British provinces. If the administrative units of new India had remained over five hundred in number, the problem of governing would have been enormously complex. The internal map of India needed to be simplified. First, through consolidation, the number of states was reduced to twenty-seven. This number included the former "provinces" of British India, which now came to be known as states also. Later a further reduction took place, followed by certain other changes. Today there are seventeen states in the Indian union.

Few had expected that new India could both swallow and digest the princely states. The unexpectedly smooth and successful integration of these states was one of the first great accomplishments of Nehru's government.

Trouble broke out, however, over the integration into India of the two largest princely states: Hyderabad in the very center of India, and Kashmir to the north bordering on both India and Pakistan.

Long after most of the other princes had made their decision about acceding to India, the Maharaja of Kashmir vacillated. Then in the autumn of 1947, Muslim tribesmen from Pakistan territory invaded his state. The Maharaja hastily announced that he would accede to India, and thereafter the Indian army was flown to Kashmir to defend it. India took the case of Pakistan aggression to the United Nations which, in January, 1949, finally succeeded in getting the two nations to agree to a cease fire on the basis of the territory actually held by their respective armed forces at the moment. The western and northern portions of the state—about a third of its area—fell on the Pakistan side of the cease-fire line demarcated by a U.N. commission. India was in control of two-thirds, which included the lovely lake-filled central valley, or Vale of Kashmir.

Since then Pakistan has repeatedly asked that the people of Kashmir themselves should be given a chance to indicate through a plebiscite whether they wish their state to be part of India or of Pakistan. Most of the Kashmiri population is Muslim, and Pakistan has expected that such a vote would favor Pakistan.

At first Nehru agreed to a plebiscite provided Pakistan withdrew her troops. (Although Pakistan had claimed at first not to be responsible for the invasion since the invaders were unorganized tribesmen, not within Pakistan control, she had sent organized troops into Kashmir as early as the spring of 1948.)

The United Nations, however, did not think that troop withdrawal by Pakistan was sufficient. It recommended that both India and Pakistan draw back. India did not think this just, since Pakistan had been the aggressor in a territory over which India considered her sovereignty legitimate because of the Maharaja's accession. When Pakistan refused to withdraw her troops, India did likewise. Time passed. India integrated the part of Kashmir she held into the Indian union, while Pakistan continued to protest that a plebiscite, which the U.N. had also recommended, should be held. After 1955, Nehru took the position that a plebiscite in Kashmir was now out of the question. Conditions had changed. Too much had happened since 1947 to reopen the question.

In the West, Nehru's refusal to hold a plebiscite was often ascribed to the fact that his ancestors came from Kashmir. Actually a plebiscite there came to seem to him a threat to the very foundations of the Indian nation. If he were to keep religious communalists from fighting each other in the future as they had done during the bloody eighteen months between August, 1946, and Gandhi's death in February, 1948, he had to hold fast to his conviction that religion and politics were separate matters and should be kept separate. The Pakistan demand for a Kashmir plebiscite, on the other hand, was based on the idea that the people of Kashmir if given a free choice would join Pakistan precisely because of their religion. Therefore if Nehru should compromise on this matter, it seemed to him that he would be compromising a principle that he had made the very basis of his national policy. It has been suggested, furthermore, that he felt real concern as to what communal-minded Hindus might do to the forty-five million Muslims still in India at the time if he should yield to the demand for a plebiscite.

Whereas the Kashmir dispute continued over the years and grew increasingly serious, the future of Hyderabad was decided swiftly and with finality in 1948. About as large as France, Hyderabad had a population of sixteen million at the time of independence and an army of almost one hundred thousand men. Although the majority of the population were Hindus, the Nizam, or ruler, was Muslim.

Nevertheless, and fortunately for India, the Nizam did not choose to accede to Pakistan. Sarvepalli Radhakrishnan, the second man to serve as president of India (1962–67), has said that this was because Jinnah once came to see the Nizam while puffing a long black cigar. His Exalted Highness considered this so crude, gross, and disrespectful that he would have nothing to do with Jinnah thereafter.[10]

While remaining aloof from Pakistan, the Nizam nevertheless did not want to become part of India either. He gave every indication of a determination to establish his state on an independent basis. This placed India in a highly awkward situation. It had been bad enough to lose sections of old India to Pakistan, but compared to Hyderabad, those sections had been mere extremities of the body politic, as it were. Hyderabad, on the other hand, was the very heart of the subcontinent.

After a year of fruitless negotiations between new India and the Nizam, the Indian army invaded Hyderabad and quickly seized control before the U.N. Security Council even had time to consider the Nizam's complaint of Indian aggression.

At that time, many Western observers regarded India's action in the matter as highhanded, to say the least, but in retrospect it is clear that the retention by Hyderabad of independent sovereignty would have created a situation completely untenable for Hyderabad as well as for India. Entirely surrounded by Indian territory, Hyderabad would have had no access to the outside world except by permission of India.

From the Indian point of view, one major justification of the sudden seizure of Hyderabad was that communist guerrillas had managed to establish themselves in the eastern part of the state where they had forcibly evicted landlords, terrorized peasants, and exacted tributes from all classes of people. Since the Nizam proved unable to destroy this communist stronghold, it remained a menace to the neighboring states within India. The Indian army succeeded in defeating the communist guerrilla bands and in restoring law and order. The entire large state of Hyderabad has been effectively integrated into the Republic of India and given democratic freedoms which it did not enjoy under the autocratic rule of the Nizam.

In 1948 and 1949, while these and other problems pressed, the Constituent Assembly was busy drawing up a constitution for new India. Nehru did not play much part in the detailed drafting, but at the outset he had laid down its general outlines and he continued to influence what the Constituent Assembly did. In this sense, the constitution was his handiwork. The work on it was finished in the autumn of 1949.

The Indian Constitution combines British and American ideas about government. It is an American, not a British, idea that the form of government, the powers of government, and the basic rights of citizens should be clearly stated in a written constitution. Then too, like the United States, India became a federation of states. Again, like the United States, India has a Supreme Court, with power to decide whether acts of the Legislature are according to the Constitution.

India has an elected president but, in normal times, he is not the chief executive of the nation, as is the President of the United States. He is only the titular head of state, like the King or Queen of England. As in England, the chief executive is a prime minister, chosen by the majority in Parliament. As his ministers or cabinet members, the prime minister must choose members of Parliament. Together the prime minister and his ministers are responsible to Parliament. If Parliament votes against any of their recommendations, they must resign.

This system of parliamentary responsibility is very different from the American system in which the President and his cabinet are completely separate from the American federal legislature, the American Congress, and can continue to hold power even if Congress is critical of their policies.

The constitution makers of new India decided that every adult, women as well as men, should have the right to vote. In a land where only one out of five people can read, this was a brave decision. Previously only people who held property and had some education could vote. Under the 1935 Constitution, for example, only 14 per cent of the adult population were entitled to vote.

The Western type of governmental structure which the Constituent Assembly approved was not to the liking of some of Gandhi's followers. He had always insisted on the importance of India's villages, and had wanted Indian democracy to rest solidly on village democracy. Without being sufficiently specific to be effective, his followers in the Constituent Assembly generally urged that self-governing village councils or *pan-*

*chayats* be established. Some of them wanted the government of India as a whole to stem from these, presumably by indirect elections.

Gandhi's old adversary, the brilliant leader of the former untouchables, B. R. Ambedkar, had been made chairman of the drafting committee of the Constituent Assembly. He was vigorous in his opposition to a government based on village *panchayats*. He said: "What is the village but a sink of localism, a den of ignorance, narrow-mindedness, and communalism!"[11]

The Assembly voted that village *panchayats* should be set up in the future, but did not link these with the state or federal governments. It provided for direct elections instead of indirect elections to fill the seats of the state legislatures and of Parliament. In a nation with a high degree of illiteracy, this may have been a mistake. Indian peasants are generally shrewd in judging people whom they know personally. Under the system of direct elections which was adopted, however, the constituencies are so vast as to preclude personal, first-hand judgments. On the average, each member of the lower house of Parliament represents a million people.

How the individual voter in India decides under such circumstances whom to vote for is a much-debated question. Many observers think that the voters rely on caste leaders for direction. The social importance of castes may be decreasing, as many believe, but at the same time castes are acquiring new importance as potential blocks of voters, like the various politically significant groups in the United States such as Italian-Americans, Polish-Americans, and Negroes.

At Nehru's urging, various clauses to protect the untouchables were written into the Constitution. Untouchability was outlawed and a certain number of seats for untouchables were to be reserved in the legislatures for a temporary period which has since been extended by Parliament to 1970. This was to fulfill Gandhi's promise of 1934 that the untouchables could be sure of adequate representation in the government of free India.

Discrimination on the basis of caste or sex was outlawed, and also discrimination on the basis of religion. This decision to try to make India a secular state was most important. Although so many Muslims had left for Pakistan, 10 per cent of the Indian population were still Muslims and another 5 per cent belonged to other minority religious groups. It was of the utmost importance that everything possible be done to prevent their being treated as second-class citizens.

One feature of the Indian Constitution which Westerners may find odd is the extremely strong "emergency powers" placed nominally in the hands of the president of India, but clearly to be exercised by his prime minister unless political instability is such that no prime minister can be found capable of commanding a majority vote in Parliament.

Whenever a situation arises within any Indian state which, in the president's view, makes the normal functioning of representative government impossible, he may declare "President's Rule." Then the central government takes the government of the state out of the hands of the state legislature and the ministry responsible to it, and rules it directly. If a national emergency exists, the president, or the prime minister, if there is one, is constitutionally permitted to assume almost dictatorial powers. These emergency clauses have proved significant in practice.

By a very close vote the Constituent Assembly decided that Hindi, the regional language of a large area in North India, should be the official language of the central government, though English was still to be used for a transition period of fifteen years.

The Indian Constitution is one of the longest in the world. It includes a list of "fundamental rights," such as freedom of speech and the right to hold property. It also includes a long list of "directive principles," which many considered at first merely a list of pious hopes, since they were not legally binding. One of these reveals with startling clarity the conflict of cultures in India. For it combines in a single sentence the directive that animal husbandry should be organized on modern scientific lines with the contrary directive that the slaughter of cattle should be prohibited. Another directive principle states that there should be free and compulsory education for all children under fourteen, a goal so far beyond India's resources at the time as to seem utopian. Still other directive principles cover Gandhian ideas such as the importance of promoting cottage industries or ideas of Nehru such as land reform, equality of economic opportunity, and the prevention of the concentration of wealth.

Although the Constituent Assembly declared India to be a sovereign independent republic, it also decided that it should be a member of the British Commonwealth of Nations. Interestingly enough, Nehru who had fought so hard against dominion status in 1928 now agreed to this. Having attained for India full independence, he found Commonwealth membership a useful link with the ouside world rather than a fetter.

By 1950, Nehru had brought under control problems which many predicted could never be solved. Order had been restored in the Punjab, refugees had been settled, princely states had been absorbed, and the Constitution had been agreed upon.

The new Constitution went into effect January 26, 1950, just twenty years after that first "Independence Day" on the eve of the civil disobedience campaign of 1930, when no one yet saw a chance of winning independence. Now India called this date her first "Republic Day." The day was celebrated with the same colorful pageantry that the British rulers had displayed on ceremonial occasions, and which they in turn had borrowed from the great Moguls who had preceded them.

At 10:45 A.M. Nehru and the new titular head of state, President Rajendra Prasad, took the oath of office in the great audience hall of what had been the British viceroy's mansion and was now to be the residence of the presidents of India. This ceremony was followed by a 21-gun salute.

Then a red-coated cavalry guard of honor, armed with lances, escorted the new president of India down Rajpath, the broad magnificent axial avenue of New Delhi, which had previously been called King's Way (Rajpath is its Hindi translation). The president took his place on the reviewing stand, seated under a gold umbrella, the ancient symbol of royalty in India. The titular head of the new republic watched a magnificent parade which included battalions of bearded Sikhs, camel cavalry, and elephants decked in gold cloth. At the end, the recently established Indian Air Force saluted with a "fly-past." Ever since, January 26 has been celebrated as "Republic Day." It has become a more important national holiday than the blood-stained August 15 on which India attained independence.

# 12.

# Father and Daughter
# After Independence

INDEPENDENCE brought great changes in Nehru's life, and also in that of his daughter. The police who had beaten and arrested Nehru so often were now under his direction, as was the entire vast bureaucracy of India—the professional Indian civil servants who had been trained by the British and had served the foreign rulers faithfully even if it meant taking action against fellow Indians who were nationalists.

Now instead of long months in prison with more than enough time to read, write, and meditate, Nehru had endless government papers to go over, decisions to make, political leaders to see, sessions of Parliament to attend. Parliamentary democracy of the British or the Indian type is especially taxing because the prime minister, in addition to being the chief executive, must be constantly in contact with his Parliament. If he fails to carry the legislators with him and receives even a single "no confidence" vote, his leadership is ended. His party in Parliament then chooses a new parliamentary leader. If his party still commands a majority vote, the new leader

automatically becomes prime minister. Because of the separation of the executive and legislative powers in the United
States, an American president, on the other hand, can concentrate far more on his executive duties. Even though the Congress occasionally refuses to enact laws which he requests, he
remains in office until the end of his term, whereas a prime
minister under similar circumstances would be replaced.

When Nehru came out of jail in 1945, he went back to live
in Anand Bhawan briefly, moving to New Delhi in 1946 when
he became interim prime minister. There he lived in a four-room
house in which he tried to accommodate altogether fourteen
or fifteen people,[1] including Indira, Feroze, and their first son,
Rajiv, who had been born in August, 1944. Feroze was working at the time as a journalist; Indira became her father's
hostess and in effect the first lady of the land.

In December, 1946, Indira's second son, Sanjay, was born
prematurely. Fortunately, he became a healthy baby but her
own health suffered and she did not feel well again for almost
a year. As late as the autumn of 1947, when Gandhi asked her
to investigate the Muslim areas of Delhi, he felt the need of
apologizing to her for making such a request in view of her
poor health.

The birth of Sanjay increased the congestion in the tiny
Nehru house to the point where it became necessary to erect a
tent outside the house in which Feroze could sleep, while the
mother, the baby, and the nurse stayed in the bedroom indoors.

Shortly after independence, Nehru moved into the palatial
building in New Delhi which had traditionally been the residence of the British commanders-in-chief of the armed forces
in India. It was at this time that Feroze moved to Lucknow to
become general manager and director of the *National Herald*,
a newspaper founded by Nehru himself to support the cause of
Indian freedom. For some while Indira spent half of the time
looking after her father's house and the other half in Lucknow

with her husband, taking her two children back and forth with
her to each place. Again and again her father summoned her to
act as his hostess when visiting dignitaries came. It was she who
had to decide what menu should be served to foreign guests,
what Indians should be invited to meet them, and how the
guests should be seated, a delicate question in diplomatic
circles where a faulty seating arrangement can lead to tensions
between two governments.

It soon became apparent that her father needed her in New
Delhi not only when some visiting potentate was expected, but
more continuously—to choose and train servants, to supervise
the housekeeping of the large house where he was now living,
and to ease his loneliness when the long hours of work were
over. She began spending almost all of her time in New Delhi
with her father. Some of her close friends have said that she
would have preferred to live in a small house of her own with
Feroze, that she acted as official hostess not just out of love
of her father, but also out of a realization that it was important
to her country that her father should have a hostess.

In the 1950's, Feroze was elected to Parliament and moved
back to New Delhi. As a member of Parliament, he was allotted a house of his own. He lived in it most of the time and
entertained his own guests there. He and his wife gradually
drifted further apart. They were never divorced, nor ever
completely separated. When their sons were in boarding school,
they were sometimes reunited at the time of the boys' vacations, but otherwise they usually lived apart.

Tensions between them had developed. Indira told an American writer, "It was not an ideally happy marriage. We were
very happy at times. We quarreled tremendously at times. It
was partly because both of us were so headstrong and partly
circumstances."[2] Far from wanting to take advantage of the
fact that he was Nehru's son-in-law, Feroze was touchy on the
subject. To him it was important to have a career of his own

and not to be overshadowed by his father-in-law. He became a hardworking and outstanding member of Parliament.

In December, 1957, he accused the giant government-owned life insurance company of buying $3,267,000 of worthless stocks "that no sane investor would touch with a tadpole's tail." He charged that this was a corrupt deal to promote the financial welfare of one particular Indian speculator who had been indicted for issuing fraudulent securities. The charge was investigated and led ultimately to the resignation of the Finance Minister T. T. Krishnamachari much against the will of the prime minister. The entire episode was a dramatic and successful attack by the young man on the government which his father-in-law headed.

Mrs. Gandhi's own entrance into politics in the 1950's strained her relations with Feroze perhaps even more than did his ambivalent attitude toward his father-in-law, whom he appears to have admired as well as criticized. She has said that her success in politics hurt Feroze's male ego which is the "biggest sin in marriage."[3]

When he had a heart attack in December, 1958, however, she rushed to his side, but after he had apparently recovered, she went off to her own work again. Her husband lived until September, 1960, when he had a second and fatal heart attack. The pair were very close at the end. She later said they seemed to have gotten beyond the earlier differences which had separated them and that during the summer before he died, they had a nearly perfect holiday.[4] She was with him when he died and was deeply disturbed by his death.

Meanwhile, since 1947, father and daughter had had contact with all the important political leaders of the world and had made innumerable visits to foreign countries. Before World War II, international visits by prime ministers or heads of state had not been frequent. Following World War II, however, one major airline after another inaugurated regular round-the-world air flights. As air travel became routine, so too did international travel by persons high in government. Face-to-face contacts over world issues seemed definitely preferable to the older system of negotiations only through the medium of ambassadors. When Indira and her father were not entertaining in New Delhi such foreign dignitaries as Khrushchev and Bulganin, Nasser, Chou-en-lai, Eisenhower, the King of Saudi Arabia, Mrs. Franklin D. Roosevelt, Mrs. John F. Kennedy, the Dalai Lama of Tibet, and many others, they were often themselves visiting foreign capitals.

Nehru, during his period as prime minister, made some twenty-four trips abroad for official visits. On most of these, his daughter accompanied him. Almost every year Nehru attended the Conference of Prime Ministers of the British Commonwealth of Nations in London. Each time he did so, he tried to include visits to several other countries as well.

In 1948, Mrs. Gandhi went with her father to Paris where he addressed the General Assembly of the United Nations held there that year. In 1949 she came with him on his first trip to the United States. Between 1949 and 1955, father and daughter paid official visits to some sixteen countries, ranging the world from the United States to Indonesia. Although the daughter said little, she was almost always present while her father negotiated or discussed world problems with the head of the nation they were visiting.

In April, 1955, they attended the Afro-Asian Conference held in Bandung, Indonesia. It has been frequently said that at a particular moment during that conference, Nehru was so irritated that he lost his temper, and that Indira helped him regain composure by saying quietly to him, "Father, control yourself." Indira had clearly emerged as more than a housekeeper and hostess. She was also Nehru's most valued and most valuable friend, adviser, and confidante.

In 1956, father and daughter, beside attending the Commonwealth Conference of Prime Ministers and making a second trip to the United States, also visited Ireland, West Germany, France, Egypt, Lebanon, and Saudi Arabia. In 1957, they went to Syria, Denmark, Finland, Norway, Sweden, and Japan. So it went.

After 1959, Indira made a number of foreign trips on her own in addition to one or two more with her father. In November, 1961, she and her father made their third trip in common to the United States. A reporter for the *New Yorker* magazine who interviewed them at their hotel in New York, the Carlyle, heard a secretary tell the prime minister that the great violinist, Yehudi Menuhin, had telephoned hoping to have a chance to see him. The secretary told the prime minister that the schedule was so full that it seemed possible only to give him five or ten minutes the next afternoon. Instead, Nehru directed his secretary to invite the violinist and his wife for breakfast the next morning. This small event was characteristic of the strong affinity Prime Minister Nehru, and perhaps even more especially his daughter, felt for the world of artists of many nationalities.

When he was not traveling, Nehru worked incredibly long hours—seventeen or eighteen hours a day. He was not only prime minister, but also minister of External Affairs, chairman of the Planning Commission, the National Development Council, and the Department of Atomic Energy. For three years, he was also his own defense minister, and briefly his own finance minister as well. He had a compulsion to know the details of what was taking place in every department of government. Indeed, one of the chief criticisms of him was that he did not know how to delegate authority or rely on and thereby develop his subordinates. Many people compared him to the widespreading Indian banyan trees, which grow long hanging tentacles from the tips of their branches. When the tentacles reach the ground they take root and then develop into full-fledged tree trunks themselves, so that the original tree gradually becomes an ever increasing group of tree trunks topped by ever spreading branches. Under the shade of a banyan tree, nothing can grow. So too, under the shade of the all-encompassing Nehru, the development of younger men in government or in the Congress party was retarded.

He maintained an office at the Parliament building, another in the Ministry of External Affairs, and still another in his home. In all three offices he kept several secretaries busy typing his dictation around the clock. After an hour off for dinner—or perhaps two hours if it were a formal state function—he usually worked on his papers until after midnight, sometimes as late as 1:30 A.M. Then he would be up again by 6:30 A.M. After a half hour of Indian *yoga* exercises to keep in good physical condition, he dressed and was ready for work by 7:30 A.M.

Indira and her sons, if they were not at school, always had breakfast with him. Sometimes guests were invited too. The meal seldom lasted longer than fifteen minutes, but it was a time of day when Nehru was relaxed, chatty, and companionable. Lunch, for which he paused about an hour, was at 1:30 P.M. Often he used this time and the dinner hour at night to discuss matters with his colleagues.

Now and then, particularly when his grandchildren were little, he took off brief periods of time to play with them on the spacious lawn behind his residence. He loved children and when he was with them his face shed the careworn expression which was so often there after he became prime minister.

During the years that Nehru was prime minister, his daughter was almost as busy as he. The list of her interests and undertakings is so long that it is almost inconceivable that one person could have dealt with them all.

Yet, particularly before her children went off to school, she spent much time with them. Her friends have commented on the unusual degree of interest and attentiveness with which she listened to whatever they said. Her reputation of being an unusually good mother was such that she won the Mother's Award of 1953 in the United States. She also took a keen interest in the cooking and the interior decoration at their home.

She believes, however, that women should have interests outside the home. Her interests fall into four main categories: the arts, social welfare, education, and politics. She has read widely and has always tried to keep up with developments in all the arts, Western as well as Indian. Before she became prime minister she seldom missed a good motion picture or a new art exhibit. She became vice president of the Federation of Indian Film Societies. She has shown special interest not merely in the revival of classical Indian dance, but also in folk dancing as well. Since 1950, a large colorful folk dance festival, which she helped to initiate and organize, has been held in New Delhi each year in connection with the Republic Day celebrations of January 26. At that time, troupes of dancers brought from various parts of India give performances before crowded audiences. Many of these dancers come from primitive tribes never assimilated into the rest of Indian society. Each has its own traditional bright-colored costumes which differ sharply from the clothing of nontribal Indians. Their folk dances tend to be symbolic expressions of the daily life of the tribe, whether in agriculture, in hunting, or in warfare. Many of them are wild and exuberant, quite different from the more formal stylized Indian classical dance.

Mrs. Gandhi's interest in music is apparently at least as great as her interest in the dance. She has said that in times of stress and strain music has helped her to relax and renew her strength and energy, that she considers music essential for the full harmonious development of one's personality.[5] She was made head of the Indian Academy of Music and Dance, an agency organized to stimulate these arts, and she was active in a society for the promotion of Western music.

Early in the 1950's, when her children began going to school, she became increasingly active in social welfare work. Her special interest was child welfare, but she was interested in women's welfare also because of its effect on the children. In the rural districts outside of Allahabad she established a residential training center for rural women, naming it after her mother.

In 1952, Mrs. Gandhi started the Indian Council for Child Welfare, a nonofficial organization affiliated with the International Union for Child Welfare. This Indian Council organizes child welfare services and demonstration projects on child welfare, sets up holiday homes and camps for poor children, and awards national prizes for children between twelve and sixteen who have shown outstanding gallantry and courage.

Mrs. Gandhi was the moving spirit behind the first International Study Conference on Child Welfare, organized in Bombay in December, 1952, and the leader of another, purely Indian, conference on the same subject in New Delhi in 1956.

In 1953, Mrs. Gandhi founded the Central Social Welfare Board. Throughout the country she had seen that much excellent social welfare work was being done by individuals and voluntary agencies in certain places. She wanted this work spread to every part of the country and felt that a central board would help to bring this about. Today this Board channels government grants to a large number of voluntary welfare agencies, and its branches in the states inspect institutions in order to advise the Central Board which institutions deserve help.

Gradually over the years, private welfare agencies have come to depend more and more upon the financial support of the government, a trend which Mrs. Gandhi has deplored. She has urged people interested in social welfare to continue to look for private funds instead, pointing to the additional freedom to experiment which this gives them.

Not content with promoting social welfare on a national scale, Mrs. Gandhi, in the 1950's, established open-air clubs for poor children in Delhi. These had reading rooms and gave some training in crafts, supplied free milk and some medical services, organized games, picnics, and outings. She soon found that some of the children who came to the clubs had no homes whatever and needed institutional care. In New Delhi, as in most Indian cities, there are many vagrant children who make a precarious living for themselves selling odds and ends, offering to call taxis, or doing other minor services which might bring a tip. The home for children which she founded, Bal Sahyog, was an attempt to prevent these vagrant children from drifting into juvenile delinquency. The home has no locked doors. Boys can leave if they choose. But if they stay, they receive three years of training in some craft, as well as education in language, arithmetic, and social science.

A 1964 press release, listing some of her other activities, details her involvement in everything from the founding of a children's museum to the founding of a bird-watching society. Clearly one of her essential gifts, revealed especially during the period before she became prime minister, was her ability to organize, to interest other people in things she believed should be done, then to leave the detailed work to them while continuing herself to supply leadership and ideas.

Her interest in education led her to become a member of the Central Advisory Board of Education of the government of India, a board that attempts to correlate the policies of the various Indian states regarding education. In 1960, she was a member of the Indian delegation to the annual conference of the U.N. Educational, Scientific, and Cultural Organization (UNESCO), and was elected by the conference to the Executive Board of the organization for a term of four years.

The success of the main activities which she started greatly increased her self-confidence. Earlier she had felt a sense of inferiority compared to her father. Some say that she still does, that all her life she will be trying to prove to him what she can do.

During the 1950's and early 1960's, while active in the arts, social welfare, and education, she also was emerging as a political figure in her own right. Just how she did this can be considered better against the background of her father's accomplishments in office, which will next be considered.

# 13.

# Nehru and the Politics of Independent India

NEHRU REMAINED prime minister to the end of his life. His popularity with the masses became so great that his Congress party won more than 70 per cent of the seats in the central Parliament in each election (1952, 1957, 1962)—automatically guaranteeing that he, as leader of the majority party, would be chosen prime minister.

The first general elections under the new Constitution were held early in 1952. Prior to the elections, Nehru campaigned hard for Congress candidates, just as he had done in 1937 and 1946. (At independence, the Indian National Congress had become the Congress party.) He traveled over thirty thousand miles and spoke to so many vast crowds that it is believed that thirty million people must have heard him. By now the people had begun to worship him much as they had worshiped Gandhi. He was not only the outstanding, the indispensable political leader, he was regarded by the people as almost a saint.

Since India's Constitution had given the vote to all males and females over twenty-one, the electorate was no longer a small body of educated persons, as it had been in the elections held during British rule. In 1952, millions of illiterates went to the polls for the first time. To help these people, the Election Commission decided to assign symbols to each party and also to each independent candidate. Instead of marking his ballot, the voter simply had to place it in the box bearing the symbol of the candidate of his choice. The symbol of the Congress party was a pair of bullocks. Symbols of other parties included a tree, a lamp, a boat, an ear of corn and a sickle —an appropriately Indian variation of the hammer and sickle which is the symbol of the Communist party in most countries.

It turned out that many illiterate workers took these symbols literally. "They had expected to offer their ballot to a living animal, or place it in an actual lamp or boat. . . . Some voters brought grass to the polls to feed the 'bullocks'. . . . Some women voters, finding no bullocks within the booth, kept their ballots and placed them on the backs of the first cow or bullock they met on their return home."[1]

Mrs. Gandhi, who also made some speeches on behalf of Congress candidates during that election, has told of another kind of confusion which she found in people's minds at the time. One day she went to speak in a village where the leader of an opposition party had spoken just the day before. After she ended her speech, an elderly man got up from the audience and said that he had listened carefully to what she had said, but that just the day before another man had told them just the opposite. He wanted to know which of them was telling the truth. Mrs. Gandhi tried to explain that the whole point of democracy is that everybody should say whatever he thinks is the truth and that the people must judge which is the correct version, or the right thing for them. The villagers found this hard to understand. They insisted that it was the government's business to see to it that no people came to tell them incorrect things. Although her schedule called for only ten minutes in that village, she stayed for two hours trying to argue out with them the whole question about freedom of expression. She has added that today no one in India would put such questions as those villagers did in that first election. "Certainly, from election to election they have shown a great maturity,"[2] she has said.

In the remaining two general elections held during Nehru's lifetime (1957 and 1962), Mrs. Gandhi again campaigned vigorously on behalf of Congress candidates, but Nehru himself made fewer speeches. By then he was so well known that the mere fact that he was the leader of the Congress party ensured its success. In recognition of this, on at least one occasion, an opposition party went so far as to print Nehru's picture on their campaign posters alongside the picture of their candidate for Parliament. The author of this book has seen illiterate peasants almost refuse to put their ballots in the ballot box because an election official could not assure them that those very pieces of paper would be placed in the hands of Nehru himself.

Although the masses loved him, some of the party leaders did not. The "Old Guard" conservatives who had been horrified by his radical policies in 1937, still wanted to restrain him. In the first years after independence, they controlled much of the machinery of the party. They wanted him as their nominal leader because they knew he could win votes, but they did not want his socialist policies. Some of them also were opposed to his ideas about the secular state. But just as Gandhi, because of his popularity with the people, had been able to make his policies prevail even when his lieutenants did not like them, so did Nehru.

He had a showdown with the Old Guard in 1951. They had elected a Congress Working Committee which was too conservative for his liking. He asked that its membership be changed to include more members who believed in his policies.

The conservatives refused. He and some of his closest associates then resigned from the Congress. They asked to be relieved of their governmental responsibilities. Many urged Nehru to make peace with the conservatives, but he would not do so. The man who was both president of the Congress and leader of the conservatives at that time, Purshottamdas Tandon, then resigned from the Congress presidency. Nehru was again elected president. He held that position as well as the prime ministership until 1954, then passed it on to a man of his own choosing. By then Nehru had had altogether seven terms as Congress president.

In the 1951 struggle within the party, he had scored an important point. If Congress wanted him as its leader, it must not oppose his policies. From then on, the Congress presidency and the membership of the Working Committee went to persons of whom he approved. His was the final word on every matter, large or small, within the party as well as the government. He did not use his vast authority dictatorially, however. He took pains to consult advisers and tried to reconcile differences of opinion among his followers. No political leader could have been more skillful in doing this than he was.

The fact that he faced not one opposition party, but many —fifteen other parties officially recognized in the elections of 1962—made his position easier. There was political thunder to his right and to his left. But the various thunders never mingled. He governed so long not only because of his own ability and skill at leadership, but also because the opposition was badly divided.

To the left of him were various socialist parties who found his policies—once he attained power—not sufficiently socialistic for their taste. They struggled to gain support from the voters on the plea that he was going too slowly toward the "socialistic pattern of society" which he advocated and which became the avowed Congress goal only in 1955. But Nehru was sufficiently socialistic to make it hard for the socialists to lure votes away from him. Also, they quarreled among themselves and lost strength thereby.

Still further to the left were the communists. Nehru had been impressed by the Soviet Union, but he was a strong foe of communism in India. For one thing, he thought communists were ruthless and doctrinaire. Also, in 1943, they had urged that any region of India that desired to be separated from the rest should be allowed to form a nation of its own. Unless combatted, this proposal could have led to the fragmentation of India.

When he saw the communist menace stretching out into India from Hyderabad state in 1948, he used all the powers which the Constitution gave him to destroy communism in the subcontinent. He not only sent his army into Hyderabad, he also imprisoned great numbers of communist leaders.

Finding that guerilla tactics met such forceful response from the Nehru government, the Communist party of India announced in 1951 that it would contest the 1952 elections within the framework of the government of India. The government then released many of its communist prisoners.

In those elections the Communists received about 9 per cent of the popular vote. This percentage increased slightly in subsequent elections. They received 10 per cent in 1962, and were the chief opposition party.

In the southwestern state of Kerala, the Communist party won enough votes in 1957 to form the government of the state. This Communist state government was the first in any country of the world to receive power through true democratic processes. After some months it became more than clear that it was using its position as the governing party to prevent any other party from taking its place by democratic means subsequently.

Local Congress leaders in Kerala decided to fight the communists along Gandhian lines. Congress party members lay down in the streets by the thousands, making it impossible for Communist cabinet ministers even to get to their offices, let alone govern. Using the emergency powers provided for in the Indian Constitution, the central government took over the government of Kerala, displacing the Communist ministry. New elections were held the following February in which the Congress party formed a coalition with the Praja Socialist party and with the local Muslim League, which had not been dissolved at the time of independence as had the Muslim League in North India. This coalition won and a coalition ministry was installed in the state.

In the early 1960's, the differences between communists who followed the lead of the Soviet Union and those who followed China became acute the world over. This resulted in an outright split in the Communist party of India. The left-wing communists, influenced more by China than Russia, showed signs of reverting to guerilla tactics.

To the "right" and more conservative than Nehru's Congress party were the various parties representing Hindu communalists and the policies of the Old Guard. The Hindu communalists were conservative in cultural matters. The economic conservatives organized themselves into a Swatantra or "Freedom" party in time to contest the 1962 elections. They won a little over 8 per cent of the popular vote.

In addition to parties that were nationwide in scope, there were many that were purely regional. The Akali Dal, strong in the Punjab, was the mouthpiece of the Sikhs of the Punjab. The D.M.K., a Madras party, spoke for those in that state who thought that the south was treated badly by the northern-dominated government. There were numerous other regional parties in addition to these.

One of Nehru's greatest battles as prime minister was against the Hindu extremists, the communalists. More than anything else he wanted to establish a secular state where religion and politics were not mixed, where all religions would be treated equally, and where religious practices would not interfere with progress.

Nehru fought for a secular state in a number of ways. Whenever riots broke out between Hindus and Muslims, he had the police take firm measures quickly. He was also careful to appoint to his central cabinet members of the minority religious groups. He entrusted the important Ministry of Education to a distinguished Muslim scholar, Maulana Abul Kalam Azad, until the latter's death in 1958. That same year, when he established a Ministry for Scientific Research and Cultural Affairs, he entrusted it to another Muslim, Dr. Humayun Kabir. He supported still another Muslim, Dr. Zakir Hussain, for the Vice Presidency of India in 1962. Muhammad Ali Chagla, Ambassador to the United States in September, 1958, later minister of education in the central cabinet, and still later, minister for external affairs, was also Muslim. Many other Muslims have held important positions in the government services or as judges and ambassadors. So, too, have members of the other minority religious groups.

It is particularly significant that Nehru should have entrusted education and cultural affairs to Muslims. It illustrates his strong belief that the culture of India is composed of many strands, and that only by interweaving them, not separating them as the Hindu communalists would do, can India attain lasting unity.

A "secular state" may sound like a natural and even an easy objective to attain. But in India, where such contrasting religions exist side by side and where religion is so important to the masses, a secular state can by no means be taken for granted.

Nehru's aim of establishing one strongly influenced his policy on the much disputed question of the former princely state of Kashmir. Pakistan had again and again urged that Kashmir should belong to it because 77 per cent of the Kashmiris are Muslims. At first sight, this argument made sense to many people in the West, but to Nehru it was an argument that he had to fight with all his power if his much cherished secular state were not to vanish. He could not agree to the idea that religion should determine statehood. If he did so in the case of Kashmir, he believed that his struggle for a secular state within India would be undermined.

Although the Congress party itself contained some communal-minded Hindu extremists, several opposition parties have been organized especially for the purpose of pressing communalist or, at the very least, Hindu ideas. These are the Hindu Mahasabha, the Jan Sangh, and the Ram Rajya Parishad. The slogan of V.D. Savarkar, long president of the Hindu Mahasabha, gives some indication of the nature of Hindu communal thinking, "Hinduize all politics and militarize Hindudom." Savarkar believed that the Hindus should be considered not merely a religious group, but also a nation. Like Muhammad Ali Jinnah, he believed in the "two nation" theory: the idea that the Hindus and Muslims in India were two antagonistic nations living side by side.

The Hindu Mahasabha has asked that the Constitution of India be changed so that India should become a truly Hindu rather than a secular state. It has never fully explained exactly what changes it wanted, nor what would be the positions of non-Hindus in a Hindu nation. The Hindu communalists have repeatedly accused Congress of appeasing Muslims and of creating thereby a "fifth column" of enemies within India. They have also argued that Christian missionaries should not be allowed into India and that those already there should not be permitted to make more conversions. Other points they have asked for include a complete ban on the slaughter of cows, a far sterner policy toward Pakistan, and compulsory military training.

In addition to their political parties, the militant Hindu communalists have a highly disciplined national youth organization, which was formed in 1925 to fight for the Hindu cause in communal riots. It is generally known by the initials of its Hindu title, RSS. Its members meet regularly for military drill, calisthenics, religious ritual, and ideological training. Gandhi's assassin had been a member of both the RSS and the Hindu Mahasabha. The leaders of the RSS were immediately arrested after his death, and the organization was banned. But the government could not prove that the RSS itself had had a part in the terrible act. After nineteen months it was allowed to hold meetings again.

In 1948, Nehru told the Constituent Assembly that "the alliance of religion and politics in the shape of communalism is a most dangerous alliance, and yields a most abnormal kind of illegitimate brood."[3] He also said that Hindu communalism was the Indian equivalent of fascism and nazism. He had vigorously opposed those twin evils; he opposed their Indian equivalent with equal vigor.

In 1950, a proposal was made in Parliament that the Muslims remaining in West Bengal should be sent to Pakistan and that the Hindus in East Pakistan should be sent to India. Nehru opposed this strongly, saying, "such proposals shame us in the eyes of the world. They show that we are narrow, petty-minded, parochial bigots who talk of democracy and secularism but who in fact are totally incapable of thinking in terms of the world or of this great country. They put us in a position in which we have to say to people who are our own fellow citizens, 'we must push you out because you belong to a faith different from ours.' This is a proposition which, if it is followed, will mean the ruin of India and the annihilation of all we have stood for."[4]

In Parliament, Nehru fought a number of other battles over matters on which he differed from the Hindu communalists. They exerted steady pressure on him to agree to a federal law to prohibit the slaughter of cattle. A committee appointed to consider the subject reported that a total ban on the slaughter of cattle would not be in the best interests of the country. India has a large number of old, over-age, worthless cows, which yield little or no milk, and of bullocks no longer strong enough to pull a plow or bullock carts. Hindus do not kill these animals themselves, but they sometimes sell them to members of minority religious groups who want them for their hides and meat. Thus, in the absence of an outright national ban on cow slaughter, there is at least this check on the number of useless cattle. Nehru declared that he would resign from the prime ministership if the cattle preservation bill should be passed. Parliament rejected it, but several members of his own party voted for it, in spite of his opposition.

Another of his parliamentary battles against orthodox Hindus had to do with his efforts to codify the personal law of India. Strange as it may seem to some foreigners, even today Hindus, Muslims, and Christians in India are governed by different laws regarding marriage, divorce, the inheritance of property, and other such personal matters. There is no uniform civil code of personal law. At the time of independence, even Hindus were subject to different personal laws in different parts of the country.

On Nehru's urging, the Constituent Assembly had provided in the Constitution that the government should endeavor to draw up a uniform civil code. As a first step toward this, Nehru considered it most important that uniformity should be attained at least in regard to Hindu law. He wanted also to change all Hindu law where he regarded it as outdated or unfair to women. For example, daughters received no part of their father's estate. Nehru fought successfully for a law to change this. Another law which he sponsored prohibited bigamy and permitted divorce and intercaste marriage. Still another law permitted marriage between members of different religious groups without requiring the marriage partners first to give up their faiths in order to be married to each other, as had previously been the case.

All these changes in Hindu personal laws were vigorously opposed by the Hindu communalists. Why, they asked, should Hindu personal law be changed when the personal law governing other religious groups was not under consideration. Nehru's answer was that only if a statute reflecting modern thinking were adopted for the majority religious group could a uniform civil code covering all people of India ever be reached. He felt, however, that India was not yet ready for a uniform civil code, that all he could do for the present was to prepare the grounds for it.

Clearly he faced a dilemma. He realized how important it was to give the religious minorities the confidence that they would have fair treatment in a nation where the majority were Hindus. He knew that some of their most cherished religious beliefs were contrary to the new Hindu code which he had pushed through. For example, under Muslim religious thought, it is quite right to have more than one wife. Muhammad had married repeatedly.

This posed and still poses a real dilemma. How can a state which wants to keep its religious minorities content, challenge their cherished religion-based laws on matters such as inheritance and marriage? How, on the other hand, can it remain secular if different laws apply to different religious groups?

A second dilemma has to do with education. In India, as in other countries, it is natural that considerable attention be devoted in schools and colleges to Indian history and Indian classical literature. In Indian history there was a long Hindu period followed by a period of Muslim dominance that began around 1200 A.D. and lasted in certain parts of the country until the British conquest between 1757 and 1848. In Indian literature the old Sanskrit religious writings are the most prominent classics. Therefore, it is not easy to teach Indian history or Indian literature in school fairly and without raising strong objections on the part of one religious group or the other.

Did Nehru succeed in his great aim in establishing a secular state? In a sense, no nation is *completely* secular. Nehru did, however, succeed in checking the worst forms of religious bigotry, and this was no simple task.

Nehru encountered one group of interrelated problems which proved to be a veritable hornet's nest. He could find no satisfactory solution to them, nor is it easy to imagine one. These had to do with language. India has no single language known to the majority of the population. Instead, it has a large number of languages which serve as the mother tongues of peoples in different regions of India.

Of these, Hindi, the regional language of the central section of the great northern Gangetic Plains, is known to the largest number—about 40 per cent of the Indian population. In its spoken form Hindi is almost identical with Urdu, the mother tongue of the Nehrus and now one of the official languages of Pakistan. In their written forms, however, the two languages use different scripts. Hindi is written from left to right and contains many straight lines. Urdu is written from right to left—as is the Arabic language which strongly influenced it. Like Arabic, it is composed of many bold curving strokes.

Because they were so alike, Hindi and Urdu in their spoken form used to be called by a single name, Hindustani. Since independence, however, the emotions connected with partition have tended to make them increasingly different from each other. The more educated speakers of Hindi have made a deliberate attempt to replace words of Arabic or Persian origin by words of pure Sanskrit lineage. Likewise in Pakistan, the speakers of Urdu have tried to replace words derived from Sanskrit by words of Arabic and Persian origin.

Usually we do not think of politics as something that can change language, but on the Indian subcontinent it has done just this.

Apart from Hindi, there are about nine major regional languages in present-day India. Except for the North, where a number of states share Hindi, each of the present states of the nation has a language of its own.

Since independence India has gone through a curious, indeed a potentially tragic three-way struggle between Hindi and the other regional languages and English. Before independence, English was generally recognized as the common language for the educated elite, learned as a matter of course. All higher education was given with English as the medium. English was the language of the government and of the higher and lower courts also. Even so, at independence, less than 2 per cent of the population knew English.

The spirit of nationalism brought with it a popular revolt against the use of the language of the imperialistic rulers. In the period immediately following independence, it was considered not quite right to continue to urge the use of English.

More and more young people of lower income brackets have come to aspire to university degrees. Many of the young people lack the English language knowledge to enable them to take in English the matriculation examinations which must be passed before entering a college or university. They and their parents have objected strenuously to the requirement that this examination has to be written in English.

First, therefore, there was a demand that the examinations be held in the regional languages. This was followed by a demand that education at the university level itself be conducted in the regional languages, instead of in English.

The pressure for the increased use of the regional languages had been great. Since the state governments play a large role in the financing of higher education, universities have had a hard time withstanding the demand that they teach in the regional languages instead of in English. Yet there are almost no textbooks in the regional languages and these languages are badly equipped to express scientific concepts.

As the pressure for education in the regional languages has increased, the teaching of English has suffered. Almost everyone in India agrees that English is spoken (and understood) less well today than at the time of independence.

The progressive loss of this common link language can be seen at any national conference—whether of political parties or of trade union leaders or of women's organizations or of other groups. Those present cannot understand one another. Often the use of interpreters is necessary. Scholars educated in one region cannot use their talents in another. The immense dangers that this poses for the future of communications within India can scarcely be exaggerated.

If the struggle were merely between the minor regional languages and English, some way might be found to resolve it. Perhaps in that case, everyone would agree that English, the language of the long detested rulers, might be better than a Tower of Babel with everyone speaking a different tongue.

The existence of Hindi confuses the issue. Hindi is not spoken by the majority. Still it is spoken by far more persons than ever spoke English or any other single one of the regional languages. The people who speak it claim that it should be the recognized single official language of India.

By a narrow margin, the Constituent Assembly decided to continue the use of English as the official language until 1965, after which Hindi would take its place. Many Indians were against this decision to shift eventually to Hindi. Those who came from language areas which did not use Hindi opposed it because they would clearly be at a disadvantage in a nation where a knowledge of Hindi was necessary for holding government office or for communicating with the government. Others opposed it because they believed English to be an essential common medium for the nation, and an essential "window on the world"—a channel through which to understand the major trends of thought in the world at large.

Then too, Hindi is far from a developed language. Compared to such other languages as Bengali (spoken to the east in Bengal) and Tamil (spoken in the important southern state of Madras), it was relatively late in taking form. Both Bengali and Tamil have proud old histories and literatures.

The opposition to the change to Hindi was so great that Nehru had to promise that the deadline would not be adhered to, that English would be used even after 1965. After his death, the attempts of some Hindi enthusiasts to ignore his oral promise and to press for the use of Hindi in government communications to the states immediately led to much violence and disturbance, particularly in the state of Madras. Trains were derailed, telephone lines cut, local offices of the central government sabotaged. The feeling there ran so high that Nehru's first successor, Prime Minister Lal Bahadur Shastri, had to agree that English would still be used along with Hindi in the government communications.

It is an expensive matter for a nation as poor as India to publish all documents in two languages. This requires not only much extra paper (and India is short of paper); it also requires trained manpower to make and verify the necessary translations. Yet this is what is now being done.

What is worse, people belonging to a number of the other language groups have begun demanding that their language also should be regarded as official, that it too be used in government publications.

Language differences and the agitation over them that followed independence led to a redrawing of the boundaries of the Indian states in 1956. As early as 1920, the Congress had organized its provincial divisions on the basis of the regional languages. When independence came, many asked why state boundary lines within India should not be made the same as the Congress party boundary lines. Everyone knew that some reorganization of the states would be needed. The hundreds of princely states and the various provinces of British India had somehow to be consolidated. To continue having hundreds of states in the federation of new India was clearly unwieldy. Then too, the old boundaries were far from logical. They often had been drawn for no reason more weighty than British convenience.

The makeshift consolidation of states, worked out immediately after the princely states were absorbed, reduced their number from several hundred to twenty-seven. It still seemed to many, however, that the boundaries needed to be redrawn. The Indian Constitution gives Parliament the power to do this—a power far greater than the federal government of the United States has.

In the first years of independence, pressure mounted for the redrawing of the state boundaries on the basis of language. Nehru resisted this at first. Agitation mounted, particularly in the southern state of Madras, where the predominant language was Tamil. A very large minority, however, spoke another language—Telegu. Believing themselves to be at a disadvantage in a state ruled by speakers of Tamil, the Telegus agitated for a state of their own. One of their leaders, Potti Sriramulu, resorted to a Gandhian technique to achieve his aim. He fasted. He announced that he would not end his fast until the government had promised to cut off the part of Madras state where the Telegu-speakers lived and make it into a new state to be called Andhra, in memory of an old kingdom which had once flourished there. Nehru refused to make this promise. The Telegu patriot continued to fast. Still Nehru did not yield. Finally, Potti Sriramulu died of fasting. He had made himself a martyr to the cause. The agitation of the Telegu-speakers now became so great that Nehru granted the establishment of Andhra.

This led to a chorus of demands from linguistic minorities in other states. Finally in 1956, there was a general redrawing of Indian state boundaries, chiefly on the basis of language. Since then, further agitation has resulted in certain additional modifications. Today the number of Indian states is seventeen. There are also a number of centrally administered "Union Territories."

From the administrative point of view, the reorganization was convenient, but it has the disadvantage that groups with strong regional loyalties now have states of their own. These regional loyalties often seem greater than the loyalty to the nation as a whole. Many have wondered what effect this will have in the long run on Indian unity.

In the state of Madras in the 1950's, there arose a movement for secession from the Indian union. The Tamils of Madras were strongly opposed to the adoption of the northern language, Hindi, as the national language. They also thought that far too great a share of the large sums of money being spent by the central government on development was being spent in the North. The central government has banned discussion of secession.

Realizing the various threats to national unity resulting from linguistic and regional loyalties, as well as from caste and religious loyalties, Nehru established in 1961 a National Integration Council to consider ways of working for a national outlook that would overcome the divisive forces of language, region, caste, and religion, and integrate the nation. No spectacular results have flowed from it; perhaps none could or can. Much hinges upon how well or how badly India's economic programs work out. If the Indian people see some signs of economic progress as a result of the activities of the central government, they will become far more national-minded than they would if poverty should increase, thus tempting every state, every linguistic area, every caste, every religious group to blame the hard-pressed national government.

# 14.

# The Fight Against Poverty

FROM HIS YOUTH, Nehru had wanted to improve the conditions of the Indian poor and reduce the inequalities of wealth. Now he had his chance to try. He and those around him were to find, however, that the fight against poverty was infinitely more difficult and complex than their earlier fight for independence. Believing as he did that Indian poverty was in large measure the result of British rule, Nehru appears to have underestimated at first the economic task ahead of him.

In addition to the long-term undertaking of modernizing and industrializing the Indian economy, he faced, at the time of independence, acute immediate economic problems. There were millions of homeless refugees to support and relocate. The new international boundary between India and Pakistan had cut across the old established lines of trade within the subcontinent. The chief cotton growing areas fell to Pakistan, while the cotton textile factories were in India. Jute was grown chiefly in East Bengal which now was part of East Pakistan, but the factories which manufactured burlap from this jute were in India. This separation of raw materials from the plants which processed them led to a serious depression in the Indian processing industries. The jute factories of Calcutta, the chief employers of industrial labor in that great city, the second largest in the British Commonwealth, had to shut down since they could no longer receive their needed raw materials. From causes such as this, unemployment rose.

India's food supply was also affected by partition. The chief wheat-growing area was in the part of the Punjab that went to Pakistan. Partly because of this, India has had to struggle hard for self-sufficiency in food grains, although agriculture is the occupation of 70 per cent of her population.

Another reason why the economic situation was grave at the time of independence was that the subcontinent had not yet recovered from the impact of World War II. Having used India as a base for operations against the Japanese in Burma, the British had bought large quantities of food, cloth, and other products in India. This resulted in such shortages and rising prices that the British imposed a system of price controls to prevent inflation. These controls were still in effect at the time of independence. Nehru believed they should be retained. Gandhi, however, was influenced by the business community which hoped to profit by inflation. In the autumn of 1947, he urged that the controls be removed, and Congress followed his lead as usual. Against his better judgment, Nehru removed the controls. Inflation resulted, and the general price level rapidly rose by about 30 per cent, while prices of certain commodities even tripled. Because wage increases did not keep pace with prices, this was especially hard on labor, and many strikes resulted.

Meanwhile, the business community remembered Nehru's earlier speeches in favor of socialism. Worried that he might nationalize industry, they hesitated to start new industries or other undertakings, or to invest more money in existing ones.

This also caused unemployment to rise. The country was in a major economic crisis.

To improve the situation, Nehru took three decisive steps. In the first place, he managed to secure a three-year truce regarding wage disputes. Secondly, he issued a statement regarding socialism and the public ownership of industry which pleasantly surprised the business community. Only three industries were to be entirely in the hands of the government: the railroads, atomic energy, and munitions. He announced that the government might possibly start new undertakings in a number of other fields, but that all existing privately owned factories, mines, shipyards, and the like would remain in private hands. The entire field of consumer goods was to remain "normally" open to private enterprise.

This first industrial policy statement suggested the nature of Nehru's particular brand of socialism. Like the socialism advocated by the British Labour party, his was to be gradual and incomplete. In his own words, India was to have a "mixed economy" in which "the private sector" (private enterprise) would exist side by side with "the public sector" (government-owned industries and other government operations). In general, under his leadership, the government went into lines of activity which private enterprise had not entered and which required especially large capital investments.

Later Nehru subjected private industry to more detailed government regulations than exist in most countries. Even so, private industry generally flourished during his period in office.

The third major step which Nehru took to combat the economic crisis of the first years of independence was to decide that India would adopt a system of national planning. He had been impressed by the results achieved in the Soviet Union through a series of five-year plans. It seemed to him that economic planning was the best way of harnessing all the nation's resources for the fastest possible development of the economy.

Unlike the Soviet leaders, however, Nehru did not think that economic plans should be imposed autocratically from above. On the contrary, he believed that they should be the outcome of discussion at various levels of government, and then subject to approval by Parliament.

In 1950, he set up a six-member Planning Commission with himself as chairman. Its function was to draft successive plans and supervise continuing research on matters bearing on Indian development. The Commission was made responsible to the Indian Cabinet, which made the final policy decisions before submission of the plans to Parliament. To tie the state governments more closely to the planning process, a National Development Council was organized in 1952. The chief ministers of the states were made members of it, as well as the members of the original Planning Commission.

It was Nehru's idea that planning should provide for balanced development, and that the plans should therefore deal not only with industry and agriculture, but also with such other important matters as irrigation, power, communications, transportation, education, and social welfare.

The First Plan (1951–56) focused especially on agriculture. At its outset the shortage of food was already serious. Anxious to be independent economically as well as politically, India had not wanted to ask for economic aid from abroad. But crop failures due to drought forced her to do so in 1951. That year, India received the first of many food grain loans from the United States. By that time it was already clear that agricultural improvement was of major importance, but the obstacles to it were great.

The Indian soil had been worked for centuries. Much of the nourishment which crops need had been used up. In the case of most crops, the yield per acre in India was among the lowest in the world. The situation was made all the worse by the fact that very little artificial fertilizer was available to add food to the soil. The most important natural fertilizer, cow dung, was, and still is, customarily used in India not in the fields, but as the household fuel for cooking purposes. Wood for fuel is scarce in most parts of the country, since the woods have been largely cut down as population expanded. Coal and kerosene are too expensive. Electricity and gas are likewise expensive and in many places unavailable. As late as 1951, only 3,600 of India's 570,000 villages received electricity. Over one-third of even the major cities with populations of over 100,000 also lacked electricity.

Even today, though steel plows are being introduced as rapidly as possible, the characteristic plow remains nothing more than a crude pointed stick with only a tiny tip of steel. It is so light that it can barely scratch the surface of the land. At harvest time, the men and women cut the grain in handfuls with crude sickles. Threshing is done by hitching together several pairs of oxen and driving them around the threshing floor on which the grain has been laid. The pounding of their hoofs separates the kernels from the stalk. Then the stalk is lifted off and the grain is brushed into piles. It is a wasteful way of threshing, but few Indian peasants can afford modern threshing machines.

Knowing that experience has shown that the application of science to agriculture can lead to a great increase in output, Nehru determined to stimulate a scientific revolution in Indian agriculture. He wanted to teach peasants modern methods, to make available to them improved equipment, and supply them with fertilizers and new varieties of scientifically improved seeds. This was a large undertaking. New research was needed to produce improved seeds that would thrive in Indian soils and in the hot Indian climate. Then ways had to be found of reaching scores of millions of agricultural families, most of them unable to read and write. Many spoke dialects unfamiliar to the educated people from the cities. At first they were suspicious of the government officials sent out to make contact with them. Until independence, whenever officials came near their villages, it had been to collect more taxes. The peasants were still suspicious and could not believe that the government was now sending its employees to help them.

Then too, most of the peasants had so little money that they could not buy the equipment or the fertilizers they needed. Most of them were heavily in debt to money-lenders and could not borrow more except at exorbitant rates unless the government supplied cheap credit.

Peasants the world over tend to be conservative in their point of view and hesitate to try new methods until the value of these has been proved to them beyond doubt. With no savings to fall back on if the new should fail them, as it sometimes does, the risk seems to them too great to take.

In the early years of independence, the government promoted the seed of a new strain of wheat producing a heavy yield, but the stalks of the new plant proved too weak to hold upright their heavy heads. The government then promoted a still newer strain. Its stalks were strong but so tough that the cattle could not chew them. The government had failed to give consideration to the fact that the peasant must rely on his wheat not only for grain, but for fodder for his cattle.

During the 1950's, the attempt to increase agricultural output was combined with an attempt to improve village living in general, to teach villagers about hygiene, sanitation, better housing, better cattle breeding, and many other matters. The total program of village uplift was called the Community Development Programme. Young men known as Village Level Workers were employed by the government to take to the villagers all the information they might need on a wide variety of subjects. Usually between five and ten villages were assigned to one Village Level Worker and he was given a bicycle with which to go from one to another.

At the "Block" headquarters to which the Village Level Workers of a given area reported, they could turn to experts in each of a number of fields for the answers to special problems which might arise, but they were expected to know a great deal about many subjects.

On the whole, the task assigned to these young men proved too great for them. The Indian villagers were not ready for many of the new ideas. Except when a Village Level Worker proved to have exceptional abilities both as a diplomat and as a teacher, the villagers resisted change.

Here and there some changes in village living did take place. In some villages, new wells for drinking water have been built which are far more sanitary than the old-fashioned type of well, into which polluting surface water could run back. Some village lanes have been paved with bricks so that they will no longer become mires of mud in the rainy season. It is in terms such as these that one must visualize the changes in village living accomplished under Nehru in the 85 per cent of India that is rural.

Meanwhile Nehru had attempted to implement his promises of land reform first made in 1928, and again more vigorously and systematically in his 1937 election campaign. It seemed to him that one reason for India's low agricultural yield was that the peasant had little incentive to improve the land he tilled by fertilization, leveling of slopes or other means, since he normally did not own it.

Under the Constitution, control over land policy was placed in the hands of the states, not the central government. At Nehru's urging, the states adopted laws dealing with the matter in various ways. Because landowners were politically powerful, particularly in the early 1950's, none of these laws went as far as Nehru would have wished. In general, they did abolish the system of *zamindari* or tax farming, and took away from the *zamindars* all the land from which they had derived income except for their home farms which were not limited in size. They placed ceilings on the size of holdings that could be acquired in the future but not on present holdings. To forestall loss if ceilings should be placed on existing holdings, large landholders parceled out tracts of land to members of their own families.

Altogether the laws created no marked change in the peasants' situation. Land reform under Nehru has often been called woefully inadequate. Most of the actual tilling continues to be done by landless agricultural laborers employed for so few days in the year that they are almost unemployed. Indians call them "under-employed."

For the purpose of helping impoverished peasants to secure loans at reasonable interest rates so that they might finance farm improvements which might lead to increased yields, the government created a network of cooperative credit associations in rural areas and gave them financial backing. Evidence seems to indicate that this network also largely failed to achieve its purpose, as large landowners and men of substance managed to secure control over the cooperatives, to borrow the government money intended for the really poor, then to lend it out to the latter at the old usurious rates of interest.

By the late 1950's, it came to be realized that land reform and cooperative credit had not yet proved helpful so far as improved agricultural yield was concerned. Nor had the Community Development Programme succeeded in this direction. Little could be accomplished if one district adopted new seeds, while another received aid in irrigation, and still another began using fertilizers. A far greater crop increase would result if these and other needed "inputs" were brought together in one place. A new intensive program, the "package program," was then adopted. Certain districts were selected to receive special help, including irrigation, fertilizers, seeds, pesticides, technical advice, and anything else required. Within three years a quick rise in production had been accomplished in these districts. From the political point of view, the selection of certain districts for favored treatment was a dangerous and hence a courageous step. It was a fine demonstration of what could be done under the best conditions.

Apart from the increases in these selected districts, India's output of food grains on an overall basis also increased during the seventeen years when Nehru was prime minister. It is impossible, however, to say exactly by what percentage. Indian agriculture has always fluctuated greatly from year to year depending on whether the annual rains, the monsoons, have been good. Therefore, it can be misleading to compare one crop year with another. In some of the years of the early 1960's, India suffered from poor monsoons and resulting crop failures. But in one year of good weather, 1961–62, the food grain output was 81 million tons. In 1950–51 it had been only 50 million tons. This would indicate an increase of 64 per cent in that period. Although this was an accomplishment, the Indian planners had begun to realize that population growth might soon outstrip increased yields.

The Indian census is taken every ten years. The 1960 census showed a population increase of 21.6 per cent since 1951: that of 1951 had shown an increase of only 13.3 per cent in the previous decade. Improvements in health facilities had clearly decreased the death rate, while the birth rate had not yet fallen. Nehru's daughter inherited the major problem of how to keep crop yields growing faster than the population, and how to keep the population from growing still faster than it has in the past.

In India, irrigation is of particular importance. In most of

India, the rainfall is concentrated in a three-month period. The rest of the year is predictably rainless. Yet during those rainless months, the weather is warm enough so that a second crop can be grown at that time, providing that water can be brought to the land from time to time. The kings of ancient India realized this and built many large storage tanks, particularly in South India. These tanks collected water in the rainy season and released it in the dry season through canals which fanned out into ever smaller canals leading to the fields. Later the British developed a splendid network of canals in North India, one of their real contributions to Indian welfare. Most of these canals came from reservoirs fed by rivers which had their source in the snows of the high Himalayas. Hence they could be counted on more surely than the rivers of South India, which tend to dry up during the dry season.

At independence, it seemed to the Nehru government that still more reservoirs were needed. Like people in many developing nations, the Indians were impressed by the Tennessee Valley project in the United States. The basic idea of TVA is that a number of different purposes can and should be accomplished at once in the development of a river valley. The high dams which create the reservoirs for irrigation also make it possible to generate electricity by the power of the falling water, and the flow of the water can be regulated so that floods are controlled also.

Particularly in the first ten years of planning, India embarked on a number of large "multi-purpose" river valley developments. The increase of electricity generated was great but, so far as irrigation was concerned, it was realized by 1961 that large dams were not the answer. More might be accomplished at a lower cost by smaller projects. Canals from the big dams can reach only the land that is low enough for the water to flow there by gravity. Also, peasants need to be educated as to how to use canal water successfully. In the late 1950's, the planners discovered with dismay that only a small fraction of the flow from the expensive new dams was being used.

On the other hand, from time immemorial, Indian peasants have known how to irrigate their fields from wells in their own fields. Any field can be watered from local wells providing it has been leveled. Traditionally, these wells have been shallow. Until recently, the methods used for raising the water have scarcely changed in two thousand years. One method is the "Persian Wheel." Over the mouth of the well is suspended a wheel from which a loose circular chain hangs down into the water of the well. Attached to the chain are many small buckets. As the wheel revolves, the buckets come up to the surface full of water and dump their contents into a little channel. From there the water is guided first to one part of the field, then to another by human labor—by digging together mud obstacles to guide it where it is needed.

To make the wheel over the well mouth revolve, a set of rusty gears is used. They connect the wheel and its chain with an upright pivot, far enough away to one side of the well so that a pair of bullocks or a camel can walk around and around it, pulling a beam attached to the pivot. As the animals and the central pivot go around, the gears and the wheel translate this motion into the continual rising of the little buckets in the well. Boys as young as ten spend hours on end, often all their days in the dry season, keeping the animals moving so that the water will rise and the family crop will not fail.

Crude though a Persian Wheel is, it is more advanced and efficient than some of the other ways in which poorer peasants raise water from their field wells. If they cannot afford the gears which are necessary for the Persian Wheel, they simply erect a crude wooden pulley near the well mouth, dig a slope going down from it, place a rope over the pulley, attach one end of this to the yoke of their bullocks and the other to a cowhide bag which they drop down the well hole. As they drive the bullocks down the slope, the bag comes up and is dumped to one side. Then they back their bullocks up the slope and the bag drops down for more water. To back bullocks up a slope again and again all day is strenuous work. It is much easier to operate a Persian Wheel.

Some Indian peasants even in the recent past used a still more arduous way of raising water. If a man had no bullocks or if he needed them for other work, he built over his well a beam like a high seesaw. A bucket was attached to one end. By walking back and forth across the beam, two men working together could raise and then lower the bucket by dint of their own human energy.

One difficulty with raising water in any of these three ways is that animal or human power by itself can raise water only from shallow wells. Often in a period of bad drought these wells would run dry.

After the Indian planners began to see that large dams were not producing the results in proportion to their cost, attention was paid to helping the peasants dig much deeper wells and install simple kerosene or electric pumps capable of bringing up more water and irrigating much larger pieces of land than could be irrigated from the old shallow wells by the old methods.

These new "tube wells" are growing rapidly in number. Although the Persian Wheel and the inclined slope have not entirely disappeared, one seldom sees the old walking beam well. As one motors along a country road these days, one hears repeatedly the high beep-beep-beep of the little one-cylinder kerosene engines of the tube wells. The countryside in many places is dotted with the little white boxlike concrete buildings in which the kerosene or electric pumps are generally housed. Progress is occurring in the countryside, though more slowly than Nehru desired.

In the Second Five-Year Plan, emphasis shifted from agriculture to industry. This was perhaps partly because the Indian planners had not yet realized fully how difficult and how pivotal agricultural improvement would be. It was also because Nehru and the men around him saw that India had an alarming surplus of underemployed agricultural labor and that new industries would be needed if they were to find jobs which really supported them. Then too, government officials saw that the industrialized nations of the world were more prosperous than the nonindustrial ones. There seemed to be a magic about industrialization which might cure many ills.

The steel industry, of course, is basic. Steel, and machines made out of steel, are essential to the development of all other industries. India has one of the largest reserves of high-grade iron in the world and ample supplies of coal nearby. With such natural resources, it seemed obvious to Nehru and his Planning Commission that India should build up her steel industry. The two existing plants, both privately owned, were encouraged to expand their operations greatly. With Russian, German, and British aid, three great new plants were built by the government in the "public sector." The government also developed a number of other basic industries in the public sector: a locomotive factory, a fertilizer factory, three factories to make heavy electrical equipment, and factories to make machines, including machines capable of making machines.

Both in the private and the public sector there has been a tremendous expansion of production in existing industries and the development of a host of new industries. Automobiles, locomotives, railway coaches, telephone equipment, cables, industrial chemicals, antibiotics, electrical equipment, fans, radios, light bulbs, ball bearings, rayon, razor blades, linoleum, air conditioners, fertilizers, and many new kinds of machines and machine tools are among the products that were formerly imported, but are now being made in India.

Privately owned plants have sprung up by the score on all

the roads radiating out from the great cities. Total industrial production in India is almost three times as great as it was in the beginning of the 1950's.

While the Indian economy continued to remain "mixed," however, the proportion of socialism in the mixture gradually increased under each successive plan. In 1951, as has been noted, Nehru freed himself from the more conservative Old Guard who had largely controlled the Congress party machine until then. Thereafter, opposition within India to increasing socialization came to be more and more difficult as government regulation of every detail of private industry increased. Indian businessmen had to turn to the government for permits to start new enterprises, to invest additional capital, to import machinery or raw materials, and to take any other step of significance.

From Nehru's point of view, there were good reasons for this tight regulation. Capital was scarce in India. Therefore, it was important that it be used in lines of production which would help India's basic economic growth, rather than in non-essential lines. It seemed clear to Nehru that only the government could decide what was best for the country as a whole. Then too, especially after 1956, there was a shortage of foreign exchange, the kind of purchasing power which makes it possible for a nation as a whole, or individuals within it, to import goods from abroad. Again it seemed obvious that the limited foreign exchange should not be wasted, but should be used in ways likely to help Indian development. A businessman who depends on the government for permits may hesitate to criticize that government for fear of reprisals from it. Even among Indian businessmen, the small group which would otherwise probably have fought socialization, there came to be a reluctance to oppose Nehru's policies too vigorously or too openly. Then, too, certain private industrialists acquired near monopolies over the production of particular kinds of products, by reason of the government's reluctance to grant permits for starting enterprises which would duplicate existing ones. The protected position of these industrialists was highly enjoyable to them. Not having to worry about competition, some businessmen were sincere in their support of Nehru's economic policies.

As the opposition to socialization weakened, Nehru was able to persuade the Congress party at its annual session in 1955 to adopt a resolution strongly favoring socialism and advocating for India "a socialist pattern of society."

The following year, he followed this up with a new industrial policy statement which specifically allotted to the government a much larger sphere of business operations than had the earlier statement of 1948.

In the Third Five-Year Plan, 1961–65, it was contemplated that 60 per cent of all new industries should be government owned and operated, and only 40 per cent by private enterprise. Yet by then the government itself had discovered that the efficiency at the plants it owned and operated was not high, and that they usually ran at less than their maximum capacity.

The pressure for the quickest possible industrialization, at a pace far faster than took place in Western countries, produced a vicious circle. It required ever higher taxes, hence threatened to dry up the source of private savings without which private investment is impossible. The increasing shortage of private capital in turn provided more basis for the argument that the government itself should take over an ever increasing role in industrialization.

Still another difficulty arose from the large role that the government played both in the direction of its own industries and in the regulation of those privately owned. These activities placed a heavy burden on the all-too-small staff of trained government administrators. Many forms of delay resulted which caused economic loss. Private businessmen often had to wait months for permits to import items they needed immediately if they were to operate efficiently. Then, too, the danger of corruption increased, as businessmen perhaps sought to minimize these delays by bribes. Corruption on the part of government employees has been known to exist in countries other than India. How much of it exists there cannot be stated, but the cynical feeling is spreading in India that corruption is widespread, deep-rooted, and perhaps even customary.

If Motilal had been alive, he doubtless would have said to his son, "I told you that socialism would hurt our cause, not help it." It is impossible to say, however, whether India would have made greater economic progress with less socialism. Some economists argue that it would not have, that the amount of capital which the Indian government managed to secure for the starting of new industries could never have been raised by private Indian capitalists. In any event, it is clear that what led Jawaharlal to adopt socialism was his sincere and troubled sensitivity to the poverty he saw around him.

Aside from the rapid growth of new industries and some improvement in agriculture, progress was made under Nehru's leadership in a number of other ways. The multiplication of educational opportunities, to be treated in the next chapter, and the increase of the potential supply of electricity, basic to many aspects of modernization, were fully as striking. The installed capacity of electric generating plants (both hydro and steam) increased from 2.3 million kilowatts in 1950–1951 to 10.2 million kilowatts in 1965–66—far more than a threefold increase. By the time of Nehru's death, almost every city or town with a population of more than 10,000 was electrified, in the sense that electricity was available to those who could afford to use it. Some 36,000 of India's 570,000 villages with a population of less than 10,000 had power lines running to them, a tenfold increase since independence. Few villagers could afford to use the new electricity for domestic purposes, but they could and did use it to help pump water from the ground. The amount of electricity used for irrigation increased fourfold during Nehru's seventeen years in office.

Similar indications of real progress could be cited in many other areas as well. As against 145,000 kilometers of paved or black-top roads in the entire nation in 1947, there were 235,000 kilometers in 1961. For unsurfaced roads, the corresponding figures are 242,000 in 1947, and 400,000 in 1961. Over a hundred major bridges had been built during this period. These replaced such unsatisfactory arrangements as pontoon bridges which became unusable during the monsoons, or slow ferries, propelled by oars.

Roads, bridges, air transport, communications, port facilities, and electric power potential are often grouped together by economists and spoken of as the "infra-structure" of a nation's economy. The infra-structure includes all the basic facilities which must be developed before there can be any rapid general economic development or rise in the standard of living. India, under Nehru, made marked progress in developing her infra-structure, but the fight against poverty itself had made little progress.

Per capita income at the time of independence was only slightly over $50 a year—a figure so low that it is almost incredible to those in the West who take for granted a standard of living which includes not merely the bare necessities of life, but many comforts, conveniences, and luxuries as well.

Income stated in money terms cannot, of course, give an adequate picture. The Indian prices for food and clothing are lower than those in the West, and in the villages many transactions still take place by barter without reference to money standards, so that cash income is usually far smaller than total real income.

The average Indian had just barely enough food to prevent starvation, perhaps a few new yardages of cheap unsewn cloth per year for clothes, plus housing of a standard below that of even the worst slums in the West. He could spend money on almost nothing else.

By 1964, per capita income had gone up slightly—by about 16 per cent—though increased taxes and rises in prices had partly offset this increase. More Indians had begun wearing sandals instead of going barefoot. Many more men had acquired bicycles so that they no longer had to walk long miles to their work. Although the average Indian was not yet adequately nourished and the vast majority were not eating a balanced diet containing sufficient proteins and vitamins, nevertheless the consumption per person of the better food grains, wheat and rice, had risen. Then, too, more people were buying kerosene lanterns and using light more often at night.

Compared to the expectation of rapid economic betterment which many had had at the time of independence, these small changes in the standard of living were disappointing. Worse than that, many danger signals loomed ahead. Although industry had been expanding, it had not been expanding fast enough to absorb the constantly increasing surplus of manpower from the rural districts. By 1964, according to one estimate, both unemployment and underemployment had increased to such an extent that about 25 per cent of the working days of the total working population of the nation was wasted in idleness. No nation can prosper if so large a percentage of its population is unproductive.

Meanwhile, as the government of India became increasingly conscious of the scale of the task ahead of it, it had almost doubled the size of each successive Five-Year Plan. Beside raising taxes sharply to pay for these plans, the government had borrowed heavily from foreign governments. From the United States it received more than $5 billion in foreign aid, most of which had come in the form of food loans, to be repaid in Indian currency (rupees), not American dollars. Foreign aid had also come from the Soviet Union, the World Bank, West Germany, the United Kingdom, Japan, Canada, and France. The order in which these are listed indicates, in decreasing size, the amount of this aid.

In the mid-1950's, Indian spokesmen had talked hopefully of a future "take off point," a time when the Indian economy would no longer need large loans from abroad. They expected it soon to become "self-generating," able to supply from within the capital and equipment needed for further development. In the 1960's, however, Nehru saw the old hope for a take off point grow dim. It became clear that India would continue to need foreign aid for some time to come. An important reason for this was India's shortage of foreign exchange, already mentioned.

Basically no nation can buy from abroad more than she sells abroad unless loans or grants make up the difference. If a nation does not sell abroad enough goods or services at least to equal what it buys, then it cannot earn foreign currencies and its own currency loses value in the international market. In spite of India's severe governmental restrictions on all nonessential imports, it would not have been possible for the government or private businessmen to import the machinery, spare parts, and raw materials needed for industrial progress if India had not received ever increasing foreign loans.

To place in perspective Nehru's record in the economic field, it should be noted that India was not the only underdeveloped nation during that period to fall short of hopes and expectations on the economic front.

Economists tell us that in recent years per capita incomes have been rising more slowly in the relatively poor countries than in countries such as the United States that were relatively rich to start with. Economists see many reasons why wealth tends to lead to greater wealth, and why poverty tends to continue. One of these has to do with education. A rich land can afford high-grade schools and colleges in which the young people can learn, if they choose, advanced technology and other physical or mental skills that will enable them to become more productive than their parents. A poor land cannot afford enough schools or colleges, or ones of adequate quality. It cannot give enough young people the kind of education which would enable them to make full use of the technological knowledge available in modern times.

Another reason why rich lands grow richer and poor lands grow poorer has to do with the accumulation of the capital needed for economic progress. In rich lands, capital is accumulated almost automatically. Not needing to spend all they earn, people tend to save. Through their banks or through their own direct purchases of stocks or bonds of industrial concerns, their savings become available for economic expansion. On the other hand, in a land where the majority are desperately poor, few can save and the supply of capital is not sufficient for the nation's needs, even when capital is forceably accumulated by the government through high taxation.

What will happen in the long run if the gulf between rich lands and poor lands continues to widen? This is a question of real concern not only to government policymakers, but also to every thinking citizen.

# 15.

# Progress in Education

In 1959, an American correspondent asked Nehru what he regarded as the most encouraging development in India. In his answer, he placed first the development of education.[1]

Quantitatively, the increase in educational opportunities under Nehru's leadership was tremendous. By the time of his death, the number of primary schools in the country had doubled since independence. Most of these new schools were simple one- or two-room buildings in rural areas which had never had a school before. The enrollment in the first five elementary grades had risen from 14 million to some 35 million. The percentage of children between six and eleven years of age who were in school had increased from 35 per cent to 61 per cent.

The number of secondary schools increased still more, and their enrollment rose from 2 million to 6 million, a threefold increase. The percentage of young people between eleven and fourteen attending school rose from 9 per cent to 23 per cent. Although the increase is great, even today three out of every

219

four young people between the ages of eleven and fourteen are not in school.

More than a fivefold increase has occurred in school attendance at high school age, yet only 18 per cent of that age group are in schools.

In 1947, there were only 200,000 students enrolled for higher education. By 1964, the number had soared to a million and a half—a sevenfold increase in seventeen years. The number of colleges and universities had greatly increased. Even so, less than 3 per cent of the young people of college age were receiving higher education.

The tremendous, if still inadequate quantitative expansion of educational opportunities at every level unfortunately was not accompanied by much improvement in the quality of the education offered. The teachers were and are so poorly paid that the teaching profession seldom attracts people with sufficiently good minds to get another job. Many teachers are untrained as teachers and a considerable number have not even finished high school themselves. The vast majority of the teachers, especially in the rural districts, are men, since few village women are sufficiently educated to teach, and since educated women from the cities would hesitate to move into an Indian village. This creates a vicious circle, for village families do not like to have their daughters taught by men. At the time of Nehru's death, only forty girls were enrolled in school for every one hundred boys. In the rural districts, most of these remained in school only in the lower grades.

Indian schools lack the abundant educational resources available to Western schools. Visual materials of any kind are often entirely lacking. In a school in a city slum, where few if any students have ever seen even a blade of grass growing, a teacher may drone on about the growing of rice—without a single photograph to illustrate what a rice field looks like—or about the various steps of cultivation which he describes only in words. Textbooks, normally handed down from one class to the next until they fall apart, are not only dog-eared and dirty, but often unsufferably dull.

Students in the West who are accustomed to question the all-mighty wisdom of the teacher would find the Indian classroom strange, with its marked authoritarian atmosphere. Students are seldom encouraged to discuss or to think for themselves. They must learn by heart what the teacher tells them.

The problem of drop-outs, recognized even in the United States as serious, is many times more serious in India. Out of every five children who enter the first grade, only one reaches the eighth grade. This is partly because, in the rural districts where most of the population lives, children are often needed at home, to help with farm work or to watch over baby brothers and sisters. It is also partly because there is no tradition among the lower classes that an education is a useful thing to have, essential in the long run to the best welfare of the young student. Probably also it is in part due to the dull character of much of the teaching. Yet an odd and moving aspect of the drop-out situation in India is that if one visits an "adult" literacy class, held after dark and usually lighted only by a single oil lantern, one may find that most of the adults in it are young men between fourteen and sixteen who had to abandon their schooling earlier because their families needed them for work, but who still care enough for an education to try to learn what they can, after an eight- or ten-hour day in fields and factories. Between 1921 and 1961 the rate of literacy rose from 8.3 per cent to 24 per cent.

Although the Indian government has attempted to increase the proportion of technical and vocational training in the schools, it has made only limited progress in this regard, due to the difficulty of finding teachers capable of teaching such subjects.

At the university level special problems arise. Some universities are so crowded that their classrooms are in use eighteen hours a day. The number of hours which a professor or instructor must teach is far greater than in the West, leaving them little time to prepare their lectures, let alone do original research to keep their minds keen and fresh. Most of the students are so poor that they live at home if they can, rather than in dormitories or student hostels. At home, conditions are often so crowded and the light so bad that they have difficulty doing their homework.

About three out of every four students drop out of the universities because of failing their examinations before securing their B.A. degree. One reason is doubtless that at this level the teaching emphasis is still on memorizing rather than thinking, yet the examination system is one that is particularly hard on students who have docilely memorized and have not thought and read further on their own account. The examination questions are drawn up, and the student papers are graded, not by the persons who teach the students in their colleges, but by the universities of which the various colleges are members. Unless a student has a truly agile mind, he finds it hard to deal with questions posed by someone other than his own teacher.

Another problem for the students is that of language. In spite of political pressures to shift from English to some Indian language for teaching purposes, the universities still use English as the medium of instruction. This is partly because textbooks at this level have not been translated into the regional languages, and partly because higher education today needs words and terminology for which the Indian languages have no equivalents. Unfortunately students come to the universities with little if any knowledge of English, since the teaching of English at school level has greatly decreased since independence. It cannot be easy to learn subject matter taught in a foreign language with which one is not familiar.

In his great ambition to improve educational opportunities, as in his desire to raise the standard of living, Nehru made some progress, but he also encountered difficult problems. Colossal tasks lie ahead if Indian education is to be made adequate (qualitatively as well as quantitatively) for the needs of this developing nation.

# 16.

# Nehru's Foreign Policy

NEHRU'S LONG INTEREST in foreign nations and international relations made it natural that he personally should decide on India's foreign policy.

Since his participation in the Congress of Oppressed Nationalities in Brussels, Nehru had been particularly interested in the emerging nations of Asia and Africa. In 1947, even before independence was won, he invited representatives from a number of these nations to come to New Delhi for a conference. He called together a second conference in 1949, and took part in the organization of the larger Afro-Asian Conference of 1955, held at Bandung, Indonesia. For some years he was regarded widely as the leader of the Afro-Asian nations, many of whom followed India's lead in voting on resolutions at the United Nations.

The keystone of Nehru's policy toward the major powers was "nonalignment." At first, people in the West were critical of this. They thought India should line up with the West in the "cold war" between the West and the communist nations which was particularly intense in the early years of Indian independence. Nehru insisted, however, that it would be better for world peace if a group of nations should stand aside from the enmity of the two opposing blocs of great powers. A nonaligned bloc, he believed, should be able to mediate usefully between these opposing powers. Again and again he tried to do so.

To Westerners, it often seemed that India's nonalignment was somewhat nominal, that actually the Nehru government leaned more toward the Soviet Union than toward the West. Nehru appeared to criticize the policies of Western nations more often or more vigorously than he criticized those of the Soviet Union. In 1956, for example, he was indignant when the British and the French took action against Egypt over the Suez. Yet when Soviet tanks subdued a rebellious Hungary shortly afterward, he said relatively little.

If he was slightly pro-Russian, there were logical reasons for this. As he had pointed out in the book on the Soviet Union which he wrote in 1928, that great nation was very near India's borders and could easily be a "thorn in India's side" if relations became strained.[1] Then too, the Soviet leader, Khrushchev, strongly supported the Indian position on two controversial questions of great importance to India: the Indian seizure in 1961 of the Protuguese enclave of Goa on India's West Coast and the Kashmir question which continued to embitter Indo-Pakistan relations.

On the other hand, the United States had antagonized Indian opinion in 1954 by beginning a large program of military aid to India's chief enemy, Pakistan, and by entering into two military pacts with Pakistan, the SEATO Pact of 1954 and the Bagdad Pact of 1955.

Meanwhile, the Soviet Union gave India not only diplomatic support, but also economic aid, which included a Russian-built steel plant and three oil refineries. The total economic aid received from the West has been far larger than that received from Russia, but it has not been concentrated on projects which are so clearly visible as the Russian showpieces in India.

In short, from an Indian point of view, Nehru's policy of nonalignment made sense. It had the strong backing of almost all the people of India with sufficient education to be aware of the outside world.

For India, foreign relations with her neighbor, Pakistan, are particularly important. Partition left ugly wounds, some of which have not healed. Relations between the two nations over the millions of refugees were long strained. Hindu refugees from Pakistan naturally brought with them horror stories of how they had been treated in Pakistan. Muslim refugees from India had similar stories to tell. As these stories were circulated public hatred of its neighbor increased in each of the new nations.

A major problem in the early years after independence was the division of the essential waters of rivers that have their sources in India, but feed the irrigation canals of Pakistan, and are part of the Indus Valley river system. India temporarily cut off the flow of these western-flowing waters in the spring of 1948. The crops of hundreds of thousands of acres of Pakistan were ruined. India later restored the flow, but argued that she was entitled to more of this water for her own canals. Controversy on this matter was sharp until 1959 when the World Bank succeeded in drawing up a compromise plan satisfactory to both nations. In return for a loan from the World Bank, Pakistan agreed to build new storage reservoirs and canal links. As these were finished, she would give up the claim to some of the water originating in India. India agreed to pay a substantial part of the cost of the new water projects within Pakistan.

By far the most serious problem between the two nations, however, had to do with the disputed state of Kashmir. After the U.N. cease-fire of 1949, which ended the first war between India and Pakistan there, the armies of the two nations for years faced each other across the cease-fire line which now divided the state. Each nation laid claim not only to the part of Kashmir which it actually held, but to the whole state. At first Nehru said he would be willing to have the people of Kashmir themselves vote in a plebiscite whether they wanted to be part of India or of Pakistan. But he laid down an important proviso, which many people in the West soon forgot. He said that before this plebiscite could be held, Pakistan, which had been the aggressor, should withdraw its troops. Pakistan never did this.

Because the accession of Kashmir to India was regarded as provisional at the time that India's Constitution was being drafted, Kashmir was given a special status under it and was exempted from some of its clauses. After 1955, however, Nehru took the position that a plebiscite was now out of the question. Gradually Indian-held Kashmir was put on a parity with the other states of India and thoroughly integrated into the Indian union, and the government embarked on a number of expensive development projects there. Pakistan watched anxiously and kept demanding a plebiscite.

So strong is Indian feeling about Kashmir that it may well be that if Nehru had yielded to Pakistan he might have been forced out of office.

New Pakistan intrusions across the cease-fire line occurred after Nehru's death, in the summer of 1965. These led to a second armed conflict between India and Pakistan. Mrs. Indira Gandhi, by then a member of the Cabinet, was the first cabinet minister to fly to the front to see the actual conditions there.

As it turned out, full-scale fighting between India and Pakistan at this time lasted only a few weeks. Both nations saw they did not have the resources to continue full-scale fighting much longer. For some months the troops remained facing each other in battle readiness. Then in January, 1966, the Soviet Union brought pressure on both sides to agree to troop withdrawal and a formal end to hostilities. At a conference in the Russian city of Tashkent, the Pakistan representative and Prime Minister Lal Bahadur Shastri of India finally signed this agreement. Only a few hours later, Shastri, who had apparently been overtaxed emotionally and physically by the negotiations, suddenly died of a heart attack.

Peace of a kind returned to Kashmir, but the fact remains that in spite of Nehru's great belief in peace, he left in Kashmir the seeds of war.

One tragic aspect of Nehru's foreign policy was that he long relied on the friendship of neighboring China. He sent delegations of agricultural experts, women, cultural leaders, and others to China. He received delegations from China to India. Again and again he and the men under him repeated the slogan, "China and India are brothers." But in the autumn of 1962, the Chinese army invaded North India in several places, badly defeated the unprepared Indian army, then stopped hostilities of its own accord as unexpectedly as it had begun them.

Both the United Kingdom and the United States rushed military aid to India at that time. This greatly improved India's relations with the West. After a delay, the Soviet Union also began to help India in her new, more vigorous attempt to build up her defense forces. She sent India a number of the newest type Russian fighter planes and she arranged to help India begin building these planes for herself. India, however, continued to remain "nonaligned." Needing foreign aid now more than ever, it seemed necessary to keep on the best terms with both power blocs. With as much foreign aid as she could secure, she hastily built up her armed forces in fear of a new attack.

To Nehru, the Chinese invasion was a major shock and disappointment. Some commentators have said that in some sense he died the day it occurred. To him it was more than an invasion. It was a revelation that something had been wrong in the very essence of his philosophy of international relations and world peace. He had believed in Asian solidarity. He had believed that a peaceful approach would lead to a peaceful response. Then, through no fault of his, these beliefs were disproved. He had regarded the Indians and the Chinese as brothers. The Chinese had listened, had applauded, had echoed the slogan—and then had attacked.

Worse than that, the new defense effort now so obviously needed would be expensive. It could not fail to undermine the effort to raise the standard of living about which he cared so much.

The burdens he had been carrying had already been too great. He had assumed responsibility for dealing with all the problems of a desperately poor country. Everyone in government, it seemed, had leaned on him, had gone to him with whatever difficulty seemed incapable of solution.

By April, 1958 he had felt so tired that he announced he would like to resign as prime minister, that he needed a chance to rest and to think. This startling news was greeted by a storm of protests. Many felt that his resignation would bring disaster to the Congress and to the nation. They had depended on him so long that they did not see how they could do without him. "Panditji,"* cried one member of Parliament, "you are leaving us orphans."[2] So great was the pressure on him that he withdrew his resignation and wearily went on with his work.

---

* *Pandit* is both a last name, as in the case of Ranjit S. Pandit, Jawaharlal Nehru's brother-in-law, and a title of honor meaning a learned man. Nehru himself was generally called by this title until he specifically repudiated it shortly after independence.

Although he did not abandon his followers in 1958, the time came six years later when he had no choice. At a mass meeting of the Congress party in January, 1964, he slumped in his seat and collapsed. His daughter, who was by his side, helped lift him off the platform. He had had a stroke. Although he partially recovered, he was never well again. He died on May 27, 1964, at the age of seventy-four.

On the following day, a million and a half Indians lined the streets of New Delhi to do him honor, as the gun carriage on which his body rested was drawn for six miles through the streets of New Delhi to a spot by the Jumna River near the place where his beloved Gandhi had been cremated. His body was surrounded by flowers. He was dressed in a white home-spun jacket, with a rose in his third buttonhole, long his personal insignia. Soon after independence, a woman who admired him had begun waiting each day at the entrance to his grounds in order to give him a rose. Then his gardener, who saw that he always accepted the gift, himself saw to it that a fresh rose was ready for Nehru each day.

In a Hindu funeral the oldest son has a major part to play. Since Nehru had no sons, it was his seventeen-year-old grandson, Sanjay, who struck the match and lit the fire which consumed his grandfather's body. Two years later Mrs. Gandhi told a newspaper correspondent that after her father's death she felt numb for weeks.[3]

The great man had died and India did not know how it could go on without him. Yet people and nations do go on. Before Nehru's death, Indira had been mentioned as a possible successor to him, but when he died, she said she would not want to be chosen.

It is not certain that she would have been chosen at that time, even if she had been willing. To Kamaraj Nadar, the forceful southerner who was president of the Congress party at that time, it seemed of overriding importance to find what leader commanded the greatest degree of support within the party in Parliament and then to persuade other candidates to withdraw so that there would not be an open contest for the position—a contest which might have led to bitterness and undermined the unity of the party.

Privately he ascertained the views of each Congress member of Parliament, and found that Lal Bahadur Shastri was acceptable to many or most of the members, and did succeed in persuading other possible candidates, including Morarji Desai, former finance minister, to withdraw. Shastri was elected unanimously.

He did well and became especially popular in the summer and autumn of 1965. At that time, he was highly applauded for the strong stand he took, when, as already mentioned, several thousand armed infiltrators from Pakistan entered Indian-held Kashmir, apparently in an attempt to foment an uprising of the people against India. Shastri ordered the Indian army to seize posts on the Pakistan side of the line to prevent more infiltration, and also sent other detachments of the army across the international boundary which divides the Indian Punjab from the section of the Punjab which Pakistan acquired at partition. The Pakistan army retaliated. The fighting escalated. Both sides used tanks and planes.

Although the war was a popular one in India, neither side could continue fighting at full intensity for long. Each knew of its own weaknesses, whether in regard to spare parts, ammunition, or other supplies. Therefore, after three weeks of hard fighting, both India and Pakistan yielded to pressure from the United Nations and agreed to a cease-fire. By then India had seized some Pakistan territory and Pakistan had seized some Indian territory.

For several months thereafter the two hostile armies continued to face each other at close range across the new cease-fire line, and both sides repeatedly charged that the other had violated the cease-fire.

Finally, under pressure from the Soviet Union, which clearly wanted peace restored between the two nations, Shastri agreed to meet with Muhammad Ayub Khan, the president of Pakistan, in the Russian city of Tashkent. After a number of days of intense negotiations there an agreement was finally reached between them. They would withdraw their armed forces to the positions held before the beginning of the fighting in the summer. They would resume diplomatic relations and telephone, telegraph, and postal communications. Also trade, railway, and air services between the two countries would be resumed.

On January 10, 1966, within a few hours of signing this agreement, Shastri died of a heart attack, and was greatly mourned. Once again India had to look for a new prime minister.

# 17.

# The Emerging Daughter

In 1956, Nehru had said to a foreign correspondent whom he had long known, "Did you know, Indu has gone into politics! Yes, and she is doing quite well!"[1] He seemed incredulous. Many years before, when she had been only thirteen, he had told her that he expected her to play a part in Indian history. But now that she was thirty-nine, he found it hard to believe that his prophecy had come true.

Although in one sense Indira had actually been in politics all her life, she gradually came to play a more and more positive political role in the 1950's. While consistently refusing to become a candidate for office herself, she spoke frequently on behalf of other Congress candidates. Also between elections she traveled widely within India, speaking before groups of women and organizing a Women's Division of the Congress party. In February, 1955, she was elected to the twenty-one-member Working Committee of the Congress. Later that year she was elected a member of its small powerful Central Elections Committee, which selects the party's candidates for Parliament. If there were a parallel to this Committee in the United States, which there is not, party committees sitting in Washington would have the power to decide what Republican or Democratic candidates could run for office from each of the states of the Union. Being on this committee put Mrs. Gandhi in the very center of Congress party politics.

When she was elected Congress president, Nehru was surprised and apparently a little upset, but he decided not to interfere in the matter, although he felt there were disadvantages in this apparent dynastic succession. Indira herself was on a political walking tour when she received the news. She accepted the job without consulting her father, saying simply that if the party wanted her it was her duty to do what she could. [2]

Some members of Congress were worried that she would be too subservient to her father. This proved not to be the case. She dropped several of his old colleagues whom she believed to be corrupt from their high positions in the party. She reorganized the Congress Working Committee, putting her father's name off the list of its members, though allowing him to attend its sessions. It is said that while presiding over one of its meetings, she banged the gavel down to stop him from speaking after he had exceeded his time limit. It is generally believed that it was she who made the most important decisions of the year—those regarding policies toward the Communist ministry which was ruling the state of Kerala at the time she took office.

She flew to Kerala to see at first hand how the Communists were governing the state and was shocked by many things which were brought to her attention, such as textbooks in which high praise was paid to Karl Marx instead of to Gandhi. Then in May she made a speech to a Congress meeting warning that the Communists were taking steps to prevent other parties from ever defeating them again in Kerala. She urged the people of the state to resist Communist rule. This led to the nonviolent Congress campaign already described. It was apparently she who then persuaded the president of India to use his emergency powers, declare President's Rule, and take over the government of the state from the Communists. Her father, it is said, had been hesitant to advise this action. She then formed an alliance with two other parties, which succeeded in defeating the Communists in the next state election in February, 1960.

Although she declined to run for reelection to the Congress presidency the following year, she continued to be politically active. She remained on the Central Elections Committee, was active in screening the Congress candidates for the 1962 elections as she had been for those in 1957, and served on several other important party committees as well. She continued to go to many places on what might be called political errands. In the spring of 1961, when new communal rioting broke out in Madhya Pradesh, she flew there immediately in an attempt to ease the tensions between Hindus and Muslims, as she had done in Delhi in 1947.

That autumn, when her father established a National Integration Council to advise on ways by which caste, religious, and regional differences could be bridged and a feeling of national unity promoted, she became its chairman. She also became chairman of a committee of the Congress party dealing with the same subject.

In 1961 and 1962, when it seemed desirable to create a better image of India in the United States, she made a number of speeches there, undertaking in March, 1962, a nationwide tour under the sponsorship of a prominent American lecture bureau.

When the Chinese invasion of India occurred in the autumn of 1962, she immediately flew to the front, spoke with the soldiers, organized welfare services to bring them some comforts, and became chairman of the Citizens' Council for Defense and the National Relief Committee which helped the families of the soldiers at the front.

In 1963, when a contact needed to be made between India and the states of East Africa which had recently gained freedom or were about to do so, it was she who went there on a goodwill tour.

Over the years she had acquired in India the reputation of being a person who pounced on any problem that she saw, and dug as fast as she could to the heart of it. On one election tour, some villagers who were entitled to food rations told her that they had not eaten for three days. She asked them why not? Where were the rations? She proceeded to look into the matter thoroughly and found that the accredited supplier was in a distant town and had sold the grain nearby for a higher price instead of delivering it to the relatively inaccessible village where he would have had to sell it at a price fixed by the government.[3]

At least two years before her father's death, she had been frequently mentioned as a possible successor to him. Writing of her at that time, the American journalist Welles Hangen said:

> *She has probably been involved in more top-level decisions than any other member of India's present ruling hierarchy except her father. . . . Her power is vast, amorphous, and indefinable. No one doubts that she has easier and more frequent access to her father than any other Indian, but no one really knows the extent of her influence on him. No Congressman dares defy her. . . . No public figure in India disclaims political ambition so insistently and none is more disbelieved.[4]*

Many others, however, believed that if she were ever to become prime minister, Nehru himself would have to express his approval of the idea before he died, that otherwise her

The adversaries: Nehru and
Muhammad Ali Jinnah (left)

Crowds at the Red Fort,
Delhi, celebrating inde-
pendence in 1947 (below)

Muslim refugees in Delhi crowd into
train leaving for Pakistan, 1947
(upper left)

A refugee camp in Delhi, another result
of Partition (upper right)

The ancient Persian Wheel used for
irrigation (left)

A tube well, new electric
pump for better irrigation
(upper left)

Tribal dancers from Kerala
State (lower left)

The great new hydroelectric
dam at Bhakra, the Punjab
(upper right)

Bridges, old and new
(lower right)

Symbol of the Congress party painted on a village home (upper left)

Election Day (lower left)

Indira and Jawaharlal campaigning (right)

Indira and Jawaharlal on a state visit to England (upper left)

Jawaharlal enjoying his grandchildren (upper right)

Lal Bahadur Shastri, Nehru's successor (lower left)

Madame Prime Minister—Indira Nehru Gandhi (lower right)

political importance would vanish with his death. Nehru, however, carefully avoided endorsing her. He once said that he was neither grooming Indira nor ruling her out, that she had won the Congress presidency in her own right and that she might win the prime ministership likewise, but that he certainly did not want to encourage "some sort of dynastic arrangement."[5]

After Nehru's stroke in January, 1964, and before his death the following May, she was with him constantly. As he recovered slightly it was she who decided what few questions should be given him to consider. During that period, she was in effect the acting prime minister of India.

After his death, she indicated she did not want to be a candidate to succeed him. When Shastri became prime minister, he asked her to be his minister of external affairs, a post for which she was highly qualified because of her many contacts with high officials the world over. She asked instead for a lesser post and was appointed minister of information and broadcasting in June, 1964. As such, she decided that the policies of the All-India Radio, run by her department, should be reviewed, and set up a committee to make such a review. She chose a talented man as the director of the radio, and tried to persuade the government that it would be wise to allot money for the development of television in order to improve communications with the illiterate masses. The project seemed to the Shastri Cabinet too expensive and was not approved. Only a limited pilot project in TV exists in India.

As minister of information and broadcasting, another of her projects was to organize an international film festival in India in January, 1965, taking pains to see that the films shown would be of the highest quality from the artistic standpoint. She also liberalized the ultra-moral film censorship that India had previously had.

During Shastri's period as prime minister, she continued to travel widely. She attended on his behalf the Conference of

Commonwealth Prime Ministers in London in July, 1964. She made a trip to Moscow soon after Kosygin succeeded Khrushchev, and secured from the new Soviet leadership the assurance that it would continue its foreign aid to India. She also visited many places in India, including villages, where thousands flocked to see and hear her. She rushed to any trouble spots; when riots broke out in the state of Madras in the winter of 1965 in protest against the changeover from English to Hindi as the language of communication between the government and the states, she immediately flew there, and when in September, 1965, war broke out with Pakistan she was the first member of the government to fly to the front. One prominent Indian called her "the only man in the cabinet."[6]

After Shastri's death, Kamaraj Nadar, who was still party president, again tried, as he had done after Nehru's death, to find a candidate for prime minister who could be elected unanimously by the members of Congress in Parliament. This time he did not succeed. The election was contested. But it was Kamaraj Nadar who decided that, in the interest of national unity, Mrs. Gandhi would be the best candidate. He persuaded her to run. Most of the other contenders were closely associated with one region or another and would have proved unacceptable to people in other regions. Only Mrs. Gandhi seemed to have the much needed all-India point of view and appeal. Kamaraj Nadar mobilized majority support for her and worked hard to persuade the other candidates to withdraw from the contest. All but one did. The exception was Morarji Desai, from Bombay, former finance minister, a conservative, a strong believer in the prohibition of alcoholic drinks, undoubtedly a capable man, but one with many other rigid beliefs as well.

On January 19, 1966, the Congress members of Parliament met in the circular, high-domed central hall of the Parliament building to decide between this man and Mrs. Gandhi. She came to the meeting with a red rose pinned to her sari which recalled the rose that her father had worn in his third button-hole for so many years. The waiting crowds, loving her for herself, as well as for this gesture, cheered her enthusiastically. When the votes were counted in the Parliament building, Mrs. Gandhi had received 355; Desai, 169. She walked to the platform and said briefly in Hindi, "As I stand before you, my thoughts go back to the great leaders: Mahatma Gandhi at whose feet I grew up, Panditji—my father—and Mr. Lal Bahadur Shastri. . . . These leaders have shown us the way, and I want to go along the same path."[7] She emphasized especially the policies of democracy, socialism, secularism, and nonalignment.

A few hours after her election, she quoted to a friend a poem of Robert Frost which begins:

> The King said to his son: 'Enough of this!
> The Kingdom's yours to finish as you please.
> I'm getting out tonight. Here, take the crown.'
>
> But the Prince drew away his hand in time
> To avoid what he wasn't sure he wanted.[8]

She told her friend that she was reminded of the poem because that was the situation that she had found herself in. She was not sure she wanted the job, and she had accepted it with a shade of reluctance, adding, "I'm always reluctant when I enter into something, but then I give it my best."[9]

On January 24, 1966, the President of India, Sarvepalli Radhakrishnan, appointed her prime minister as a matter of course. She thus became the first woman in modern times to rule a major nation.

Her emergence as such immediately raised a number of questions in Western minds. Could a woman succeed in such a job? What was Mrs. Gandhi like as a person? Would she be controlled entirely by the party bosses, particularly by Kamaraj Nadar, or would she follow policies of her own? Had she been chosen merely because, as her father's daughter, she might be an effective vote-getter in the election due the following year? Would she be therefore dropped after the elections or would she again be chosen?

The first question—the ability of a woman to lead India—clearly irritated Mrs. Gandhi. To various interviewers, she repeatedly said in effect that it was not a matter of being a woman or a man, that like many other Indian women in the nationalist movement she had gone through the same hardships and faced the same dangers as the men, that she had been beaten by the police, had faced bullets, had been imprisoned, as had they. No question had been raised then about sex; why should such a question be raised now? When an American writer asked her if being prime minister didn't frighten her, she answered, "It hasn't frightened me yet. . . . All the things I've done were big challenges that I'd never met before, but I grew up with the idea that courage was the most important thing."[10]

To the question of what she was like as a person, commentators gave diverse answers. It seemed clear at least that she was a highly complex individual with many inner contradictions, for example, as between personal warmth and coolness. One writer spoke of her as "forbiddingly regal." He noted her "Brahmanical self-assurance" and said that she reminded him of a Hapsburg empress. Yet he added that her smile was warm and disarming.[11] Another writer spoke of her "forbidding aloofness, which keeps a visitor on edge and appears to some to be arrogance."[12]

Though she has friends all over the world, many of them have said that in some sense she always holds herself aloof, that even when she is warm she is also reserved. When the *New York Times* correspondent in India wrote his first feature article about her, he chose as his title, "She Stands Remarkably Alone." It may be that the loneliness of her childhood became an ingrained tendency so that even after she gained friends she still could not be close to them. It may also be that it is this very aloneness which has generated in her the energy to accomplish so much, to undertake so many lines of endeavor.

She is an unusually good-looking woman, small, thin, apparently frail, but lovely and abounding in energy and vitality. She has a long, thin, well-chiseled face, an arched nose, luminous dark eyes with heavy shadows under them, and short, slightly waved hair with streaks of white running through its blackness. She is knowledgeable on a host of subjects, sensitive to beauty, urbane, sophisticated, cosmopolitan, and rational in her outlook. She seems to have the directness and practicality of her grandfather, rather than her father's tendency to introspection and to theorizing.

When critics accused her of being pragmatic, of making decisions on the basis of what works rather than on the basis of theory or of an ideal concept of society, she welcomed the charge and retorted that a prime minister should be pragmatic and practical continuously.

She has a modern, progressive, scientific, rational outlook on the world. She believes that it was India's isolation from world thinking which caused her slavery and plunged her into poverty, and that Indians "must break through the blinding walls of nationalism and obscurantism."[13] When she took the oath of office she decided not to "swear in the name of God" as did most of her ministers, but instead to "solemnly affirm" her allegiance to the Constitution. She has said that religion as understood by most people is a crutch, that she does not need that kind of crutch. Yet she often carries the *Bhagavad Gita* with her in her handbag and has said that she does have a faith: that each person has God within him, as the *Bhagavad Gita* proclaims.[14]

Although she was forty-eight years old when she became prime minister, she seemed to many Indians a member of a new and much younger generation than those who had held power before her. She kept many members of Shastri's cabinet, hence was surrounded at the top level by people of sixty or over. But to the secondary level and below, she appointed many bright young men and women and quickly attempted to infuse new life into the vast, slow bureaucracy of the government.

No prime minister ever entered office with such prior training for the position as she. She had not only traveled widely both in her own country and abroad, but also listened to top level discussions about politics and government policies. She had watched her father make decisions and had had a chance to judge which were wise and which were not. Having worked long to build bridges between quarreling factions within her country, she knew more than did anyone else about the regional, linguistic, and religious sensitivities of the diverse peoples of India. Also, no one was better known than she. Not only had people in every part of India seen her, but also she had a name to remember. As one American correspondent put it, "It is . . . as if the daughter of Jefferson had married someone called Washington, and been nominated for the Presidency by both parties."[15] The last half of his sentence referred to the fact that both the right and the left wings of Congress had endorsed her.

Mrs. Gandhi is an intense person, passionately dedicated, as was her father, to the welfare of her country. From many of her speeches it is clear that she finds it hard to understand how anyone can be primarily interested in his own personal happiness. In her experience, she has found that it is only by concerning oneself with something larger than personal satisfaction—indeed, by often sacrificing that satisfaction for the larger cause—that one becomes truly and vividly alive. Her father and grandfather before her had discovered this same paradox.

When Mrs. Gandhi assumed office, the government faced perhaps a more difficult situation than at any time since the year that her father took office. The worst drought of the century had led to a massive crop failure. In four Indian states millions of people were on the borderline of famine. In a number of Indian cities, food riots were occurring. Hoping for political gain in a pre-election year, the communists of India were apparently encouraging these riots.

The brief war of 1965 with Pakistan had not only left a dangerous residue of bitter feelings between the two countries, but also had resulted in a stoppage of foreign aid from Western nations, including the United States. This had made even worse India's chronic shortage of foreign exchange, necessary for the purchase of imports. Many industries dependent on the import of spare parts or raw materials had come to a standstill.

Then, too, tribal peoples in northeastern India were in a state of rebellion. India believed they had been egged on by neighboring Pakistan. Not content with the creation of a separate state for them within the Indian union—Nagaland—one of these tribes, the Nagas, continued to press for complete independence. Another tribe in the Mizo Hills of Assam also demanded an independent state—Mizoram—which would be only 8,000 square miles in size.

Still another political problem, which had been seething for a decade, came to a head shortly after Mrs. Gandhi took office. One-third of the population of the state of Punjab, as it existed at the time that she came into office, were the Sikhs, who claim that their language, Punjabi, is different from Hindi, the official language of the state. Ever since 1956, when other state boundaries were redrawn largely on the basis of language, their leaders had demanded the formation of a separate Punjabi-speaking state. Judging that the difference between Sikhs and non-Sikhs in the Punjab was religious rather than linguistic, Nehru refused their demand. In March, 1966, the Sikh leader, Sant Fateh Singh, announced that he would fast for two weeks, then burn himself to death unless a separate Punjabi-speaking state was formed. Reversing her father's policy, Mrs. Gandhi agreed to divide the Punjab. Violent Hindu demonstrations resulted. In a tragic reminder of British actions in 1919, the police in Amritsar found it necessary to fire into a crowd of demonstrators. Fortunately only one boy was killed. A number were wounded. Altogether one thousand people were imprisoned.

Violence again spread to the capital city where extremist Hindus chanted "Death to the Sikh state of Punjab. Death to Indira Gandhi." Besieged by a mob of Hindus, the Sikh guards in front of Delhi's main Sikh temple drew their swords and charged the mob. More rioting followed. Acting swiftly, Mrs. Gandhi ordered the police to suppress the riots and punish those who had provoked them. To the surprise of many who did not expect a woman prime minister to go to dangerous areas, Mrs. Gandhi went to that part of Delhi where the Sikh temple stood, in order to find out for herself what members of the police had allowed the riots to break out. Speaking of these riots, she told an audience, "There are no tears in my eyes: there is anger in my heart. Is it for disharmony that so many freedom fighters have sacrificed so much?"[16]

The partition of the Punjab to which she had agreed was carried out. The name "Punjab" was kept for the part where the Sikhs are most numerous. The remaining part of the state was given separate status under the name Haryana.

Mrs. Gandhi dealt with the uprising of the Mizos with equal firmness, ordering the air force to bomb concentrations of rebels. Only six weeks after taking office, she made the long trip eastward to Assam by plane, helicopter, and jeep, to discuss the problem of the Mizos and the Nagas with the governor of the state. On the way she stopped at Calcutta to investigate the food riots there.

This two-thousand-mile trip became a part of her next election campaign as well. She spoke to large meetings where as many as half a million came to see her, at least at a distance, and to countless other smaller meetings. Through village after village, she rode standing in the back of an open jeep so that no one would miss the *darshan,* or personal sight of her, which the Indian people traditionally expect of their rulers.

At the end of March, as soon as she had brought problems at home at least partially under control, she accepted President Johnson's invitation for a visit to the United States. It was a matter of top priority that she do everything possible to lead to a resumption of aid from the United States. Other Western countries had resumed their aid to India—cut off briefly during the Indo-Pakistan war of 1965—as soon as the warfare ended. The United States had not.

In four major speeches and several television interviews in the United States, Mrs. Gandhi made a highly favorable impression. Her grace and smiling shyness charmed the crowds. In New York City, Mayor Lindsay gave her a reception, appropriately at the Lincoln Center for the Performing Arts. Toasting her, he said, "She has fitted into our community with ease and grace and style. She gives us luster just by being here."[17] She replied that she had discovered that she and Mayor Lindsay had something in common: "We like people to provoke us. We are at our best under fire."[18]

She was not only charming but also persuasive. She made an able and forceful appeal for continued American aid to India, pointing both to the progress already made, the problems ahead, and to the importance of the Indian experiment to future democracy the world over.

Yet President Johnson did not immediately indicate what

would be done about the resumption of foreign aid. He merely proposed the establishment of an Indian-American Educational Foundation, using for it Indian rupees to the value of $300 million. The U.S. government had received these rupees in payment of American "wheat loans" to India. Some American aid to India was resumed in June, 1966, but as this book goes to press the United States has not come near fulfilling the aid pledge made before the Indo-Pakistan war.

Before Mrs. Gandhi became prime minister, she had been generally regarded as a member of the left wing of the Congress party. This was partly because of her close association with left-wing Krishna Menon in the past and partly because she had encouraged the "Ginger Group," a group of young radicals within the party who felt that her father was moving too slowly toward socialism. Particularly in the months after her visit to the United States, however, she took a number of steps which surprised and delighted the more conservative portion of her party and correspondingly disappointed her socialist followers. She lifted certain government controls, agreed to liberal concessions for foreign private investors, and removed certain restraints on imports. Western observers had long felt that steps such as these were needed if India was to make faster economic progress, but socialism has such a strong hold on the imagination of the Indian public that she was vigorously criticized in Parliament not only by the left-wing opposition, but also by members of her own party.

President Johnson's proposed Indian-American Foundation was also criticized, as an attempt by the United States to dominate the Indian educational system. Another step, which Mrs. Gandhi took in June, caused still more of an uproar against her.

Unexpectedly and suddenly her government lowered by 36 per cent the value of the Indian unit of currency, the rupee, in terms of foreign currency. Whereas previously 4.76 rupees had been equal to a dollar, now it took 7.5 rupees to equal a dollar.

Devaluation of a currency tends to discourage imports and make it possible for the country to sell more goods abroad. Therefore the International Monetary Fund and the World Bank had advised India on this step in order to improve her foreign exchange situation. In India, however, devaluation was unpopular. It led to an immediate rise in prices which hurt consumers, and Indians resented the fact that India had apparently allowed outside agencies to "dictate" its policies. The communist press called the step "the gravest betrayal of national interest by the government of India at the dictates of the United States imperialism since the attainment of national independence."[19] Since devaluation had been undertaken in the hope that full American aid would be immediately resumed, there was much resentment when devaluation did not lead to this.

Twice already she had been severely criticized in Congress party meetings. At the first such meeting held after she became prime minister the hostility from the floor apparently unnerved her to such an extent that when she went to the microphone she managed only a few mumbled phrases, then sat down embarrassed. It was a poor performance. On the second occasion, in Bombay in May, she had done better. When party members criticized her for alleged failure to follow her father's policies, she retorted with spirit that she was indeed following his policies to the extent that circumstances permitted, but that new problems call for new solutions. Without bending or giving an inch, she said flatly, "If you disapprove of my approach, then change your leadership, remove me."[20]

As the summer wore on, however, she apparently decided that it would be wise or necessary to try to placate the opposition within her party. Rumors had spread that the party boss, Kamaraj Nadar, had decided to split with her. If the Congress was to do even passably well in the elections in February, 1967, more party unity was clearly needed. Accordingly, she took a number of steps to satisfy the left-wing faction. She quietly dropped the much-criticized proposal of President Johnson for an Indian-American Educational Foundation. In July, she made a state visit to Moscow and there signed a statement demanding a halt in American bombing of North Vietnam, and denouncing "aggressive actions by imperialists and other reactionary forces."[21] She approved of a very large ($31.6 billion) Fourth Five-Year Plan, which included provision for the heavy investment in government-owned industries which the socialists demanded. She also announced that she did not agree with certain aspects of recent agreements with Western companies for private investment in India and said that she wanted a thorough investigation of these.

Were her reversals of policy an indication of weakness of character or were they no greater than the compromises which any political candidate must make in an election year? The question was debatable.

When the Congress met in September to agree on a platform for the coming elections, there was at least a show of unity— plus many indications from outside that the food situation and continuing poverty had led to so much widespread impatience that the Congress faced the danger of losing control of at least some state governments. In Kerala, for example, the Communists seemed certain to win again.

During the summer and autumn of 1966, Mrs. Gandhi campaigned throughout the country with incredible vigor, increasing her tempo still further in the first five weeks of 1967, when she made at least two major speeches a day, plus countless impromptu talks before smaller gatherings.

As election day approached, the heckling of Congress candidates during their speeches became common. Many candidates allowed themselves to be shouted down and gave up speaking, or even canceled speaking engagements in advance. Not Mrs. Gandhi. To a jeering mob in Rajasthan she shouted, "I am not going to oblige you by cutting short my speech. I must have my say." As the noise continued, she said: "I am surprised that even the people of Rajasthan do not realize what fire and strength a woman can have. . . . When the time came for me to take responsibility, I took it without hesitation or fear . . . because I was sure that the people of the country were with me and would share my burdens. I am still confident."[22]

At her subsequent appearances, disorder increased. On February 8, a member of a large audience in the state of Orissa threw a rock which hit her nose. Bleeding profusely, she left the platform. With a broken and bandaged nose, she fulfilled her next speaking engagement on the following day, then was ordered by her doctors to stop campaigning.

The elections were held during the last week of February, 1967. As expected, Mrs. Gandhi was elected to Parliament from her own district by a handsome majority.

The Congress party as a whole, however, suffered a major setback in most of the country. It lost over seventy of the seats it had formerly held in the central Parliament, retaining only a slim majority there. In the state legislatures its reverses were even worse. Whereas it had previously maintained control of all the state governments except Kerala, it emerged this time with a majority in only eight out of the sixteen state legislatures for which elections were held.

Clearly, large sections of the Indian electorate had become tired of the Congress, disappointed at the slow progress toward economic improvement, angered by food shortages and soaring prices, convinced that there was corruption in government —in short, decidedly ready for a change.

In previous elections the Congress had benefited from its long record of leadership in the independence movement and from the fragmented nature of the opposition, as well as from

Nehru's incomparable prestige. By 1967, most of the heroes of the independence movement were dead, and the memories of that movement had grown dim. More than that, the opposition parties in many of the states banded together to select candidates whom they would support jointly.

Then, too, factionalism within the Congress itself greatly weakened it. In vain had Mrs. Gandhi struggled to give her party a new sense of unity and new vitality. In seven states, dissatisfied members of Congress had gone so far as to form separate, rebel Congress parties of their own that sided with the other opposition parties against regular Congress candidates. As a result of this cooperation among opposition parties, many of the oustanding men of the Congress party were defeated, including four prominent members of Mrs. Gandhi's pre-election Cabinet, plus Kamaraj Nadar, the party boss himself.

In most of the states, the parties that gained at the expense of the Congress were the conservative Swatantra, the Hindu extremist Jan Sangh, or the rebel Congress parties. In Madras, the regional-minded D.M.K. became dominant; in Kerala, the Communists again.

After the elections, non-Congress governments were quickly set up in five states. Their ministries were all coalitions of parties with widely different views. In Haryana and the great state of the U.P.—the Nehrus' own state—governments formed by the Congress party split apart after only a few days in office. They were replaced by coalitions headed by Congress rebels. In one state, Rajasthan, such violence broke out in the streets when the Congress party tried to form a government that an emergency was declared and the state placed under President's Rule, India's unique system of constitutionally sanctioned dictatorship.

The entire Ganges Valley, from Amritsar to Calcutta, had passed out of Congress control, as had the two southernmost states: Kerala and Madras. Furthermore, the very success of the Congress rebels had led other members of the Congress party to consider defecting, also.

Meanwhile, in the central Parliament where the Congress still had a slight majority, it was entitled to choose the new prime minister. Party chief Kamaraj Nadar again maneuvered behind the scenes to ensure that the election would be unanimous. Mrs. Gandhi was chosen after it had been arranged that her chief rival, Morarji Desai, would not run if he were given the post of deputy prime minister.

With the elections and the long campaigning behind her, Mrs. Gandhi still faced her real test: Could she demonstrate convincingly her ability and effectiveness as a prime minister? Could she deal successfully with the non-Congress governments in the states—or, still worse, with the problem of what to do if any of them split apart and toppled, leaving no group capable of commanding a majority? Could she stem the tide of defections from her party?

Many predicted that her government would fall—would fail to secure majority support in Parliament—within a year. Some gave her not more than eight months in which to prove herself.

In May 1967, however, she scored what most observers regarded as a very significant victory. The candidate whom she had supported for the Presidency of India was elected by a wide margin, although a Muslim, and although seven opposition parties had agreed to support one particular Hindu candidate. The new President was Dr. Zakir Hussain, the prominent educator who had been Vice-President. His victory was a direct endorsement by India of Mrs. Gandhi's leadership.

Yet, whatever her political future may be, and however her abilities may finally be judged, one thing is clear: so far as courage, conviction, dedication, and energy are concerned, she has proven herself to be truly her grandfather's granddaughter and her father's daughter.

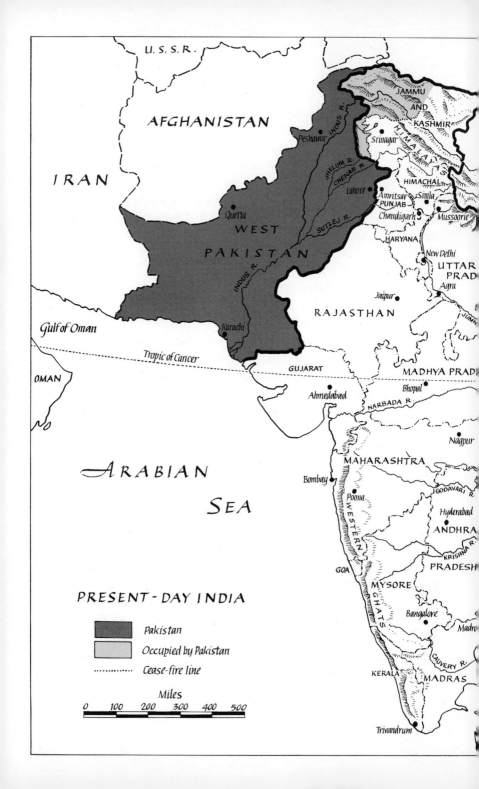

U.S.S.R.

AFGHANISTAN

IRAN

Peshawar INDUS R.

JAMMU
AND
KASHMIR

Srinagar

HIMALAYAS

JHELUM R.

CHENAB R.

HIMACHAL

Lahore

Amritsar Simla

Quetta

WEST

PAKISTAN

PUNJAB

Chandigarh

Mussoorie

SUTLEJ R.

HARYANA

New Delhi

UTTAR
PRAD

INDUS R.

Agra

Jaipur

RAJASTHAN

JUMN

Gulf of Oman

Karachi

Tropic of Cancer

OMAN

GUJARAT

MADHYA PRAD

Ahmedabad

Bhopal

NARBADA R.

Nagpur

ARABIAN

MAHARASHTRA

Bombay

SEA

Poona

GODAVARI R.

Hyderabad

ANDHRA

KRISHNA R.

PRADESH

GOA

PRESENT-DAY INDIA

MYSORE

Pakistan

Bangalore

Madr

CAUVERY R.

Occupied by Pakistan

Cease-fire line

KERALA

MADRAS

Miles

0    100   200   300   400   500

Trivandrum

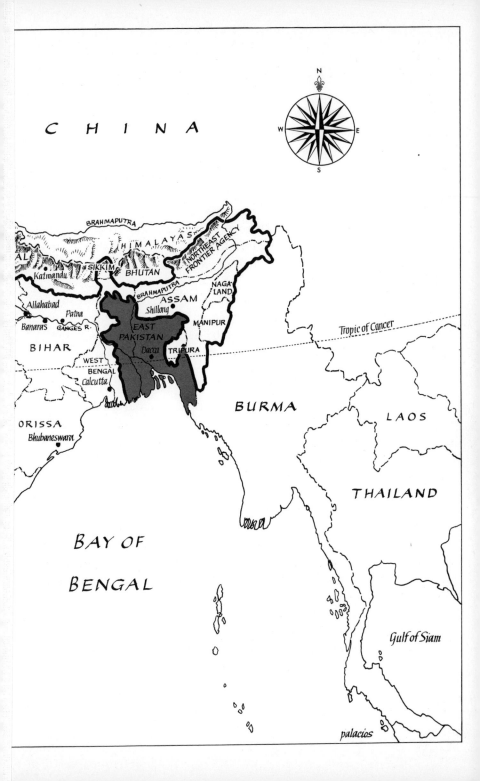

# For Further Reading

Before listing, alphabetically, suggestions for further reading, it may be helpful to make a few comments on them.

Jawaharlal Nehru's own vivid writings are highly recommended, particularly his readable autobiography, *Toward Freedom*. Although his *Discovery of India* and *Glimpses of World History* may seem forbiddingly long, they should at least be sampled. Nehru himself once recommended to his daughter that when she had a long book she should open it at random and read as much or as little as she felt like reading. The abridged version of *Glimpses of World History,* entitled *Nehru on World History* (edited by Saul Padover), omits the personal material that provides much of the original book's appeal.

The best treatment of Motilal Nehru is contained in *The Nehrus: Motilal and Jawaharlal,* by B. R. Nanda, which deals with Jawaharlal only up to the time of his father's death. Nanda is also the author of an excellent and readable biography of Gandhi, though a more accessible and equally readable biography of Gandhi is the brief paperback by Louis Fischer.

Of the many biographies of Jawaharlal Nehru, that by Michael Brecher is probably the most careful and authoritative.

The interesting biography of Nehru's sister, Madame Pandit, written by Miss Guthrie for young adults, throws some additional light on the three Nehrus treated in the present book, as does the autobiography of Nehru's second sister, Krishna Nehru (Mrs. Hutheesingh), *With No Regrets*.

As this volume goes to press, material on Mrs. Gandhi is only beginning to be available in the West. Over the past ten years she herself has written a number of brief autobiograph-

262

ical pieces for Indian magazines and has told audiences of various episodes in her life. The author of the present book has relied heavily on this material.

Since the books and articles on Mrs. Gandhi published in India are not easily available in the West, only some of the better accounts of her life and temperament published in the West are included in this list.

For additional background reading about India's history and modern India's policies and problems, my volume, *India, A World in Transition,* may prove helpful. Although written primarily for college undergraduates, it has also had wide use as an adult trade book, and as a book for use in senior high schools. A completely revised edition appeared in 1966. My shorter book, entitled *India,* though designed primarily for a younger age group, has also been listed below. Well illustrated, it could be useful for any age level.

BRECHER, MICHAEL. *Nehru: A Political Biography.* New York and London: Oxford University Press, 1959.

FISCHER, LOUIS. *Gandhi, His Message and Life For the World.* New York: New American Library of World Literature, 1954.

FRIEDAN, BETTY. "How Mrs. Gandhi Shattered 'The Feminine Mystique'," *Ladies' Home Journal,* May, 1966.

GANDHI, INDIRA. "India Today," *Yale Review,* Spring, 1961.

GUTHRIE, ANN. *Madame Ambassador: The Life of Vijaya Lakshmi Pandit.* New York: Harcourt, Brace & World, 1962.

HANGEN, WELLES. *After Nehru, Who?* New York: Harcourt, Brace & World, 1963. Pp. 159–84.

LAMB, BEATRICE PITNEY. *India.* New York: The Macmillan Co., 1965.

———. *India, A World in Transition.* 2d rev. ed. New York: Frederick A. Praeger Co., 1966.

"India's Boss Lady," *Life Magazine*, March 16, 1959.

LUKAS, J. ANTHONY. "She Stands Remarkably Alone," *New York Times Magazine*, March 27, 1966.

MICHAELIS, ARNOLD. "An Interview with Indira Gandhi," *McCall's*, April, 1966.

NANDA, B. R. *The Nehrus: Motilal and Jawaharlal*. New York: John Day Company, 1963.

————. *Mahatma Gandhi*. Boston: Beacon Press, 1958.

NEHRU, JAWAHARLAL. *Glimpses of World History*. New York: John Day Company, 1942.

————. *The Discovery of India*. New York: John Day Company, 1946.

————. *Toward Freedom*. New York: John Day Company, 1941; Boston: Beacon Press, 1958.

NEHRU, KRISHNA. *With No Regrets, An Autobiography*. New York: John Day Company, 1945.

NORMAN, DOROTHY. "Mrs. Indira Gandhi, Prime Minister of India," *Vogue*, March 1, 1966.

PADOVER, SAUL K. (ed.). *Nehru on World History*. New York: John Day Company, 1960. An abbreviation of Nehru's *Glimpses of World History*, with an introduction by Saul K. Padover.

"Interview with Mrs. Indira Nehru Gandhi, Head of Congress Party," *U.S. News and Word Report*, November 16, 1959.

ZIN, MARVIN. "Lady Who Now Leads India," *Life Magazine*, January 28, 1966.

# Notes

*Chapter 1*—Motilal and His India

1. R. C. Majumdar, H. C. Raychaudhuri, and Kalinkinkar Datta. *An Advanced History of India* (London: Macmillan & Co., 1950), p. 80.
2. P. L. Rawat. *History of Indian Education*, 3rd ed. (Agra: Bharat Publications, 1956), p. 216.

*Chapter 2*—Three Influences

1. P. L. Rawat, *History of Indian Education*, p. 177.
2. Government of India, *A Review of Education in India, 1947–61*. p. 949.

*Chapter 3*—Jawaharlal's Youth

1. Jawaharlal Nehru, *Glimpses of World History* (New York: John Day Co., 1942), p. 464.
2. Quoted in B. R. Nanda. *The Nehrus: Motilal and Jawaharlal* (New York: John Day Co., 1963), p. 46.
3. Jawaharlal Nehru, *Toward Freedom: The Autobiography of Jawaharlal Nehru* (New York: John Day Co., 1942), p. 30.
4. Nanda, *The Nehrus,* p. 90.
5. Nehru, *Toward Freedom,* p. 37.
6. Quoted in Louis Fischer, *Gandhi, His Life and Message for the World* (New York: New American Library, 1954), p. 39.

*Chapter 4*—A Marriage and a New Slogan

1. Jawaharlal Nehru, *Toward Freedom,* p. 333.
2. Jawaharlal Nehru, *Unity of India* (London: L. Drummond, 1941), p. 223.
3. Article by Mrs. Gandhi for the magazine of a Montessori School, Nov., 1957, supplied in mimeographed form by the Prime Minister's Secretariat.
4. B. R. Nanda, *The Nehrus,* p. 148.

*Chapter 5*—New Leader, New Way of Life

1. *Bhagavad Gita,* chap. II, verses 38, 71, translated by S. Radhakrishnan. Quoted in Sarvepalli Radhakrishnan and Charles A. Moore, *A Source Book in Indian Philosophy* (Princeton, N. J.: Princeton University Press, 1957), pp. 109, 112.
2. Jawaharlal Nehru, *Toward Freedom,* p. 72.
3. *Report of the Committee Appointed by the Government of India to Investigate the Disturbances in the Punjab, etc.* (Command Paper No. 681, 1920) pp. 112–13.

4. *London Times,* April 19, 1919.
5. *Ibid.,* May 23, 1919.
6. *New York Times,* July 17, 1919.
7. Nehru, *Toward Freedom,* p. 110.
8. *Ibid.*

*Chapter 6*—Jail for the First Time
1. From a mimeographed copy of an article of Mrs. Gandhi's for the magazine of a Montessori School, Nov., 1957, supplied by the Prime Minister's Secretariat.
2. Jawaharlal Nehru, *Toward Freedom,* pp. 56–57.
3. Quoted in B. R. Nanda, *The Nehrus,* p. 196.
4. Krishna Nehru, *With No Regrets, An Autobiography* (New York: John Day Co., 1945), p. 36.
5. Welles Hangen, *After Nehru, Who?* (New York: Harcourt, Brace & World, 1963), p. 165.
6. Krishna Nehru, *With No Regrets,* p. 38.
7. From a mimeographed copy of an article by Mrs. Gandhi in *Women on the March* (New Delhi), August, 1957, supplied by the Prime Minister's Secretariat.
8. Article by Mrs. Gandhi for the magazine of a Montessori School, Nov., 1957, supplied to the author in mimeographed form by the Prime Minister's Secretariat.
9. Nanda, *The Nehrus,* p. 214.
10. Exact dates of these imprisonments are given in Michael Brecher's *Nehru: A Political Biography* (London: Oxford University Press, 1959), p. 81.
11. Nehru, *Toward Freedom,* p. 92.
12. Quoted in Nanda, *The Nehrus,* p. 227.
13. *Ibid.,* p. 241.

*Chapter 7*—European Interlude
1. Quoted in Dorothy Norman, *Nehru, the First Sixty Years* (New York: John Day Co., 1965), I, 129.
2. *Ibid.,* p. 130.

*Chapter 8*—Forward Again
1. Quoted in Michael Brecher, *Nehru: A Political Biography,* p. 123.
2. *Ibid.*
3. *New York Times,* January 22, 1928, sec. 9, p. 4.
4. Jawaharlal Nehru, *Letters from a Father to His Daughter* (Allahabad: Kitabistan, 1930), pp. 33–34.
5. Speech of Mrs. Gandhi before the Conference of All-India Voluntary Organizations, May 26, 1965, supplied to the author in typewritten form by the Prime Minister's Secretariat.
6. B. R. Nanda, *The Nehrus,* p. 303.

7. *Ibid.*
8. Jawaharlal Nehru, *Toward Freedom*, p. 140.
9. Nanda, *The Nehrus*, p. 309.
10. Quoted in Brecher, *Nehru*, p. 138.
11. Quoted in Nanda, *The Nehrus*, p. 325.
12. Quoted in Nehru, *Toward Freedom*, p. 389.
13. *Ibid.*, p. 151.
14. *Ibid.*, p. 154.
15. Welles Hangen, *After Nehru, Who?*, p. 166.
16. *Ibid.*, p. 164.
17. Quoted in Nehru, *Toward Freedom*, p. 181.
18. Quoted in Nanda, *The Nehrus*, p. 332.
19. Nehru, *Toward Freedom*, p. 184.
20. *Ibid.*, p. 185.
21. Arnold Michaelis, "Interview with Indira Gandhi," *McCall's*, April, 1966.

*Chapter 9*—In and Out of Jail
1. Jawaharlal Nehru, *Toward Freedom*, p. 223.
2. Jawaharlal Nehru, *Glimpses of World History*, p. 327.
3. Nehru, *Toward Freedom*, p. 224.
4. *Ibid.*, p. 225.
5. *Ibid.*, p. 198.
6. Nehru, *Glimpses*, p. 1.
7. Welles Hangen, *After Nehru, Who?*, p. 164.
8. Nehru, *Glimpses*, p. 3.
9. *Ibid.*, p. 953.
10. Rabindranath Tagore, "Gitanjali," XXXV, from *The Collected Poems and Plays of Rabindranath Tagore* (New York: The Macmillan Company), p. 13.
11. Michael Brecher, *Nehru: A Political Biography*, p. 196.
12. Khwaja Ahmed Abbas, *Indira Gandhi, The Return of the Red Rose* (Bombay: Popular Prakashan Press, 1966), p. 50.
13. *Ibid.*, p. 51.
14. Jawaharlal Nehru, *Discovery of India* (New York: John Day Co., 1946), p. 342.
15. Abbas, *Indira Gandhi*, pp. 61–62.
16. *Ibid.*, pp. 64–65.
17. Article by Mrs. Gandhi in *Roshni*, Nov., 1959, supplied to the author in typewritten form by the Prime Minister's Secretariat.
18. *Ibid.*
19. *Ibid.*
20. *Ibid.*
21. Nehru, *Toward Freedom*, p. 312.
22. *Ibid.*, p. 353.

23. *Ibid.,* p. 334.
24. Quoted in Brecher, *Nehru,* p. 206.
25. Quoted in Abbas, *Indira,* p. 68.
26. Jawaharlal Nehru, *Bunch of Old Letters* (London: Asia Publishing House, 1960), p. 187.
27. Krishna Nehru, *With No Regrets,* p. 120.

*Chapter 10*—Toward Partition
1. Quoted in Jawaharlal Nehru, *Toward Freedom,* p. 390.
2. Quoted in Michael Brecher, *Nehru: A Political Biography,* p. 8.
3. *Ibid.,* p. 597.
4. Quoted in Welles Hangen, *After Nehru, Who?,* p. 166.
5. *Ibid.,* p. 167.
6. Quoted in Brecher, *Nehru,* p. 258.
7. Jawaharlal Nehru, *Bunch of Old Letters,* p. 408.
8. Quoted in Brecher, *Nehru,* p. 282.
9. *Ibid.,* p. 286.
10. Jawaharlal Nehru, *Discovery of India,* p. 46.
11. *Ibid.,* p. 144.
12. Krishna Nehru, *With No Regrets, An Autobiography,* pp. 145–146.
13. Khwaja Ahmed Abbas, *Indira Gandhi, The Return of the Red Rose,* p. 92.
14. Arnold Michaelis, "Interview with Indira Gandhi," *McCall's,* April, 1966.

*Chapter 11*—Independence, Slaughter, and Survival
1. Jawaharlal Nehru, *Independence and After, Collection of Speeches 1946–49* (New York: John Day Co., 1950), pp. 3–4.
2. *Ibid.*
3. Michael Brecher, *Nehru: A Political Biography,* pp. 365–66.
4. Speech of Mrs. Gandhi for the Council on Communal Harmony, May 23, 1963, supplied to author in typewritten form by the Prime Minister's Secretariat.
5. *Ibid.*
6. Indira Gandhi, "My Reminiscences of Bapu," typed statement supplied by the Prime Minister's Secretariat.
7. Indira Gandhi, article from *Women on the March,* August, 1957.
8. *Ibid.*
9. *Ibid.*
10. Author's interview with President Radhakrishnan, London, April, 1965.
11. Quoted in C. H. Phillips, *Politics and Society in India* (New York: Frederick A. Praeger, 1963), p. 159.

*Chapter 12*—Father and Daughter After Independence
1. Welles Hangen, *After Nehru, Who?*, p. 169.
2. Betty Friedan, "How Mrs. Gandhi Shattered 'The Feminine Mystique," in *Ladies' Home Journal*, May, 1966.
3. *Ibid.*
4. *Ibid.*
5. Speech by Mrs. Gandhi at Indira Music University, October 14, 1956, supplied to the author in typewritten form by the Prime Minister's Secretariat.

*Chapter 13*—Nehru and the Politics of Independent India
1. Margaret W. Fisher and Joan V. Bondurant, *The Indian Experience with Democratic Elections* (Berkeley: University of California Press, 1956), p. 6.
2. From Mrs. Gandhi's speech in Washington, D.C., March 28, 1966. From a typed copy of the speech supplied by the Indian Consulate, New York City.
3. Jawaharlal Nehru, *Independence and After*, p. 47.
4. *Jawaharlal Nehru's Speeches, 1949–53* (Government of India: Publications Division, 1954).

*Chapter 15*—Progress in Education
1. Article by William Stringer, "Nehru Scans the World," *Christian Science Monitor*, January 7, 1959.

*Chapter 16*—Nehru's Foreign Policy
1. Quoted in Dorothy Norman, *Nehru, The First Sixty Years*, p. 130.
2. As quoted in *New York Times*, April 30, 1958.
3. Quoted by J. Anthony Lukas, "She Stands Remarkably Alone," *New York Times Magazine*, March 27, 1966.

*Chapter 17*—The Emerging Daughter
1. Conversation between Nehru and Phillips Talbot in New Delhi at which the author was present.
2. *Asian Recorder* (New Delhi), January, 1959.
3. *New Statesman* (London), February 11, 1966, p. 190.
4. Welles Hangen, *After Nehru, Who?*, p. 160.
5. Quoted in Khwaja Ahmed Abbas, *Indira Gandhi, The Return of the Red Rose*, p. 14.
6. Quoted in *Newsweek*, January 31, 1966.
7. Text supplied by the Prime Minister's Secretariat.
8. Robert Frost, "How Hard It Is to Keep from Being King When It's in You and in the Situation," *In The Clearing* (New York: Holt, Rinehart & Winston, 1962), p. 74.

9. Quoted by J. Anthony Lukas, *New York Times Magazine*, March 27, 1966, p. 35.

10. Betty Friedan, "How Mrs. Gandhi . . . ," in *Ladies' Home Journal*, May, 1966.

11. Hangen, *After Nehru, Who?*, p. 161.

12. Inder Melhotra quoted in *Indira Priyardarshini* by M. Chalapathi Rau *et al.* (New Delhi: Popular Book Service, 1966), p. 43.

13. J. Anthony Lukas, *New York Times Magazine*, March 27, 1966, p. 133.

14. *Ibid.*

15. Max Lerner in *New York Post*, January 21, 1966.

16. This speech has been variously reported in different newspapers. The words quoted here were from Sharokh Sabavala in *Christian Science Monitor*, March 25, 1966, p. 14.

17. *New York Times*, March 31, 1966, p. 22.

18. *Ibid.*

19. As quoted in *New York Times*, June 7, 1966.

20. As quoted in *New York Times*, May 23, 1966.

21. As quoted in *New York Times*, Sept. 30, 1966.

22. *Indian Express*, January 20, 1967.

# Index